A HISTORY

OF THE

GREAT WESTERN RAILWAY

BEING

The Story of the Broad Gauge

BY

G. A. SEKON

AUTHOR OF 'THE EVOLUTION OF OUR RAILWAYS'
A HISTORY OF THE SOUTH EASTERN RAILWAY'
ETC. ETC.

ILLUSTRATED

LONDON
DIGBY, LONG & CO., PUBLISHERS
18 BOUVERIE STREET, FLEET STREET, E.C.
1895

Publishing Statement:

This important reprint was made from an old and scarce book.

Therefore, it may have defects such as missing pages, erroneous pagination, blurred pages, missing text, poor pictures, markings, marginalia and other issues beyond our control.

Because this is such an important and rare work, we believe it is best to reproduce this book regardless of its original condition.

Thank you for your understanding and enjoy this unique book!

PREFACE

—o—

In presenting this *History of the Great Western Railway*, I would remind the reader that it is 'The Story of the Broad Gauge' that is here chronicled, so that while in the first thirty years or so of the Great Western Railway's existence the work is, *de facto*, a 'History of the Great Western Railway,' for the remaining period up to the present time it is rather a history of that part of the Great Western system which was formerly Broad Gauge; nor have I attempted in any way to chronicle the construction or development of the Narrow Gauge extensions and additions to the original Broad Gauge trunk lines and branches, although passing references have been made to some important and interesting occurrences in connection therewith.

In the ensuing pages, with much diffidence. I offer my readers the efforts of considerable labour and research, and am acutely conscious that the book is not as complete in many respects as I should like it to be; but the difficulties that are encountered in completing such a work as this, are both numerous and unexpected, and call into use a large amount of patience on the compiler's part—thus, in a newspaper or book, mention will be made of proposed engineering feats, new locomotives, improved vehicles, increases of speed, etc., and then no more information on the subject will be obtainable, and it is only after very long research, and then generally by but an indirect reference in unexpected places that I have been able to discover if the innovations or proposals were actually carried out and the expected results obtained. Much interesting matter of this description I have therefore had to reject, since, despite considerable inquiry, I have been unable to discover the result of the proposed alterations, etc. In some cases, the careful research, so kindly made by the officials at Paddington, among the documents in possession of the Railway Company, has not succeeded in bringing to light the information required.

Here is another example of wasted energy. At the commencement of the past year a discussion arose, in an engineering journal, concerning the third-class parliamentary fares charged on the Great Western Railway. I joined in the correspondence, and promised to devote a chapter of this book to the subject. After I had gone to considerable trouble in obtaining full information on the question, the Great Western Directors decided that from 1st July 1894 third-class fares on their railway should be abolished, and only one penny per mile charged for third-class passengers. This was clearly a case of 'Love's labour lost.'

Critical readers will no doubt find that some errors more or less important have crept into the work, and I shall feel indebted to any of them who will point out such slips.

Nor do I expect the opinions I have expressed in this book to pass unquestioned; indeed, one of our most notable railway officials, who did me the honour of revising the description of an incident in which he was prominently concerned, at one part of the account observed 'that is a matter of opinion only,' so that even he did not in that particular agree with me. In the railway and engineering journals to which I contribute, articles from my pen rightly receive critical treatment from the readers; nor is this criticism always of the most gentle description, as the following extracts from a critic's remarks will show :—

'Mr Sekon says that Mr —— should have profited by the experience of his predecessor, . . . and should not have brought out the class as six wheel engines. It is true that the leading axles bear a great weight, and that one has already had a bogie substituted, but we may be sure that Mr —— knew all about the "Great Western," and only brought out the new six wheeled engines after mature consideration of every detail. Besides, it is surely not for Mr Sekon, or any other outsider, to criticise . . . the locomotive superintendent of a great railway. . . . I think it would be hasty, to say the least, to attach the

blame, if blame there be, to the locomotive superintendent, as it is quite within the range of
possibility that considerations of expense, or others
of a kindred nature, may have deterred higher
authorities from sanctioning bogies originally for
these engines. . . . Now, I should have thought
that a gentleman who sets himself up to criticise
locomotive superintendents,' etc. ; but although I
answered, and, I think, convinced, or at any rate
silenced, my critical friend, I might have left the
matter in the hands of others—readers of the
journal, several of whom replied to the gentleman's
letter and soundly rated him in more forcible terms
than I could personally have used to him under
the circumstances. I am quite prepared to find
that many readers will differ from me in some
of the conclusions expressed in this book. I
would here remark that I consider the history of
the Great Western Railway of much more interest
than the history of any other railway, for no
other line (save the companies subsidiary to the
Great Western Railway) contains the materials necessary to raise the same excitement as was caused
in engineering and general circles by the construction of the Great Western Railway—for what
other railway engineer was as bold as Isambard
Kingdom Brunel? Who else proposed, let alone
constructed, a colossal railway with the numerous
and perhaps questionable innovations, which were
so successfully carried out on the Great Western

Railway? or what other line has had almost the whole railway world, and most of the prominent engineers, arraigned against it, as did the Great Western Railway during the 'Battle of the Gauges'?

It was the fate of the Great Western Railway— or, more properly speaking, of the 7 feet Gauge— to have been constructed at an inopportune time; had it been proposed a few years earlier, when railways were yet more undeveloped than they were in 1835, or even thirty or forty years later, when the evils of the Narrow Gauge had become generally acknowledged, the result would have been different, and we might have seen a general conversion of the Narrow Gauge to the more commodious Broad Gauge. Had the 'Quadruple Treaty' of 1867-72 been fully carried out, and the Broad Gauge laid down on all the Narrow Gauge lines, and *vice versa* in Devonshire and Cornwall, as was intended, we should have had in operation to-day a larger mileage of wide gauge lines than existed in the most palmy days of Brunel's conception.

My grateful thanks are due to F. G. Saunders, Esq., the Chairman of Directors of the Great Western Railway, for the honour he has done me in revising the proofs of this work, and also to G. K. Mills, Esq., the Secretary of the Railway, both for information supplied and for help he has accorded me in supplying correct dates, statistics, etc. While the great interest both these gentlemen have taken in the production of this book has been most encouraging to me.

In conclusion, I must apologise to the general reader if he finds I have written in a somewhat technical strain, for, although I have avoided railway phraselogy when possible, I fear that, being used to writing in such terms, I have at times forgotten myself and indulged in phrases perhaps somewhat unfamiliar to the general reader. The only other history of the Great Western Railway was published forty-eight years ago, and cost £4, 14s. 6d. per copy, so that I think it cannot be denied that a cheaper and up-to-date work on the subject is requisite.

And now I leave the story of the Broad Gauge to my readers' judgment, and hope it may, in some degree at least, instruct and interest them.

G. A. SEKON.

London, N.
January 1895.

ILLUSTRATIONS

———o———

CONTENTS

———o———

A HISTORY OF

THE GREAT WESTERN RAILWAY

BEING THE

Story of the Broad Gauge

———◆———

CHAPTER I.

THE INCEPTION OF THE GREAT WESTERN RAILWAY.

THE merchants of Bristol, ever in the van of improvement, and always ready to adopt any new measure
that would enlarge their commerce, were among the
earliest of those who clearly saw the great advantages
to be derived from railway communication with other
parts of the country, and especially with London ; the
usual method of transit for goods between the two places
at that time being the Avon and Thames at either end,
and the round-about system of canals connecting at
Bath with the Avon, and at Reading with the Thames.
This water communication provided only a very costly
and very tedious mode of transit, liable to be stopped
by the drought of summer and the frost of winter, so
that for want of a quicker and cheaper connection between Bristol and London, the manufacturers and
merchants of the former place found themselves shut
out of many of the most important markets for their
merchandise.

As early as 1825, the merchants of Bristol had tried
to form a company to construct a railway to London,
but at that time the general public knew nothing of
steam in connection with railways, so that no support

could be obtained, and the proposal was dropped; but in the autumn of 1832 a committee was formed which determined to proceed with the matter, and an engineer was advertised for.

Isambard Kingdom Brunel was advised to apply for the appointment, and told he was likely to obtain it, as he was known and popular at Bristol in connection with his attempt to construct a suspension bridge over the Avon at Clifton, but which had been temporarily abandoned for lack of funds. He was also told that the committee would appoint as engineer, the person who guaranteed to construct the line for the least amount of money. His answer to this was,—'You are holding out a premium to the man who will make you the most flattering promise, and it is quite obvious that the man who has either the least reputation at stake, or who has most to gain by temporary success, and least to lose by the consequences of disappointment, must be the winner in such a race.' Despite this fearless expression of his views, he was appointed Engineer March 7th, 1833, and at once commenced the survey of the country between London and Bristol. After going over the several districts through which the line might have been constructed, he chose the course now occupied by the Great Western Railway, and having finished his surveys in June, no time was lost by the Committee, for on July 30th, 1833, the Mayor of Bristol called a public meeting of the inhabitants, and it was then resolved to form a company to construct a railway from Bristol to London. A local Board of Directors was formed, the Corporation, Dock Company and Society of Merchant Venturers each having official representatives on the Board in addition to the several general merchants and gentlemen elected Directors at the meeting. A somewhat similar Board of Directors was chosen in London, and preparations were at once made to prepare a Bill for the next session of Parliament.

The prospectus first issued asked for a capital of £3,000,000 to be subscribed, this was to build the sections of the railway from London to Reading, and from Bath to Bristol. The Company was duly constituted a month after the issue of the prospectus. Mr Brunel was exceedingly busy during all this time till late in the year preparing the necessary plans to deposit in Parliament. The Bill ' to construct a railway from London to Reading, and from Bath to Bristol, as a means of facilitating the ultimate establishment of a railway between London and Bristol,' was introduced in the House of Commons on 10th March 1834. At first the line was proposed to enter London on the south side of the Thames, but afterwards the Directors altered their plans, and substituted a viaduct, 24 feet high with a parapet 6 feet 6 inches high on either side, to prevent the passengers looking into the houses as they travelled; the terminus was then to be at Vauxhall on the river bank, abutting on the north end of the bridge. The Commissioners of Metropolitan Roads offered strenuous opposition to the Viaduct crossing Piccadilly.

The second reading was carried by 184 votes to 90, and on April 10th, the Bill went before the Committee, of which Lord Granville Somerset was chairman.

On the 13th day of the sitting of the Committee, the Railway Company abandoned the idea of a terminus at Vauxhall, and instead proposed to locate it at South Kensington near the ' Hoop and Toy' Public House. This gave up that part of the line that passed through Chelsea, and by this concession the Directors would have saved £80,141 in construction, and also hoped to prevent the opposition of the noblemen who owned the property between Brompton and Vauxhall, but without effect, for the counsel who appeared for the Brompton property owners, objected to the nuisance caused by a railway being allowed at Brompton, which he described as 'the most famous of any place in the neighbourhood of London for the salubrity of its air, and calculated for retired residences.'

It was proved in evidence that three days at the very least, and under the most favourable circumstances, were required to convey goods from Reading to London (80 miles) by river, and one day under the best auspices, from Bristol to Bath. The times the railway undertook to perform the journey from London to

		h. m.	Distance
Slough	was	0.45	$18\frac{1}{2}$ miles
Reading	,,	1.25	36 ,,
Oxford	,.	2.30	$63\frac{1}{2}$,.
Swindon	,,	3.0	$77\frac{1}{4}$,.
Bath	,,	4.10	108 ,,
Bristol	,,	4.35	$118\frac{1}{2}$,,

On the London and Birmingham the trains took, to Watford, $17\frac{1}{2}$ miles, 59 minutes; Leighton, $40\frac{1}{4}$ miles, 2 hours 17 minutes; Blisworth, $62\frac{3}{4}$ miles, 3 hours and 32 minutes; Crick, $75\frac{1}{4}$ miles, 4 hours 11 minutes; Hampton, $100\frac{1}{2}$ miles, 5 hours 35 minutes; and Birmingham, $112\frac{1}{4}$ miles, 6 hours and 14 minutes. The London and Birmingham Railway only obtained their Act of Incorporation on 6th May 1833, so that, when less than 12 months after, another railway proposed to travel 6 miles more in 1 hour 39 minutes less time, it appeared to the public, whose idea of express travelling was limited to a mail coach at 10 miles an hour, that such a speed was utterly impossible of accomplishment, and when Mr Brunel, in giving his evidence, stated that he hoped to go by steam at the rate of 100 miles an hour, the incredulous laughter and the shouts of derision were appalling.

Mr Brunel was examined for eleven days, and the landowners and others who were interested in the success or non-success of the measure during this time crowded the committee-room day by day. A person who was present thus describes Mr Brunel's

manner during this searching inquiry. 'His knowledge of the country surveyed by him was marvellously great, and the explanations he gave of his
plans, and the answers he returned to questions
suggested by Dr Lardner showed a practical acquaintance with the principles of mechanics. He
was rapid in thought, clear in language, and never
said too much, or lost his presence of mind. I do
not remember having enjoyed so great an intellectual
treat as that of listening to Brunel's examination,
and I was told at the time that George Stephenson
and many others were much struck by the ability
and knowledge shown by him.'

In 1834 a certain wiseacre — Cort by name—
possessed sufficient conceit to publish a work, which
he called *Railway Imposition Detected*, in which
occurs the following specimen of his far-seeing wisdom, or, candidly speaking, of his utter foolishness.
'The Great Western, though probably it may reach
as far as Bath from Bristol, after having, like a mole,
explored its way through tunnels long and deep,
the shareholders who travel by it will be so heartily
sick, what with foul air, smoke and sulphur, that the
very mention of a railway will be worse than
ipecacuanha, especially when the only prospect they
can find the least cheering in the midst of all this
derangement of their stomachs will be a granite
tramway actually in operation alongside of their own
dose of ipecacuanha, ready to follow up the black draft,
so as to get rid of every particle of obstruction with
which the bottoms of their pockets may otherwise
be afflicted.'

All the principal engineers of the time, including
George Stephenson, were called in support of the
scheme, the engineering evidence being forty-two days
before the Committee. The principal points relied
upon for the opposition were, the impossibility of constructing the Box Tunnel, and the fragmentary nature
of the proposal before Parliament—it was described as

neither 'Great' nor 'Western,' nor even a 'railway,' 'but a head and a tail of a concern, 72 miles apart, which would never be joined by a body.' The authorities of Eton College and the University of Oxford were among the most vehement of the opposition; indeed, after the Bill was thrown out, the Marquis of Chandos presided over a public meeting at Salt Hill, Slough, to commemorate the defeat of the measure.

On the fifty-fourth day Mr Harrison, K.C., commenced his speech in reply for the promoters, and on the fifty-seventh day the Committee passed the Bill. It was then introduced into the House of Lords, and the second reading was moved by Lord Wharncliffe, when 30 contents and 47 non-contents voted, and consequently the Bill was lost, £30,000 having been spent upon the parliamentary proceedings. In this Bill the gauge was to be 4 feet 8½ inches.

The Directors were not daunted by their non-success, and they at once commenced to prepare a new scheme for the next parliamentary session. The South Kensington Terminus was abandoned, and in its place, it was proposed to join the London and Birmingham line at Kensal Green, and use the 4 miles of that line thence to Euston, which was to be a joint station. The capital was reduced to two and a half millions, with borrowing powers to the extent of £833,333, and as the last Bill, in consequence of only part of the line being proposed to be constructed, was described as no railway at all, but 'a gross deception, a trick and a fraud upon the public, in name, in title, and in substance,' upon this occasion the promoters undertook to construct the whole of the line. The second reading took place on March 9th, 1835 (the earliest allowable date, according to the standing orders). One hundred and sixty members voted in favour of the second reading, and only the tellers on the other side.

Mr C. Russell was appointed the Chairman of Committee, and a resolution was passed that no evidence was required as to the public advantage of the railway, so that the only evidence the opponents of the measure were able to bring forward was as to the bad course adopted for the railway. The Box Tunnel bogie was trotted out again and made the most of, and another route, from Basingstoke to Bath, was described as the best one possible for the railway, as such a line would avoid 'the monstrous and extraordinary, most dangerous and impracticable tunnel at Box,' but without avail, for the Bill passed the Commons again, and on May 27th was read the first time in the House of Lords. The second reading was on June 10th, the voting being 46 contents and 34 non-contents. The Bill then came before the Lords' Committee, who heard the evidence in favour of it for eighteen days. Sergeant Mereweather, who was leading counsel for the opposition, made a speech which lasted for four days in opening the opponents' case, but despite this, the Bill passed safely through the Committee stage, was read a third time on August 27th, and received the Royal Assent August 31st, 1835. The official title of the Act being 5 and 6 Wm. IV. cap. 107. The preamble of which commences :—'Whereas the making of a railway from Bristol to join the London and Birmingham Railway near London, and also branches to Trowbridge and Bradford in the county of Wilts, would be of great public advantage, not only by opening an additional, certain and expeditious communication between the cities and towns aforesaid, but also by improving the existing communication between the Metropolis and the western districts of England, the South of Ireland and Wales, and whence,' etc.

No mention of the gauge was made in the Bill, Mr Brunel purposely having omitted that item. The Provost and Fellows of Eton College obtained the insertion of a clause forbidding the erection of a station at Slough, and also requiring the Railway Company to provide policemen to patrol the line for a certain distance each side of Slough to prevent the Eton boys from straying on the line, and so possibly being run over by the trains, but the Great Western Railway was not deterred by this clause. Railway directors are as well able (and generally much better able) to drive the proverbial coach and four through an act of parliament as ordinary mortals. The Act said they were *not to build a station at Slough.* Very well, then, they did not do so, but the Act did not enact that the trains were not to *stop at Slough,* so for offices two rooms were hired in a public house adjoining the railway at Slough. And from the very first opening of the line the trains stopped there and put down and took up passengers, who were doubtless a little inconvenienced by having no platform to alight on, or depart from, but they were able to go to and from Slough nevertheless.

This quick-wittedness of the Great Western Railway made the Eton College officials furious, and on the 2d June 1838 they applied for an injunction in Chancery against the railway for breaking their Act of Incorporation in stopping at Slough, but the legal arguments of the railway counsel soon made it clear to the judge, that the *Act had been observed* and duly abided by, and the application of the College was refused. The authorities of the Oxford University also obtained the insertion in the Bill of a clause by which the station at Oxford was to be erected at a spot as distant as possible from the Colleges. Thus was the inauguration of the most colossal railway of our empire established by the law makers of nearly sixty years ago, adding a profitless burden of £89,436, 13s. 3d. to the capital of the Company.* But every *magnum opus* must be established *lex terræ.*

The original capital did not suffice to construct the line, so in 1839 an Act was obtained for raising £1,250,000 stock, and £416,000 by way of loan, in addition to the amount already authorised.

* The amount of money expended in obtaining the Act of Incorporation.

CHAPTER II.

THE CONSTRUCTION OF THE LINE.

HAVING in the previous chapter dwelt with the several parliamentary fights, which finally resulted in giving the Great Western Railway the necessary powers to construct the line, we will now proceed to chronicle the building of this remarkable railway.

We must recollect, that at this period there was no settled practice as to the mode of forming a line of railway, the only real example then existing, being the Liverpool and Manchester, which was then about four years old, so that it is not surprising that the style set by George Stephenson—which style is acknowledged by everyone—including the greatest worshippers of this truly remarkable millwright—to be of a very contracted and niggardly description,—was not followed. On the other hand, had the practice of railway construction been settled, for that very reason Isambard Kingdom Brunel, who was the last man to follow in the conventional style of other engineers, would have proceeded with his work in an entirely independent way, and with a mode of detail completely his own, as indeed he did in this instance, and which he carried out in his usual dauntless manner, well worthy of the master mind he undoubtedly possessed.

In the previous chapter we mentioned that the Great Western Railway upon one occasion proposed to use the Euston Station as a terminus jointly with the London and Birmingham Railway, the idea being that the former railway should join the latter on the London side of the present Willesden Junction, or as the Act of Incorporation defines it, 'in a certain field lying between the Paddington Canal and the turnpike road leading from London to Harrow, on the western side of the General Cemetery.'

This then accounts for the Great Western Railway approaching so closely to the London and North-Western Railway at Wormwood Scrubs, near Willesden Junction.

Most writers have stated that the difference in

THE ORIGINAL PADDINGTON TERMINUS, 1845.

gauge of the two lines caused the abandonment of the proposed joint station at Euston Square, but this is incorrect, the real reason being a difference between the two Companies as to their respective rights of using the 4 miles of line from Willesden to Euston Square. Although the Company had no Act for the construction of the line from Wormwood Scrubs to Paddington, the Directors made but little stir about such an important preliminary, but commenced to purchase the necessary land and to build the line, obtaining official sanction for their proceedings afterwards.

The Act for the extension to Paddington, and for the erection of the station 'in a certain field at Paddington,' was obtained in 1836. It will be well to describe this station at once, since it is the starting point of the Great Western Railway system. The original structure was quite a temporary one, the booking offices being under the Bishop's Road Bridge. The original station is depicted in the illustration opposite. The present station was not commenced till 1849, and was completed in 1854.

It is the Paddington departure platform that is depicted in Mr Frith's inimitable picture, and one of the principal figures there portrayed (Mr Craig, the ticket inspector,) only retired from active service at the station towards the end of 1893. This picture always had a great charm for the writer, and when as a little boy he first went to a boarding school, he distinctly remembers that, upon being ushered into the library to see the headmaster, an engraving of this picture which hung upon the wall completely engaged his attention, and in a measure drove away his sense of loneliness and natural desire to return with his father, although he had never before slept from beneath the paternal roof.

The platforms are 700 feet long, the width of the building being 238 feet; the roof is divided by two rows of columns into three spans, the outside ones being each 68 feet wide, and the middle one 102 feet. These are crossed at two places by transepts each 50 feet wide, the total area being 70 acres. The architecture is a mixture of Italian and Arabesque. The original cost of this station is stated to have been £650,000. With regard to the levels of the railway, Paddington Station is 50 feet higher than Bristol Station. For the first 2¾ miles the line rises

3 feet per mile. At 2¾ miles from Paddington the line was crossed on a level at right angles by the Birmingham, Bristol and Thames Junction Railway, incorporated 21st June 1836. This line is now known as the West London Railway, and is leased to the London and North Western and Great Western Railways jointly for 999 years, from 11th March 1845, at a rent of £1800 per annum.

At this spot the London and North Western and Great Western Railways are only a third of a mile apart. The West London line had here an unusual structure, on the lowest level of which, in a tunnel, was the railway ; on the ground level, the Paddington Canal crossing the line at right angles by means of an aqueduct, and above this a public road bridge across the canal. This level crossing existed till 1860, when the Great Western Railway, having in the previous year obtained powers, deviated the railway and substituted an over bridge for the level crossing. The line rises 4 feet in the mile till the 7¼ mile post is reached, and here we have one of the many remarkable engineering achievements for which this line is famous—the Wharncliffe Viaduct. The Great Western Railway was at the time of its construction truly described as 'the most gigantic work, not only in Great Britain, not only in Europe, but in the entire world,' and taking the Great Western Railway system in its completeness as it exists to-day, the words still remain true despite the very many stupendous engineering triumphs that have since been gained in other parts of the Universe. Nor did Brunel himself underrate the importance of the work he was engaged in, for on the 26th December 1835 he wrote in his diary this short but expressive sentence :—' I am engineer to the finest work in England.'

The first important edifice ' on the finest work in England' is this Hanwell Viaduct, called the Wharncliffe Viaduct in honour of Lord Wharncliffe, the

Chairman of the Committee in the House of Lords that passed the Great Western Railway Bill. It is to this nobleman's enlightened intelligence that railways are also indebted for the title of Wharncliffe Meeting, as applied to the principal statutory meetings of their shareholders.

The Wharncliffe Viaduct spans the valley of the Brent, which rises at Mill Hill and, proceeding by a winding course, enters the Thames at Brentford. The ravine to be crossed by the railway is 70 feet deep, and the viaduct is 896 feet long and 30 feet wide; it is supported by eight elliptical arches with a spring of 18 feet and a span of 70 feet. The piers from which these arches spring have a broad brick platform as a foundation, a pair of immense columns rise from these, and their summits are united by massive architraves, and so form single piers from which the elliptical arches spring. When first erected, an engineer thus described the viaduct :—' The shafts are brick, but the capitals are formed of large stone blocks, swelling out with a gentle sweep, and ending in a massive bold torus. The architrave is also of stone, and a second course of stone blocks above it, tapered to an obtuse angle, serves at once as a finish to the column on the side view, and as a skew back to both the arches which spring from it on opposite sides. Each column taken by itself is thus an architectural whole ; and each pair connected below by the square basement, and uniting above in the same architrave, forms a handsome and consistent pier. The string course above the arches, by which all these are connected, is of the same kind of stone—bold, similar in style, but smaller than the mouldings on the capitals of the piers, and the parapet is surmounted by a square stone coping. The abutments have a still more solid character, and the whole produces the effect of strength without heaviness, massiveness without inelegance, in such perfect harmony with the great purposes of railway construction as to render this bridge a remarkable instance of successful architectural invention.   As a piece of masonry the work is also perfect ; it is everywhere accurately formed, well put together, dry, and in good condition.   The arches consist of eight courses of brick about 36 inches in thickness.   No one should leave this bridge without going under one of the extreme arches and looking along through the openings in the piers to the other extremity, where he will see a cyclopean colonnade stretching far away in distant perspective, and carry away with him a memorable and not unpleasing impression.'

Adjoining the viaduct is an immense earth embankment—the largest on the line—being three-quarters of a mile in length and about 70 feet high, the foundation being of clay, but composed of ' all sorts of other things,' so the Great Western officials used to say.   A remarkable fact in connection with this embankment was its disappearance.   The subsoil on which the clay surface rested was of a treacherous description, and the immense weight of the materials forming the embankment caused the subsoil to give way, and the clay and other materials sunk from view, but the continual pressure of the upper part of the embankment forced the foundation along the surface of the slippery stratum, and where this cropped out again the lower part of the embankment arose on either side of its original site.   Shortly after the viaduct, the line crosses the Uxbridge Road by a skew bridge of peculiar design (one of the girders of this bridge gave way in 1839, but the contractor had to replace it at his own expense).   It was at first partly composed of wood, and a few years later was burnt down, but rebuilt afterwards, when it was made entirely of iron.

The line continues to rise 4 feet per mile till $9\frac{3}{4}$ miles from Paddington is reached, when for half a mile the line is level ; this is the first summit, and the Paddington and Grand Junction Canals are here crossed over by bridges.   The line then falls for $2\frac{1}{2}$ miles at the ruling gradient of 4 feet per mile. This brings us to West Drayton, 13 miles from London, the first principal station, and the place where the original locomotives were delivered by canal and placed upon the rails under the superintendence of Mr Daniel Gooch, the first locomotive superintendent of the railway. The line is level to the 15½ mile post. Shortly after the ' Dog Kennel' Bridge is passed through, the line falls at the usual rate till 17¼ miles are reached, it then rises 2 feet in the mile to the twentieth mile post. The first portion of the line completed was from West Drayton to the Dog Kennel Bridge. Slough Station is 18 miles from Paddington, and is the first of the first-class ones on the line. Acting on the old idea that railways and trains were only roads and coaches of an improved description, this station was built on one side of the line only, with a single platform at which both the up and down trains stopped. The station was indeed meant to be a roadside inn, and the platform the ' Pull up' for the coaches. Reading, the next important station, was also built on this principle, and is only now being modernised. The first section of the line extended to the London side of the river at Maidenhead, 23 miles from Paddington. Having reached this point, it will be well to describe the peculiarities of the original system of permanent way employed on this portion of the railway, which was of such an unsatisfactory nature that it was all taken up, resulting in a dead loss of capital of £97,267, 2s. 5d., which was the cost of relaying that part of the line ; the work was spread over several years, not being finally completed till 1846.

But before doing so, we will mention that the first great point of difference between the Great Western Railway and other railways was the gauge. No settled one had been decided, several different ones being in use, but none were so wide as the 7 feet one adopted by Mr Brunel for the Great Western Railway. The entire width of the line was 30 feet, made up as follows :—

Rails, up and down line, 7 feet
gauge, ...   14 feet
Width between up and down line,   6 ,,
Space on the outside of up and
down line, 5 feet each,   .   .   10 ,,
_____
30 feet

while the extreme width of the Manchester and Liverpool Railway was only 19 feet 8 inches.

The original reason given by Mr Brunel for adopting the 7 feet was, that it would allow of larger wheels being used, so that the bodies of the carriages fitted in between the wheels like ordinary road coaches; only one carriage, however, appears to have been built on this principle.

The bridges were 16 feet high as compared with 13 feet 6 inches on other lines; other points of difference were the levelness of the railway compared with other railways, most of the difference being collected in two places, at which it was proposed to use additional engine power; continuous timber bearings in place of stone blocks or cross sleepers; 'bridge' pattern rails; and larger radii of the curves. Mr N. Wood thus describes the original permanent way :—' The rails are longitudinal and are 14 to 15 inches wide and 6 or 7 inches thick, and are made of American pine, the sleepers are 6 inches in breadth and 7 inches deep, the transverse sleepers 6 inches in breadth and 9 inches deep. These sleepers are stretched across the line of railway, and to them the longitudinal rails are secured, the piles in the cuttings are from 9 to 14 feet in length, according to the nature of the material, and in the embankments 12 to 30 feet, or of such a length as that they will reach from the base or formation line of the railway 6 to 8 feet into the original surface of the ground. The cross ties are American pine, and the piles of beech. The piles were driven at intervals of every 15 feet, and in the middle between the longitudinal rails. In cuttings they are driven from 8 to 10 feet into the ground below the level of the cross sleepers, and on embankments they must be of such a length as to be driven about the same depth, or 7 or 8 feet into the original ground. Upon an embankment of 3 feet they must be, therefore, 10 or 12 feet long; 6 feet, 13 to 14 feet long, and so on, according to the height of the embankment and the kind of subsoil into which they are to be driven. The double cross timbers are laid down 13 inches, and the single timbers 9 inches below the line of the rails. Between the double timbers, and also at all the other points where the longitudinal rails intersect the cross timbers, a piece of wood is interposed, which is pinned to the cross timbers and upon which the longitudinal rails rest. The longitudinal rails are then laid down upon the cross timbers, the upper surface of which is 3 inches below the surface of the iron rails; they are bolted to the cross timbers with screw bolts and washers. When the timbers have all been throughly packed up, and rammed and strained to the utmost, and the general levels of the whole found to be correct, then the upper surface of the longitudinal timbers is adzed, or planed down to one uniform surface. A plank of hard wood, American elm, oak or ash, about $1\frac{1}{2}$ inches thick and 8 inches broad, is then laid upon the longitudinal timbers, the upper surface being sloped inwards at an angle of 1 in 20. This hard wood plank is laid on with a good thick bed of tar, and nailed down with 2 shilling nails, these nails being driven in two parallel rows, $2\frac{1}{2}$ and $5\frac{1}{2}$ inches apart on each timber, so as not to interfere with the bolts, the heads of the nails are well punched in, to allow of planing the wood. The surfaces of all joints and butts, and the whole of the bottom and sides of the longitudinal timbers; all bolts, washers, keys, spikes and nails, and all other ironwork are well tarred.

'The rail used weighs from 43 to 44 lbs. per yard, and which rests upon and is secured to the hard wood plank and timbers of the longitudinal sills in the following manner :—The upper surface of the hard wood is planed and levelled, the iron rails are then laid down perfectly straight, and fitting each other at the joinings correctly.   A space is allowed at each joint for the expansion and contraction, and the joints are made to correspond with each other on opposite sides of the railway.   The rail is fastened to the hard wood and longitudinal sills by screw bolts, a piece of felt being interposed between the base of the rails and the timber. The outside screws have square heads, but the inside screws are made with counter-sunk heads, on account of the flange of the wheel.   The outside screw is tightened until the rail fits close to the timber ; the inner one is next screwed as tight as possible ; a roller weighing about 10 tons is then passed two or three times along the rails, which is followed close by the screwing, and, consequently, the bolts are thus much more firmly screwed than could be done by any screw-driver alone.   The rails have a slight bevel inwards.'

As early as 1836 a section of the shareholders, chiefly those in the north of England, who, in consequence of their location, were probably prejudiced in favour of the narrow gauge, commenced to complain of the gauge of the Great Western Railway.   This was in a measure quieted by the Directors' Report, issued on 25th August 1836 ; but two years later, soon after the opening of the line, the agitations broke out with renewed vigour, in consequence of which Mr Brunel prepared an elaborate report, defending his method of construction, etc.   We give this report here, as it fully describes the state of affairs at this time.

REPORT TO THE BOARD OF DIRECTORS OF THE GREAT WESTERN RAILWAY COMPANY.

15th August 1838.

GENTLEMEN,—As the endeavour to obtain the opinions and reports of Mr Walker, Mr Stephenson, and Mr Wood, prior to the next half-yearly meeting, has not been successful, I am anxious to record more fully than I have previously done, and to combine them into one report, my own views and opinions upon the success of the several plans which have been adopted at my recommendation in the formation and in the working of our line. And in justice to myself and to these plans, and, indeed, to enable others to arrive at any just conclusion as to the result which has been attained, or as to the probable ultimate success or advantages of the system, it is necessary that I should enter very fully, I fear even tediously, into a recapitulation of the circumstances peculiar to this railway, which led to the consideration and adoption of these plans, which some call innovations and wide deviations from the results of past experience, but the majority of which I will undertake to show are merely adaptations of those plans to our particular circumstances. It will be necessary also that I should refer to all the numerous difficulties which we have had to encounter, which have necessarily prevented the perfect working of these plans in the first instance, but which have been overcome, or which are gradually and successively diminishing; and, finally, I am prepared to show that, notwithstanding the novelty of the circumstances, and the difficulties and delays which at the outset invariably attend any alteration, however necessary or desirable, from the accustomed mode of proceeding, and notwithstanding the violent prejudices excited against us, and the increased difficulties caused by these prejudices, the result is still such as to justify the attempt which has been made, and to show that in the main features, if not in all the details, the system hitherto followed is good, and ought to be pursued.

The peculiarity of the circumstances of this railway, to which I would more particularly refer, and which have frequently been mentioned, consists in the unusually favourable gradients and curves which we have been able to obtain. With the capabilities of carrying the line upwards of 50 miles out of London on almost a dead level, and without any objectionable curve, and having beyond this, and for the whole distance to Bristol, excellent gradients, it was thought that unusually high speed might easily be attained, and that the very large extent of passenger traffic, which such a line would certainly command, would ensure a return for any advantages which could be offered to the public, either in increased speed or increased accommodations.

With this view, every possible attention was paid to the improvement of the line as originally laid down in the parliamentary plans. We ultimately succeeded in determining a maximum gradient of 4 feet per mile, which could be maintained for the unusual distance before mentioned of upwards of 50 miles from London, and also between Bristol and Bath, comprehending those parts of the line on which the principal portion of the passenger traffic will be carried. The attainment of high speed appeared to involve the question of the width of gauge, and on this point, accordingly, I expressed my opinion at a very early period. It has been asserted that 4 feet 8 inches, the width adopted on the Liverpool and Manchester Railway, is exactly the proper width for all railways, and that to adopt any other dimension is to deviate from a positive rule which experience has proved correct; but such an assertion can be maintained by no reasoning. Admitting, for the sake of argument, that, under the particular circumstances in which it has been tried, 4 feet 8 inches has been proved the best possible dimension, the question would still remain—What are the best dimensions under the circumstances? Although a breadth of 4 feet 8 inches has been found to create a certain resistance on curves of a certain radius, a greater breadth would only produce the same resistance on curves of greater radius. If carriages and engines, and more particularly if wheels and axles of a certain weight, have not been found inconvenient upon one railway, greater weights may be employed and the same results obtained on a railway with better gradients. To adopt a gauge of the same number of inches on the Great Western Railway as are on the Grand Junction Railway, would, in fact, amount practically to the use of a different gauge in similar railways. The gauge which is well adapted to the one is not well adapted to the other, unless, indeed, some mysterious cause exists which has never yet been explained for the empirical law which would fix the gauge under all circumstances.

Fortunately this no longer requires to be argued, as too many authorities may now be quoted in support of a very considerable deviation from this prescribed width, and in every case this change has been an increase. I take it for granted that in determining the dimensions in each case due regard has been had to the curves and gradients of the line which ought to form a most essential if not the principal condition. In the report of the Commissioners upon Irish railways, the arguments are identically the same with those which I used when first addressing you on the subject in my report of October 1835.

The mechanical advantage to be gained by increasing the diameter of the carriage wheels is pointed out, the necessity to attain this, of increasing the width of way, the dimensions of the bridges, tunnels and other principal works, not being materially affected by this; but, on the other hand, the circumstance which limits this increase being the curves on the line, and the increased proportional resistance on inclinations (and on this account it is stated to be almost solely applicable to very level lines); and lastly, the increased expense, which could be justified only by a very large traffic. The whole is clearly argued in a general point of view and then applied to the particular case, and the result of this application is the recommendation of the adoption of 6 feet 2 inches on the Irish railways. Thus an increase in the breadth of way to attain one particular object, viz., the capability of increasing the diameter of the carriage wheels without raising the bodies of the carriages, is admitted to be most desirable, but is limited by certain circumstances, namely, the gradients and curves of the line, and the extent of traffic. Every argument here adduced and every calculation would tend to the adoption of about 7 feet on the Great Western Railway.

The gradients of the lines laid down by the Irish Commission are considerably steeper than those of the London and Birmingham Railway, and four and five times the inclination of those on the Great Western Railway. The curves are by no means of very large radius, and, indeed, the Commissioners, after fixing the gauge of 6 feet 2 inches, express their opinion that, upon examination into the question of curves, with a view to economy, they do not find the effect is so injurious as might have been anticipated, and imply therefore that curves, generally considered of small radius on our English lines, are not incompatible with the 6 feet 2 inch gauge; and lastly, the traffic, instead of being unusually large so as to justify any expense beyond that absolutely required, is such as to render assistance from Government necessary to ensure a return for the capital embarked. As compared with this, what are the circumstances in our case?

The object to be obtained, is the placing an ordinary coach body, which is upwards of 6 feet 6 inches in width between wheels. This necessarily involves a gauge of rail about 6 feet $10\frac{1}{2}$ inches to 6 feet 11 inches, but 7 feet allows of it being done easily; it allows, moreover, of a different arrangement of the body; it admits of all sorts of carriages, stage coaches and carts to be carried between the wheels. And what are the limits in the case of the Great Western Railway, as compared to those on the Irish railways? Gradients of one-fifth the inclination, very favourable curves, and probably the largest traffic in England. I think it unnecessary to say another word to show that the Irish Commissioners would have arrived at 7 feet on the Great Western Railway by exactly the same train of argument that led them to adopt 6 feet 2 inches in the case then before them. All these arguments were advanced by me in my first report to you, and the subject well considered. The circumstance of the Great Western Railway, and other principal railways likely to extend beyond it, having no connection with other lines then made, leaving us free from any prescribed dimension, the 7 feet gauge was ultimately determined upon.

Many objections were certainly urged against it; the deviation from the established 4 feet 8 inches was then considered as the abandonment of the principle. This, however, was a mere assertion, unsupported even by plausible argument, and was gradually disused; but objections were still urged that the original cost of construction of all the works connected with the formation of the line must be greatly increased, that the carriages must be so much stronger, that they would be proportionately heavier, that they would not run round the curves, and would be more liable to run off the rails, and, particularly, that the increased length of the axles would render them liable to be broken; and these objections were not advanced as difficulties which, as existing in all railways, might be somewhat increased by the increase of gauge, but as peculiar to this and fatal to the system. With regard to the first objection, namely, the increased cost in the original construction of the line, if there be any, it is a question of calculation which is easily estimated, and was so estimated before the increased gauge was determined upon. Here, however, preconceived opinions have been allowed weight, in lieu of arguments and calculations cause and effect are mixed up, and without much consideration it was assumed at once that an increased gauge necessarily involved width of way, and dimensions of bridges, tunnels, etc.

Yet such is not the case within the limits we are now treating of; a 7 feet rail requires no wider bridge or tunnel than a 5 feet; the breadth is governed by a maximum width allowed for a loaded waggon, or the largest load to be carried on the railway, and the clear space to be allowed on either side beyond this. On the Manchester and Liverpool Railway this total breadth is only 9 feet 10 inches, and the bridge and viaducts need only have been twice this, or 19 feet 8 inches; 9 feet 10 inches was found, however, rather too small, and in the London and Birmingham, with the same width of way, this was increased to 11 feet by widening the interval between the two rails. In the space of 11 feet allowed for each rail, a 7 feet gauge might be placed just as well as a 5 feet, leaving the bridges, tunnels and viaducts exactly the same, but 11 feet was thought by some still too narrow; and when it is remembered that this barely allows a width of 10 feet for loads, whether of cotton, wool, agricultural produce, or other light goods, and which are liable also to be displaced in travelling, 13 feet (which has been fixed upon in the Great Western Railway, and which limits the maximum breadth under any circumstances to about 12 feet) will not be found excessive.

It is this which makes the mininium width actually required under bridges and tunnels 26 feet instead of 22 feet, and not the increased gauge.

The earthwork is slightly affected by the gauge, but only to the extent of 2 feet on the embankment, and not quite so much in the cuttings; but what in practice has been the result? The bridges over the railway on the London and Birmingham are 30 feet and the width of viaducts 28 feet; on the Great Western Railway they are both 30 feet. No great expense is therefore incurred on these items, and certainly a very small one compared to the increased space gained, which, as I have stated, is from 10 to 12 feet. In the tunnels exists the greatest difference. On the London and Birmingham Railway, to which I refer to as being the best and most analagous case to that of the Great Western Railway, the tunnels are 24 feet wide. On the Great Western Railway the constant width of 30 feet is maintained, more with a view of diminishing the objections to tunnels and maintaining the same minimum space which hereafter may form a limit to the size and form of everything carried on the railway, than from such a width being absolutely necessary. Without pretending to find fault with the dimensions fixed, and which have no doubt been well considered upon the works or other lines, I may state that the principle which has governed has been to fix the minimum width, and to make all the works the same, considering it unnecessary to have a greater width between the parapet walls of a viaduct, which admits of being altered, than between the walls of a tunnel which cannot be altered. The embankments on the London and Birmingham Railway are 26 feet, on the Great Western 30 feet, making an excess of about 6½ per cent. on the actual quantity of earthwork. The difference in the quantity of land required is under half an acre to a mile. On the whole, the increased dimensions from 10 to 12 feet will not cause any average increased expense in the construction of the works, and purchase of land of above 7 per cent.— 8 per cent. having originally been assumed in my report in 1835 as the excess to be provided for. With respect to the weight of the carriages, although we have wheels of 4 feet diameter, instead of 3 feet, which of course involves an increased weight quite independent of the increase of width, and although the space allowed for each passenger is a trifle more, and the height of the body greater, yet the gross weight per passenger is somewhat less.

	Tons.	Cwt.	Qrs.	Lbs.
A Birmingham first-class coach weighs	3	17	2	0
With eighteen passengers at fifteen to the ton weighs	1	4	0	0
	5	1	2	0

or 631 lbs. per passenger ;

	Tons.	Cwt.	Qrs.	Lbs.
A Great Western first-class weighs	4	14	0	0
And with twenty-four passengers weighs	1	12	0	0
	6	6	0	0

or 588 lbs. per passenger ;

	Tons.	Cwt.	Qrs.	Lbs.
And our six-wheeled first-class weighs	6	11	0	0
With thirty-two passengers weighs	2	2	2	0
	8	13	2	0

or 600 lbs. per passenger ;

being an average of 594 lbs. on the two carriages. This saving of weight does not arise from the increased width, and is notwithstanding the increased strength of the framing and the increased diameter and weight of the wheels. I have not weighed our second-class open carriages, but I should think the same proportion would exist. As to the breaking of axles or running off the line, the practical result has been that, from some cause or other, we have been almost perfectly free from those very objections which have been felt so seriously on some other lines.

Far from breaking any engine axles, not even a single cranked axle has been strained, although the engines have been subjected to rather severe trials. One of our largest having, a short time back, been sent along the line at night when it was not expected, came in collision with some ballast waggons and was thrown off the line nearly 6 feet. None of the axles were bent, or even strained in the least, although the front of the carriage, a piece of oak of very large scantling, was shattered.

After ten weeks running, one solitary instance has occurred of a carriage in a train getting off the line and dragging another with it, and which was not discovered till after running a mile and a half. As the carriage was in the middle of a train, and one end of the axle was thrown completely out of the axle-guard, there must evidently have been some extra-ordinary cause—possibly a plank thrown across the railway by a blow from the carriage which preceded, and which might have produced the same effect on any railway; and, at anyrate, it was a strong trial to the axle, which was not broken but merely restored to its place, and the carriage sent on to London. The same mode of reasoning, which has by some been used in favour of the 4 feet 8 inches gauge, if applied here, would prove that long axles are stronger than short, and wide rails best adapted for curves. All that I think proved, however, is this, that the increased tendency of the axles to break, or of the wheels to run off the lines, is so slight that it is more than counterbalanced by the increased steadiness from the width of the base and the absence of those violent strains which arise from irregularity on the gauge and the harshness of the ordinary construction of rails. In fact, not one of the objections originally urged against the practical working of the wide gauge has been found to exist, while the object sought for is obtained, namely, the capability of increasing at any future period the diameter of the wheels, which cannot be done, however desirable it may hereafter be found, with the old width of rail. This may be said to be only prospective; but, in the meantime, contingent advantages are sensibly felt in the increased lateral steadiness of the carriages and engines, and the greater space which is afforded for the works of the loco-motives.

And here I wish to call your attentions particularly to the fact that this prospective advantage—this absence of a most convenient limit to the reduction of the friction, which, with our gradients, form four-fifths or 80 per cent. of the total resistance—was the object sought for, and that at the time of recommending it, I expressly stated as follows :—' I am not by any means prepared at present to recommend any particular size of wheel, or even any great increase of the present dimensions, I believe they will be materially increased ; but my great object would be in every way possible to render each part capable of improvement, and to remove what appears an obstacle to any great progress in such a very important point as the diameter of the wheels, upon which the resistance, which governs the cost of transport and the speed that may be obtained, so materially depends.'

These advantages were considered important by you, they are now considered so by many others ; and certainly everything which has occurred in the practical working of the line confirms me in my conviction that we have secured a most valuable power to the Great Western Railway, and that it would be folly to abandon it. The next point I shall consider is the construction of the engines, the modifications in which, necessary to adapt them to higher speeds than usual, have, like the increased width of gauge, been condemned as innovations. I shall not attempt to argue with those who consider any increase of speed unnecessary. The public will always prefer that conveyance which is most perfect, and speed within reasonable limits is a material ingredient in perfection in travelling.

A rate of 35 to 40 miles an hour is not unfrequently attained on other railways in descending planes, or with light loads on a level, and is found practically to be attended with no inconvenience. To maintain such a speed with regularity on a level line, with moderate loads, is therefore quite practicable and unquestionably desirable. With this view the engines were constructed, but nothing new was required or recommended by me. A certain velocity of the piston is considered the most advantageous.

The engines intended for slow speeds have always had the driving wheels small in proportion to the length of stroke of the piston. The faster engines have had a different proportion. The wheels have been larger, or the strokes of the piston shorter. From the somewhat clamorous objections raised against the large wheels, and the construction of the Great Western Railway engines, and the opinions rather freely expressed of my judgment in directing this construction, it would naturally be supposed that some established principle had been departed from, and that I had recommended this departure. The facts are, that a certain velocity of piston being found most advantageous, I fixed this velocity so that the engines should be adapted to run 35 miles an hour, and capable of running 40—as the Manchester and Liverpool Railway engines are best calculated for 20 to 25, but capable of running easily up to 30 and 35 miles per hour; and fixing also the load which the engine was to be capable of drawing, I left the form of construction and the proportions entirely to the manufacturers, stipulating merely that they should submit detail drawings to me for my approval. This was the substance of the circular, which, with your sanction, was sent to several of the most experienced manufacturers. Most of these manufacturers of their own accord, and without previous communication from me, adopted the large wheels as a necessary consequence of the speed required. The recommendation coming from such quarters, there can be no necessity for defending my opinion in its favour; neither have I now the slightest doubt of its correctness. As it has been supposed that the manufacturers may have been compelled or induced by me to adopt certain modes of construction or certain dimensions, in

other parts by a specification—a practice which has
been adopted on some lines—and that these restric-
tions may have embarrassed them, I should wish to
take this opportunity to state distinctly that this is not
the case.   I have, indeed, strongly recommended to
their consideration the advantages of having very
large and well-formed steam passages, which generally
they have adopted, and with good results; and with
this single exception, if it can be considered one, they
have been left unfettered by me (perhaps too much
so) and uninfluenced, except, indeed, by the prejudices
and fears of those by whom they have been surrounded, which have by no means diminished the
difficulties I have had to contend with.   The principal
proportions of these engines being those which have
been recommended by the most able experimentalists
and writers, and these having been adopted by the
most experienced makers, it is difficult to understand
who can constitute themselves objectors, or what can
be their objections.   Even if these engines had not
been found effective, at least it must be admitted that
the best and most liberal means had been adopted to
procure them; but I am far from asking such an
admission.   The engines, I think, have proved to be
well adapted to the particular task for which they
were calculated, namely, high speeds — but circumstances prevent their being beneficially applied to this
purpose at present, and they are, therefore, working
under great disadvantages.   An engine constructed
expressly for high velocity cannot, of course, be well
adapted to exert great power at a low speed; neither
can it be well adapted for stopping frequently and re-
gaining its speed.   But such was not the intention
when these engines were made, neither will it be the
case when the arrangements on the line are complete;
in the meantime our average rate of travelling is much
greater than it was either on the Grand Junction or
Birmingham Railway within the same period of the
opening.

I. have but one serious objection to make to our present engines, and for this, strange as it may seem, I feel that we are mainly indebted to those who have been most loud in their complaints—I refer to the unnecessary weight of the engines. There is nothing in the wide gauge which involves any considerable increased weight in the engine. An engine of the same power and capacity for speed, whether for a 4 feet 8 inch rail or for a 7 feet rail, will have identically the same boiler, the same firebox, the same cylinder and piston and other working gear, the same side frame, and the same wheels ; the axles and the cross-framing will alone differ, and upon these alone need there be any increase, but, if these were doubled in weight, the difference upon the whole engine would be immaterial. But the repeated assertion, frequently professing to come from experienced authorities, and repeated until it was supposed to be proved, that the increased gauge must require increased strength and great power, was not without its indirect effect upon the manufacturers. Unnecessary dimensions have been given to many parts, and the weight thereby increased—rather tending, as I believe, to diminish than to add to the strength of the whole. I thought then, and I believe now, that it would have been unwise in this case to have resisted the general opinion and taken upon myself the responsibility which belonged to the manufacturers ; but I need not now hesitate to say that a very considerable reduction may be effected, and that no such unusual precautions are necessary to meet these anticipated strains and resistances—such being, in fact, imaginary. It cannot surprise anybody that under such circumstances attention was more occupied in endeavouring to meet these imaginary prejudiced objections, than in boldly taking advantage of the new circumstances, and that a piece of machinery constructed under such disadvantages was not likely to be a fair sample of what might be done. I am happy to say, however, that the

result of the trials that have been made has entirely
destroyed all credit in these alarmists with the manufacturers, and that we may hope in future to have the
benefits of the free exercise of the intelligence and
practical knowledge of engine manufacturers. The
mode of laying the rails is the next point which I
shall consider. It may appear strange that I should
again in this case disclaim having attempted anything
perfectly new, yet regard to truth compels me to
do so. I have recommended, in the case of the Great
Western, the principle of a continuous bearing of
timber under the rail, instead of isolated supports—
an old system recently revived, and as such I described
it in my report of January 1836, the result of many
hundred miles laid in this manner in America, and of
some detached portions of railways in England, was
quite sufficient to prove that the system was attended
with many advantages ; but since we first adopted it
these proofs have been multiplied—there need now be
no apprehension. There are railways in full work,
upon which the experiment has been tried sufficiently
to prove beyond doubt, to those willing to be convinced, that a permanent way in continuous bearings
of wood may be constructed, in which the motion will
be much smoother, the noise less, and consequently—
for they are effects produced by the same cause—the
wear and tear of the machinery much less. Such a
plan is certainly best adapted for high speeds, and this
is the system recommended by me and adopted on
our road. There are no doubt different modes of
construction, and that which I have adopted as an
improvement upon others may, on the contrary, be
attended with disadvantages. For the system I will
strenuously contend.

But I should be sorry to enter with any such determined feeling into a discussion of the merits of the
particular mode of construction. I would refer to my
last report for the reasons which influenced me, and
the objects I had in view in introducing the piling ;

that part which had been made under my own eye
answered fully all my expectations. Here the piles
did answer their purpose, and no inconvenience resulted from their use. The difficulties which we have
since encountered, the bad state in which the line was
for a considerable time, and which is only recently improved, have undoubtedly been aggravated, if not
caused by these piles; but not as I believe from a
defect in the principle, as applied in our case, where
the line is mostly in cutting, or on the surface, but from
defective execution; for notwithstanding the determination to allow sufficient time for this most important
operation, yet, to make up for previous delays and loss
of time, it became necessary at last to force forward the
work more rapidly than was at all consistent with due
care in the execution; and during the whole of this
period I was most unfortunately prevented by a serious
accident from even seeeing the work almost until the
day of opening, when I ought to have personally superintended the whole. I do not mean that the work
was neglected by those whose duty it was to supply
my place—far from it; but in such a case a new work
cannot be properly directed, except under the eye of
the master. Following exactly the plan which had
succeeded on the first piece completed, several serious
faults were committed. A much greater density and
firmness of packing is required than was previously
supposed; the mode of packing adopted, and the
material selected, in the first instance, have proved
defective elsewhere; and over a great extent in the
line, particularly in the clay cuttings and where the
work was at last most hurried it has been badly executed. But many parts have stood well from the
commencement; others are fast improving, and I have
the satisfaction, although a very painful one, of seeing
that, if in the first instance, a foundation of coarse
gravel had been everywhere well rammed in before the
timbers had been laid, and the packing formed upon
this, we should from the outset have obtained as solid

a road as we have now over a great part of the line.

What we have been able to effect since the opening of the line has necessarily been a slow, expensive and laborious operation.   We have been compelled to open the ground, and excavate it to a depth of 18 inches under the longitudinal timbers, and this without interrupting the traffic, to remove the whole of the material thus obtained from off the line, and to replace it by coarse ballast; and not having the means of sufficiently consolidating this ballast by ramming while the timber is in its place, the packing has to be repeated once or twice after it has been compressed by the passing of the trains.   This new packing, however, does stand, and in a few weeks I expect the line will be in a very different state from that in which it has been, or indeed now is.

From what I have described as the result which can now be, and might have been, obtained from the commencement, it will be inferred that I am disposed still to defend the system of piling.   I certainly could not abandon it from conviction of its inefficiency, for I see proofs of the contrary; and I feel that under similar circumstances I could now prevent the mischief which has occurred.   Upon that portion of the line where the permanent way must next be formed, piling could not be resorted to, the ground being a solid hard chalk for many miles.   I had intended, however, recommending the same principle, but in a different form, holding down the longitudinals by small iron rods driven into the chalk; but the same objection could not exist, because the chalk cannot yield under the timbers like clay, or even gravel.   But I should wish most anxiously to avoid anything like an obstinate adherence to a plan, if the object which I believe essential can be obtained by other means, particularly when that plan being my own, I may be somewhat prejudiced in its favour.   I find that the system of piling involves considerable expense in the first construction, and requires perhaps too great a perfection in the whole work, and that if the whole or part of this cost were expended in increased scantling of timber and weight of metal, that a very solid continuous rail would be formed. For this as a principle; as for the width of gauge, I am prepared to contend, and to stand or fall by it, believing it to be a most essential improvement where high speeds are to be obtained. As regards the expense of forming the permanent way on this principle, I am quite prepared to maintain what I have on a former occasion advanced, that, even on the system which we have adopted between London and Maidenhead, the total cost does not materially exceed that of a well-constructed line with stone blocks. I did not in the outset make an exact estimate of the cost of either mode; I was unable to obtain the cost, which has actually been incurred on other lines, but a comparative estimate was made, and the result of that comparison led me to state that the one might exceed the other by £500 a mile. The actual cost of our permanent way appears, by the detailed account which has been made out, to have been above £9000, including expenses of under-draining and forming the surfaces, which cannot be included in the cost given in other cases because that drainage (though I believe generally forming part of the plan) is not yet constructed. This sum includes the sidings at the stations, switches, joints and other contingencies, and also the expenses incurred during the first month of working the line, and which, as I have before stated, consisted in removing and replacing work which had been improperly executed. These items will make a considerable reduction; and besides these, larger reductions may be effected in parts of the work which were new, and from the circumstances naturally attending a first attempt were not so economically conducted as they might be, or, indeed, as they were towards the close of the works, when the different parts were let by contract. Taking the prices at which the work was latterly actually executed, £8000 per mile would be a liberal allowance for our future proceeding, even adopting the same system ; and with a modified system, such as that suggested of simple longitudinal bearings of large scantling, and a rail of 54 pounds per yard, at the present high price of iron, the cost, calculated upon our actual past expenditure, would not exceed £7400 per mile. This I am aware is a larger sum than that which has usually been assumed as the cost of the permanent way. I cannot prove that others have cost more, or even so much as this, as I have nothing but the published accounts to refer to ; but this I can state, and prove if necessary, that rails and blocks, such as are now being adopted on the Manchester and Liverpool Railway, would upon our lines cost at least as much. The prime cost of rails and chairs delivered on the line would alone amount to half the money ; and nothing is perhaps more certain than that the experience of other lines within the last two or three years has proved that this part of the construction of a railway is unavoidably much more expensive than was ever calculated for at the time our estimates were made.—I am, Gentlemen, your obedient Servant, I. K. BRUNEL.

But the dissentient shareholders pressed for an inquiry, and Mr John Hawkshaw of Manchester and Mr N. Wood of Newcastle-on-Tyne were requested to report as to whether any advantages were obtained from increasing the width of the gauge. If any, to what extent and at what additional cost, and if the advantages (if any) were equivalent to the increased cost of forming the railway on this plan? Mr J. Walker, the then President of the Institution of Civil Engineers, and Mr Robert Stephenson were also asked to prepare a report on the subject, but both declined to do so. Mr Hawkshaw's and Mr Wood's reports were delivered in the autumn of 1838. Mr Brunel sent in an answer on 13th December 1838. Then

Mr Wood made another report which is dated 18th December 1838. Mr Brunel's answer to Mr Wood's second report was published on 27th December. The Directors thereupon addressed the circular to the shareholders which contained their opinions on the controversy, which were favourable to Mr Brunel, and they decided that 'upon a deliberate reconsideration of all the circumstances affecting the permanent welfare of the undertaking, divesting the question of all personal partialities or obstinate adherence to a system, unanimously acquiesce in the abandonment of the piles, in the substitution of a greater scantling of timber, and of a heavier rail, retaining the width of gauge, with the continuous timber bearings, as the most conducive to the general interests of the Company.'

The directors also required Mr Gooch to prepare them a report on each locomotive, which he did, condemning their construction, but pointing out that it was quite possible to build engines suitable for the Broad Gauge. His report resulted in the Directors requiring him to prepare designs for a suitable class of engines. These new engines formed the celebrated 'Firefly' class.

The meeting of the shareholders to consider these reports was held at the London Tavern, and was adjourned till 9th January 1839. The Directors proposed this resolution:—'That this meeting, deeply sensible of the disastrous consequences inevitably arising from repeated discussions as to the principles acted upon in carrying on the work, do request the Directors to adhere to the principles laid down in the report as most conducive to the permanent welfare of the proprietors.' To this proposition an amendment was proposed,—'That the reports of Mr Wood and Mr Hawkshaw contain sufficient evidence that the plans of construction pursued by Mr Brunel are injudicious, expensive and ineffectual for this professed object, and ought not to be persevered in.' On the division only 6145 votes were given for the amendment, and 7792 against it, so that the Directors' resolution was carried by the large majority of 1647 votes. Nor was any other attempt ever made to alter this decision of the shareholders. There were two circumstances which greatly influenced the shareholders in arriving at the above conclusion, one the fact that Dr Lardner had conducted the experiments on behalf of Messrs Hawkshaw and Wood, but at that time the doctor's conclusions had not much weight, for he had often publicly affirmed that it was impossible for a steam vessel to cross the Atlantic, when in 1838 several had successfully performed the voyage. He also stated that the Broad Gauge engine 'North Star' could not haul more, travelling at 45 miles an hour, than 15 tons, when, the next day, Mr Gooch travelled with her at that rate with a load of 50 tons. So no wonder the shareholders were rather dubious as to the result of his gauge experiments.

The other circumstance which influenced the shareholders was an exceedingly ingenious pamphlet written by Mr G. Clark, one of the Great Western engineers, in which he mercilessly satirised the whole inquiry. In describing the line when first opened one writer thus refers to this inquiry :—' The advantages of the Broad Gauge are :—

' 1. It gave the power of constructing more powerful engines, by which greater speed for passenger trains and greater tractive power for heavy goods trains were obtained.

' 2. It gave more space for the convenient arrangement and beneficial proportions of the machinery as well as for convenient access to it. In all these points difficulties had been found on the Narrow Gauge, and the compulsory restriction of so important a dimension as the width between the rails has been a bar to any improvements of great magnitude or comprehensive nature.

' 3. It gave, even with the overhanging carriage, the facility for obtaining large wheels, and consequently diminishing the axle friction without sacrifice of stability.

' 4. The greater width of base for the carriages to rest on gave increased steadiness and smoothness of motion, particularly at high speeds. It was the impulse given by the increase of speeed and comfort obtained without difficulty on the Broad Guage which had led to the chief improvements introduced in railway travelling.

' 5. Greater safety was secured, particularly at high speed, from the greater stability of position, due to the wider base producing increased steadiness and diminishing the chance under exceptional circumstances of the derangement of any part of the train.

' 6. While the Broad Gauge was but little more costly than the Narrow, the width of the works being determined not by the width of the rails but by the width of the carriages, and the extra cost of rolling stock being very small, the Broad Guage could not be worked more economically under parallel circumstances than the Narrow.

' 7. It gave the facility of using broader vehicles with equal steadiness in cases where the extra breadth would be useful, though the extra breadth was by no means an ' essential part of the scheme.' *

A well known engineer, writing at this time on the result of this inquiry, said :—' One great advantage results to the public from the investigation which has taken place into the merits of this railway, proving the very defective condition of the system of rail-

* While Mr Herapath, the railway authority of that time, said,—
" Experience has proved 4 feet 8½ inches to be too small, but we are not aware it has yet proved that 7 feet is too large."

ways generally, rendering it the imperative duty of railway companies to avail themselves of the suggestions and improvements of others besides their own people. If it has the effect, therefore, of breaking down the spirit of domination and exclusiveness at present existing which forbids the introduction of other methods than the crude and original ideas of Stephenson and Company, such a conclusion is well obtained at the expense and noise this inquiry has created, and must be regarded with satisfaction by every well-wisher to the railway system.'

In the Appendix will be found the various reports alluded to in this volume.

Proceeding with the description of the construction of the line, Maidenhead Skew Bridge is the next to claim attention, of this bridge and the Box Tunnel (to be considered later on) we believe it can be truthfully said that more has been written than about any other engineering success of the nineteenth century. The great peculiarity is the extreme flatness of the arch, which was erected in brickwork. Mr Hawkshaw recommended stone being used as being more likely to make the bridge secure. The bridge consisted of only two elliptical arches, each of 128 feet span, with a spring of only 24 feet 3 inches. There were also four smaller arches for the passage of flood water, the centreing from one of these being removed before the cement had set, caused the arch to give way. The opponents to this style of bridge construction made such an outcry about the accident that the contractor was so frightened that he begged of Mr Brunel to allow him to give up his contract. Mr Brunel, however, proved to him, by simple geometrical figures and diagrams, that his method of construction was quite correct. After this untoward event one of the newspapers, which prided itself upon being an authority on railway matters, each week used to send a commissioner to Maidenhead to report upon the defects of this bridge, and his emphatic statement was, ' That the bridge could not stand alone, it was only supported by the centreing, and when they were removed the bridge would fall.' One Saturday morning the paper came out with strictures much stronger than usual on the instability of the bridge ; it so happened, however, that the previous night there had been a severe storm, and the wind had blown down the wood centreing, and, as Mr Gooch says, 'before the paper was in the hands of the readers the arches were standing alone, and have stood well ever since.' Indeed, so proud are the Great Western Railway of this bridge that, after standing fifty years, they have such respect to the memory of its brilliant designer that in carrying out the widening of the line from Maidenhead to Didcot, the Company have built a similar bridge to Brunel's famous one, parallel with it ; and to insure the quality of the work, instead of it being let to a contractor as the rest of the widening was, the Company built it so as to make sure of good workmanship and unity of design. So far has the idea been carried out that, finding the original bridge has settled about an inch, the new one is not built a true ellipse, but is the same amount out of the correct form.

This widened bridge was opened for traffic on 1st February 1893. There are now four lines of rail over the bridge, the level of the rails being only 40 feet above that of the river beneath. The following is a very clear and interesting account of this famous bridge written soon after the work was completed :—'To the eye familiar with geometrical beauty, the perfect execution of an elliptical arch on so large a scale, and so high a degree of eccentricity, is no common gratification ; but when the practical mechanician considers, from his point of view, the difficulties and risks which must have attended its construction—when he reflects that this beautiful outline is wholly formed of insignificant little bricks, $4\frac{1}{2}$ inches wide by $2\frac{3}{4}$ inches thick, each course of which on this enormous span has not only to carry its own weight, but its proportion of the road and the train—when he considers the strains to which these materials are thus exposed, and remembers that in such circumstances they are subject to a pressure that must approach very nearly to the extreme limits of cohesion, then, indeed, and only then, will he sufficiently appreciate the courage and the capacity which have approached so near to the verge of possibility without transgressing its bounds.

'Let him examine the structure closely, and he will see that the most perfect execution and the soundest materials, with the most judicious arrangement, could alone have secured its success, for at certain critical points there may be observed some delicate displacements, nowhere exceeding a quarter of an inch in extent, sufficient nevertheless to show that courage carried further might have been rashness. As it is, this example is one which it is impossible not to admire, but which it would be imprudent to imitate.'

The following table gives some interesting statistics of the two great brick works on this line.

Material—Brick.	Wharncliffe.	Maidenhead.
Cost,	£40,000.	£37,000.
Total length,	896 ft.	778 ft.
Breadth,	30 ft.	30 ft.
Height,	70 ft.	40 ft.
Span,	70 ft.	128 ft.
Spring,	18 ft.	24 ft. 3 ins.
Thickness of piers at foot,	13 ft. 6 ins.	30 ft.
Thickness at spring,	10 ft. 6 ins.	8 ft.
Arch at haunch,	5 ft. 9 ins.	7 ft. 6 ins.
Arch at crown,	3 ft.	5 ft. 3 ins.

There are 4 miles of rather deep cuttings between Maidenhead and Twyford, while beyond Twyford the cutting towards Reading is about 40 feet deep. It was originally proposed to make a tunnel here, but the idea was abandoned and the deep cutting substituted. Reading was one of the principal stations built with but a single platform, which it still retains. We believe that this and Cambridge are the two remaining examples of the early desire to make the intermediate stations like roadside inns.

After Reading the line crosses the river and then runs along a narrow gorge worn out of the surface by the action of the river, shut in on one side by the water and on the other by the chalk cliffs of the gorge. Pangbourne was the next station, after which the railway recrosses the river and arrives at Wallingford Station, 3 miles from the town of that name. The next station was Steventon, 56 miles from Paddington. The first 53 miles from London exhibits one of the great advantages of this line, viz., the freeness from curves, and an almost level stretch of railway, the gradients nowhere exceeding 4 feet per mile ; the gradients beyond are not so good, for as Swindon is the summit level, and is 253 feet above the London Terminus, there remains 147 feet to be climbed in the next 24 miles, which is done as follows :—First, 4 miles from Didcot, 7 feet per mile ; $1\frac{1}{4}$ mile level ; $1\frac{1}{4}$ mile 8 feet per mile ; and from the sixtieth to the sixty-ninth mile, a uniform gradient of 7 feet ; 3 miles more have a rise of $5\frac{1}{2}$ feet ; and with the remainder at 6 feet 4 inches, the summit is reached near Swindon, where the Cheltenham Union line branches off to the North.

There was at first only one station, Farringdon, $63\frac{1}{2}$ miles from London, between Steventon and Swindon. The village of Swindon then had a population of 1742 souls, but the Great Western Railway quickly caused a new town to spring up by determining on locating its engineering works there, which now rank with the largest in the kingdom. Mr Gooch selected Swindon for the purpose, it being a convenient place to change engines, in consequence of it being the summit level of the line, and also as being the junction for the Cheltenham and Great Western Union Railway.   In 1840, when the site was selected, the whole neighbourhood was a long expanse of green fields, and the spot where the trains now wait ten minutes so that the passengers may obtain refreshments, should they feel so inclined, is identically the same as that where Mr Brunel and Mr Gooch had an *al fresco* picnic in the summer of 1840.   Rather a different view meets the eye to-day.   The liberality of the Railway Company soon built a church, schools, and an institute, for the accommodation of the workmen and their families, and also paid the stipend for the clergyman and the salaries for the school teachers out of the revenue of the Company, and provided a park and cricket ground as well.   The inhabitants of New Swindon long suffered from the circumlocution of the Government in many ways, which greatly retarded the development of the town,   All letters addressed to New Swindon, which adjoins the railway station, were sent to the post office at Old Swindon (two miles distant), and delivered from there, and the same plan was adopted with letters sent from New Swindon, resulting in a delay of about two hours each way ; while a workman who wanted to post a letter in time for the evening mail had to get a half-day off, and take it to the post office at Old Swindon before 6 P.M., although the mail did not leave the station for many hours after.

Mr Acworth truly says,—'A description of a corner of the works would furnish enough matter to fill a volume.'   We, however, append his description of a few of the secondary pursuits here carried on. ' In one place we came upon a whole gang of harness-makers diligently stitching.   They are only making head-stalls for use in the Company's stock of horse-boxes.   In another place we find that, even in the matter of economy, the Broad Gauge is not wholly without advantage.   A lattice-work girder, 124 feet long and 12 feet 6 inches high, is being riveted together, and is going to be sent down to Bristol in one piece, to form part of a new widening of the line that the

Severn Tunnel has rendered imperatively necessary.
Portable riveters, in shape and size like a horse-collar,
opening and closing at the pointed end, hang suspended from above, and are fed with water through
flexible coils of copper tubing. Each machine performs the work of a dozen lusty boiler-makers and
strikers.

'When we cross the rails into the carriage shops,
we begin to wonder whether the skilled mechanic will
not ere long be an extinct species. Here we come
across a boy of fourteen making curtain rings out of
flat discs of wood by a process somewhat similar, and
implying about as much mental or bodily exertion as
is required to squeeze oil paint out of a collapsible
tube. Close by a second boy looks on while a copy-
ing lathe reproduces, with a scrupulous accuracy that
the most skilled hand-turning could never hope to
rival, the thickenings and taperings of the oval-shaped
handle of a platelayer's pick. A little further on a file,
alone and unattended, has taken a band-saw in charge,
and is sharpening its teeth, while two studs, nudging
alternately from opposite sides, give them the requisite
"set." We turned to the foreman, and inquired how
long it would be before the saw would be taught to
get up off the table after the operation and go back to
its work. His reply was,—"Well, sir, they do say
that a man only wants a hammer and a glue pot to
build a railway carriage nowadays." But if the glue
pot has so far remained outside the range of influence
of steam power, its brother the paint pot has already
succumbed, for one shop we found in sole possession
of a small engine that was assiduously grinding and
mixing paint. It is true there was a man looking on,
or, as he would doubtless have arrogantly described
himself, "in charge;" but the engine went on with its
task with a quiet self-confidence that brooked no interference.'

The area of Swindon Works now amounts to 208
acres, and 9360 hands are permanently employed. On

the whole line there were only 10,000,000 cubic yards of cuttings—much less than on any other line of the same magnitude. Of the material excavated very little should have gone to the spoil banks; but the line was constructed at high pressure and in much less time than any other railway, between 6000 and 7000 men being constantly engaged upon it during construction. Under such circumstances as these was an embankment made just beyond Swindon Station. The Company having purchased some land, brought the wet, saturated clay to form the embankment, so that, with a change of season, it could not be made stable, till at last they drove rows of piles on each side, and chained them together with chain cables, and so confined the slippery soil. They drove these piles—tall beech trees—20 feet into the earth, and to this day every train passes over tons of chain cables hidden beneath the ballast.

In the 42 miles from Swindon to Bristol, the line falls 275 feet, most of which is concentrated in two places—Wootton Bassett and Box Tunnel. Both of these it was at first intended to work by the help of bank engines, the gradients being considered too severe for one engine. This was one great point in Mr Brunel's system. Instead of making the road up and down banks at all parts, which would check the speed, and require all the engines to have a large reserve of power to mount them, he made the whole line as level as possible, and put all the inclination together, so that it could be overcome by the slight additional cost of a bank engine. For the first 8 miles from Swindon there is a total fall of 50 feet; the Wooton Bassett Bank is 1¼ miles long, and falls 1 in 100, or 66 feet in all; for the next 4 miles the line falls 1 in 660, and then rises at the same rate till the entrance of Box Tunnel, 98½ miles from London. Chippenham was the next station to Swindon, from which place it is 17 miles distant.

We now come to the Box Tunnel, the first on the

line, 98½ miles from London.   In whose words shall
we describe it ?   So many authors have fully written
of its wonders, that we fear our one more will be *de
trop*.   The great thing in connection with it, is, that
throughout its entire length the line falls 1 in 100;
this falling gradient is in all 2 miles 660 yards in

THE BOX TUNNEL.

length.   In *Our Iron Roads*, Mr Williams tells the
following anecdote in connection with this tunnel :—
    'On one occasion some of the Directors of the
Great Western Railway were inspecting the works at
the Box Tunnel, and several of them resolved to
descend a shaft with Mr Brunel and one or two other
engineers, who mentioned the incident to the writer.

Accordingly, all but one ensconced themselves in the tub provided for that purpose—he declined to accompany them. His friends rallied him for his want of courage, and one slyly suggested, " Did your wife forbid you before you started ? " A quiet nod in response intimated that the right nail had been struck, and the revelation was received with a merry laugh. But as the pilgrims found themselves slipping about a greasy, muddy tub, jolting and shaking as the horses stopped—by whose aid they were lowered,—and how at length they were suspended some 150 feet from the bottom, till the blastings that had been prepared roared and reverberated through the " long drawn caverns," more than one of the party who had laughed before wished that they had received a similar prohibition to that of their friend above, and that they had manifested an equal amount of marital docility.'

Box Hill, through which the tunnel passes, rises abruptly to a height of 270 feet above the level of the rails, and for 2½ miles the approach is through a continuous and deep cutting. The tunnel is 3123 yards, or nearly 2 miles long ; the clear width is 30 feet, and the height 25 feet ; the surface of the land at each entrance is about 70 feet above the level of the rails. The cost of the brickwork per yard was about 43s., the cutting at the entrance contained above a million and a half of cubic yards of very various materials, and this with the tunnel formed one of the most troublesome and tedious works on the line.

George Stephenson was one of the witnesses called by the promoters of the Great Western Railway. The counsel who cross-examined him asked the railway pioneer if it would not be dangerous to travel through the Box Tunnel. George Stephenson replied, ' I wish you had a little engineering knowledge, you would not talk to me so.' Counsel, ' I feel the disadvantage.' George Stephenson, ' I am sure you must.' This counsel, however, was not crushed by Geordie's sarcasm, for in his speech he refers to this tunnel thus :—' The noise of two trains passing each other in this tunnel would shake the nerves of this assembly. I do not know such a noise. No passenger would be induced to go twice.' When the line was opened these old wives' tales as to the dangers of the tunnel had a considerable effect on timid passengers, for they left the trains at the stations each side of the tunnel, and posted by chaise to the next station on the other side, where they regained the later trains. Even when the tunnel had been safely worked for some years, a scare was raised that it was not safe, and the Government ordered an inspection and report, but this document was in every way favourable to the stability of the tunnel. When the railway mania was at its height, a prospectus writer took advantage of the then dying-out timidity of travellers, and in describing his proposed line to Bristol he states that travellers will prefer the new line, as by using it they will avoid the danger of travelling through the unsafe Box Tunnel.

In 1847, for the greater safety of the trains, the electric telegraph was laid through the tunnel, and what has since developed into the block system was introduced into the signalling of the trains through the tunnel.

In consequence of the severe falling gradient, the down rails through the tunnel were canted inwards, so that they in a measure wedged the wheels of the trains and partially retarded their progress.

Another short tunnel succeeds the Box one, the descending gradient still being 52⅔ feet per mile, but the rest of the fall to Bristol is very slight, 97 feet being spread over 17 miles, or an average of about 5½ feet per mile.

The whole of the gradients on the line are thus divided :—

	Miles.	Yards.
Level or incline not exceeding 4 feet in mile,	66	88
Above 4 feet ,, ,, 8 .,	47	110

D

Miles. Yards.

Steep inclines, Wootton Bassett, 1 in 100,   1   550
Box Tunnel incline,   1 in 100,   2   660

The Bath Station is 106½ miles from London, after which is a viaduct of 65 arches, each 20 feet span built of Bath stone. Between this point and Bristol is the most interesting part of the railway, so far as the construction is concerned. The line crosses the Avon by a timber skew bridge, the most oblique ever built of wood, and proceeds along the Twerton Embankment to the station of that name,

BATH STATION, SHOWING THE ORIGINAL BROAD GAUGE CARRIAGES.

108 miles down. Next we have the Saltford Embankment, 20 feet high and 1¾ miles long; then Saltford Station and Tunnel, the latter 480 feet long, and would have been longer but for a landslip at the commencement, which removed the necessity for a part of the tunnelling. This accident gave Brunel an opportunity of showing his artistic skill; to hide the chasm formed by the fall of earth, he built a fine Gothic arch en-

trance to the tunnel, with pseudo ruined towers each side, over which ivy was trained, and so completed the idea of a ruined castle, which the entrance to the tunnel resembles.

After Keynsham Station is the Pennant Cutting, 70 feet deep, through the hard Pennant sandstone. The Brislington Tunnel follows; it is 1049 yards long, 30 feet wide and 30 feet high. There are two other cuttings, one 158 yards, the other 350 yards long. Then crossing the Avon by a stone bridge we arrive at the Temple Meads Station at Bristol, the original terminus of the Great Western Railway.

In connection with the construction of a portion of the line near Bristol, the Company was engaged in a long and expensive lawsuit with a contractor named Ranger. Under the contract with him entered into in 1836, if the work were not proceeded with to the satisfaction of the Company's engineer, after due notice, should the work not be expedited, the Company was entitled to enter into possession of the whole of the effects of Ranger on the line and finish the work itself. In 1838 the railway gave the notice and seized Ranger's plant, valued by him at £70,000. He then commenced legal proceedings against the railway, and after going through the various Courts, the case was settled by the House of Lords in 1847.

CHAPTER III.

THE OPENING OF THE RAILWAY.

THE first experiment with a Broad Gauge locomotive was made by Mr Gooch on 9th January 1838, when the 'Vulcan' was tried on the only part of the line then completed, which was from West Drayton to the Dogkennel Bridge. The celebrated 'North Star'

THE 'NORTH STAR.' An Original Broad Gauge Engine (originally built for a Russian 6 feet Gauge Railway).

commenced her career on the 7 feet gauge on the 15th January; she was brought by barge to Maidenhead, and placed on the line there. The next day the Great Western Railway officials had a dinner party in honour of the event at West Drayton—then the headquarters of the locomotive department. Of this event, Mr Gooch remarks,—'Some Irish gentlemen took more wine than was good for them, and amused themselves by dancing an Irish war dance on our hats, which happened to be piled up in a corner of the room. I was rather disgusted with the termination of our dinner, and resolved never to have anything to do with another. I was one of the stewards.'

It was on the 31st May that the Directors made their first trip by railway over the line, and finding everything well prepared for the public opening, it was arranged that the section from the temporary station at Bishops Road to the riverside station at Maidenhead (the present Taplow one) should be opened at once.

On June the 1st, other experimental trips were made; the 'North Star' took a train containing 200 passengers the whole distance (22½ miles) in 47 minutes, or at the rate of 28 miles an hour, the return journey being made in 35 minutes, which was at the rate of 36 miles an hour.

On the same day another train performed the down journey in 44 minutes.

The next day, in preparation for the opening for general use, the full service of trains (eight each way per day) was run.

On 4th June 1838, 'the broad way that leads to destruction,' for a distance of 22½ miles, was opened to the public as the Great Western Railway. How jubilant must have been any Narrow Gauge partisans who happened to travel by the first train, and how well we can imagine the shaking of the heads, and the significant 'I told you so,' when in the morrow's newspapers the wider circle of the Coal Mine Gauge adherents read of the rather unsatisfactory result of the first trip.

Mr Gooch says of the engines that the 'North Star' and the six engines from the Vulcan Foundry were the only ones he could depend upon.

The 'Æolus' was the one chosen to draw the first

train, which consisted of seven vehicles, viz., two first-class carriages, three closed and two open second-class ones, and a truck, on which was mounted a posting-chaise; but upon arriving at West Drayton, the further progress of the pioneer train was prevented by a leaky tube, which extinguished the engine fire. This untoward accident occasioned a delay of 76 minutes, as the train had to wait till the arrival of the following one to push it forward to Maidenhead. The weight of the first train was 80,078 lbs., or about 36 tons (without the engine), the combined trains, with the propelling loco-motive in the middle, reached Maidenhead (so far as the first part was concerned) after a journey of 2 hours 42¾ minutes, or, deducting the stoppage, the actual time of travelling was 86¼ minutes, being an average travel-ling speed of 15.56 miles an hour.

Nor was the return journey without its *contre-temps*, for at Slough, the truck on which was the posting-chaise, had to be detached and left behind in consequence of one of the wheels running hot; but the rate of progression was a distinct acceleration, the whole trip only taking 62 minutes, or, after deducting stoppages, 54½ minutes, being an average speed of 24.88 miles an hour.

Mr N. Wood gives the following account of a trip from London to Maidenhead and back by one of the regular trains on the day after the line was opened :— 'Being the Eton Montem, for the convenience of the public, an extra carriage was attached to the train, which consisted of three first-class carriages, each capable of containing twenty-four passengers; two second-class close and two open carriages, containing from twenty-four to thirty passengers each; and one open carriage with six wheels, capable of holding fifty to sixty passengers. With this train of carriages, in which were upwards of one hundred and ninety pas-sengers, we started from London. The following table will show the time of performing the journey there and back :—

	DISTANCE.		TIME.	
	Miles.	Chains.	Min.	Secs.
From London to Drayton,	13	3	26	22
Stopped at Drayton Station,			3	55
,, Water ,,			3	0
,, Slough ,,			3	50
From Drayton to Maiden-head, ...	9	40	25	10
	22	43	51	32

	Miles.	Chains.	Min.	Secs.
From Maidenhead to Drayton, . . .	9	40	27	50
Stopped at Slough, . .			5	20
,, Drayton, .			2	10
From Drayton to London,	13	3	26	50
	22	43	55	40

'The average rate of travelling in both directions in the above trip is about 25 miles an hour, but it must be considered that a great loss of time was occasioned by checking the speed on stopping at the intermediate stations, and again recovering the speed at starting; the rate being upwards of 30 miles an hour when not checked.

'Considering, therefore, the disadvantage under which the above experiment was made, the number of stoppages and the short distance, that the engine had also to drag an extra carriage, and that no attempt was made to urge the engine to its utmost capabilities, it appears quite certain that, with such powerful engines, a much higher rate of speed will be accomplished upon

this railway than has hitherto been attained, especially
as it did not appear to us that any obstacle existed to
the higher rate of speed being kept up without difficulty.'

The selection of Maidenhead as the first terminus
for the railway was a capital one so far as the passenger traffic was concerned, as more stage coaches
passed through that town than any other in England.
The daily number being ninety ; and not only did the
coach passengers commence or complete their journey
by the railway, but the coaches were mounted on
trucks and came to and left London by train. The
'Beaufort Hunt,' a celebrated Bath and London
coach, used the railway between London and Maidenhead almost from its first opening.

The engines caused Mr Gooch great disappointment; he says of them :—'I had . . . to rebuild one
half of the stock. . . . For many weeks my nights
were spent in a carriage in the engine-house at
Paddington, as repairs had to be done to the engines
at nights to get them ready to do their work next
day.'

On 21st July, we have recorded another trip performed by 'Æolus,' when she took a train consisting
of three first-class carriages, two open and one closed
second-class carriages, and two stage coaches on trucks,
or a load of 96,164 lbs., or about 43 tons, and essayed
a trip to Maidenhead, but 'about 2½ miles the train was
suddenly stopped and remained in *statu quo* for 21¾
minutes. In the meantime, 'Æolus' moved slowly
away to recover his strength, and having sufficiently
exercised himself, returned after a lapse of 21¾ minutes
to lead the train forward;' but she did not appear to
have quite recovered her strength by this exercise, for
she had to stop at Slough 'where she took water.' This
journey took 150 minutes to complete; but deducting
the 34 minutes spent in four stoppages, the average
travelling rate was 11.71 miles an hour. On 6th
November 'Æolus' did better, for with three car-

riages she attained a speed of 48 miles an hour. In September 1838, the passenger traffic produced £7579, while to 31st December, or for a period of nearly seven months, the income was—

Passengers and Mails, . £61,779 14 5		
Parcels, ... 869 5 7		
Merchandise, . . . 1,620 7 1	£65,885 19 6	
Conveyance of materials for Contractors constructing the Line, . . 1,616 12 5		

while the expenditure for the same period amounted to £32,168, 14s., in which was included £3405, 18s. 5d. Government duty, and £971, 10s. 9d. for rates and taxes. It is evident at first that railways were rated in a fairly equitable manner, but not for long, for four years later, when the duty for the half-year had increased *pro rata* with the traffic to £13,625, the rates had increased out of all proportion to £12,998. With regard to the rating, the Great Western Railway for a long while waged war against the unjust assessments made on their property, and on several occasions distresses were levied on the effects of the Company for rates they refused to pay. And good cause railways had for narrowly inquiring into how their rates were calculated, for one inquiry produced the astonishing result of disclosing that the assessor had made a rate of 6d. in the pound against a railway company in his parish, while the other occupiers were rated at but 2d. in the pound; for this swindle the parish official had to take a holiday at his country's expense, which holiday we need scarcely add was spent in well-guarded confinement.

Returning to the early history of the Great Western Railway, a storm of wind on the morning of 29th October 1838 showed how extremely well the carriages were constructed for easy running. The force of the wind propelled four carriages which were at Maidenhead along the line, which has a scarcely perceptible falling gradient—the first two reached Wormwood Scrubbs, a distance of over 20 miles, before they were stopped, the other two were stayed at Slough.

On 1st July 1839, the railway was opened to Twyford—an extension of $8\frac{1}{2}$ miles, included in which was the celebrated brick bridge across the Thames already alluded to.

Early in 1839, Cook and Wheatstone's galvanic telegraph was laid down on the Great Western Railway from Paddington to West Drayton.

At first the wires were enclosed in an iron tube, $1\frac{1}{2}$ inches diameter, which was fixed some 3 feet from the side of the line, and about 6 inches off the ground. By the early adoption of this great improvement, the Great Western Railway Directors gave the public further proof that they were far ahead of all other railways in the measures they took for the safety of the public travelling by their line. The telegraph was most prominently brought into public notice by the good service rendered to justice by the Great Western Railway in connection with an atrocious murder perpetrated at Salt Hill, near Slough, from which station the criminal journeyed to London by train. The foul crime was discovered shortly after the train had started, and the railway officials courteously telegraphed the description of the murderer to Paddington, where a detective awaited his arrival. The publicity thus given to the magnetic telegraph did more for its general introduction than many years of plain unobtrusive utility would have accomplished. It is not often that a scientific invention, at the commencement of its career, gains such a good advertisement of its undoubted usefulness.

At first this new means of instantaneous communication was called magnetic, galvanic or electric telegraph, to distinguish it from the system of telegraphy used by the Government to convey orders and news from London to the naval ports, which was accomplished by semaphores similiar to those now used by the coastguards to converse with passing ships. These semaphores were placed within sight of the attendants at the next semaphores on either side, who signalled the messages from one to another.

On 12th August 1839, the 'Vulcan' made a record in railway speed, having with four carriages attained the then unparalleled speed of 50 miles an hour.

The line was further extended in 1840; in March to Reading, and in June to Steventon, while, on 31st August, the Bristol Directors, who were working independently of the London Board, opened the section between Bath and Bristol, the up trains leaving Bristol at 8, 9, 10, 11, 12 A.M., 2, 4, 5, 6, 7 and 8 P.M; the first-class fare was then 2s. 6d. against 2s. 1d. now. To meet the hourly competition of the railway, a half-hourly service of coaches was put on the road between Bath and Bristol.

When we consider that at the present day, despite our elaborate and marvellously complicated system of combined interlocking and electric block signalling, collisions are not infrequent, it is intensely surprising to find how remarkably free from accidents the Great Western Railway was in the early years of its history, when its traffic was unprovided with any of these modern safeguards; but although accidents were few, narrow escapes from collisons must have been of rather frequent occurrence, for Babbage, a leading scientist of sixty years back, in his life, thus records a narrow escape he had one Sunday, when he was about to make a trip for the purpose of taking some observations. Upon arriving at the station, he found that he was to travel down on the north or up line.

'As this was an invasion of the usual regulations, I inquired very minutely into the authority upon which it rested. Being satisfied on this point, I desired him to order out my train immediately. He returned with the news that the fireman had neglected his duty, but that the engine would be ready in less than a quarter of an hour. The officer took pains to assure me that there was no danger on whichever line we might travel, as there could be no engine but our own on either line until 5 o'clock in the evening. A messenger arrived soon after to inform me that the obstructions had been removed, and that I could now pass upon the south, which was the proper line.

'While we were conversing together, my ear, which had become peculiarly sensitive to the distant sound of an engine, told me that one was approaching. I mentioned it to the railway official. He did not hear it, and said,—" Sir," it is impossible." " Whether possible or impossible," I said, " an engine is coming, and in a few minutes we shall see its steam." The sound soon became evident to both, and our eyes were anxiously directed to the expected quarter. The white cloud of steam now faintly appeared in the distance. I soon perceived the line it occupied, and then turned to watch my companion's face. In a few minutes more I saw it slightly change, and he said,— " It is indeed on the north line." Knowing it would stop at the engine-house, I ran as fast as I could to that spot. I found a single engine, from which Brunel, covered with smoke and black, had just descended. We shook hands, and I inquired what brought my friend here in such a plight. Brunel told me he had posted from Bristol to meet the only train at the furthest point of the rail then opened, but had missed it. " Fortunately," he said, " I found this engine with its fire up, so I ordered it out, and have driven it the whole way up at the rate of 50 miles an hour."

' I then told him that but for the merest accident I should have met him on the same line at the rate of 40 miles, and that I had attached to my engine my experimental carriage and three waggons with 30 tons of iron. I inquired what course he would have pursued if he had perceived another engine meeting him upon his own line? Brunel said in such a case he would have put on all the steam he could command with a view to driving off the opposite engine by the superior velocity of his own.'

But the Great Western Railway was remarkably fortunate with regard to the safety of its passengers, for during the three years preceding Christmas Eve 1841, the Company had carried over 3,000,000 passengers, and the only accidents reported were a broken leg and a broken arm, and a few bruises.

The trouble with the locomotives disappeared early in 1840, for Mr Gooch had his 'Firefly' (the first of the class numbering 142) running in March, and others were speedily delivered and got to work.

On the 30th June 1841, the whole of the Great Western main line from London to Bristol was opened. The Wooton Bassett incline of 1 in 100 was successfully mounted by the powerful Broad Gauge engines. Mr Brunel was very anxious as to the success of the long rise for over 2 miles, including the section through the tunnel, but with a bank engine the trains were got through without any difficulty. Mr Gooch thus describes the working of trains through the tunnel for the first days of the opening :—'Only one line of rails was complete through the tunnel, and the trains had therefore to be worked on a single line. I undertook to accompany all the trains through the tunnel, and did so the first day and night, also the second day, intending to be relieved when the mail came down on the second night. At about 11 o'clock that night we had a very narrow escape from a fearful accident. I was going up the tunnel with the last up train when I fancied I saw some green lights placed as they were in front of our trains. A second's reflection convinced me it was the mail coming down. I lost no time in reversing the engine I was on, and running back to Box Station with my train as quickly as I could, when the mail came down behind me. The policeman at the top of the tunnel had made some blunder, and sent the mails on when they arrived there. Had the tunnel not been pretty clear of steam we must have met in full career, and the smash would have been fearful, cutting short my career also. But as though mishaps never come alone, when I was taking my train up again, from some cause or other the engine got off the rails in the tunnel, and I was detained there all night before I got straight again.

'Box Tunnel had a very pretty effect for the couple of days it was worked as a single line from the number of candles used by the men working on the unfinished line ; it was a perfect illumination extending through the whole tunnel, nearly 2 miles long.'

The Queen did not venture to patronise the 'iron road' till 1842, but Prince Consort early made use of the Great Western Railway between London and Slough. For the use of the royal travellers a special saloon was built, which had one remarkable feature, wooden wheels with *wooden tyres*, to prevent the noise caused by the iron tyres striking against the iron rails. This carriage was constructed in 1840, and was 21 feet long, and 9 feet wide and 6 feet 6 inches high, in three compartments, the two end ones being each 4 feet 6 inches long, and the centre one nearly 12 feet ; the centre saloon was fitted in Louis XV. style, panelled with crimson and white silk, with paintings by Parris representing Fire, Air, Earth and Water. The sofas were of carved oak. At the end of the smaller compartments, over the buffers, was a large bow window. When the Windsor line was 'narrowed,' this saloon was withdrawn from service, but it is still preserved among other relics of the past greatness of the Broad Gauge at Swindon.

We have now given an account of the opening of the several sections of the Great Western Railway proper ; in 1841 were opened 18 miles of the Great

Western Railway and Cheltenham Union Railway, and 32½ miles of the Bristol and Exeter Railway.

In 1837 the Great Western Railway leased the former in perpetuity at a rent of £17,000 a year, thus really incorporating the Cheltenham and Great Western Union Railway with its own system. While a lease of the Bristol and Exeter was taken to work each section of the line as it was opened, and the whole line for five years from the date it was opened throughout.

Our readers have now had a succinct account of the formation and early development of the most important system of railways then or now in existence in this Kingdom.

Being constructed on principles entirely dissimilar to those adopted by other lines, the Great Western Railway has always received a large amount of attention from students of our railway organisations, and that there is much to be learnt from the history of the Broad Guage every reader will readily admit.

CHAPTER IV.

THE EARLY BROAD GAUGE LOCOMOTIVES.

MR DANIEL GOOCH, who has undoubtedly done more for the development of the locomotive steam engine than any other man, was appointed locomotive superintendent to the Great Western Railway in August 1837, commencing his duties as such on the 18th. He therefore, before he had attained his majority, was appointed to this most important of all positions on a railway. We can well understand his feelings; how jubilant and happy he must have been in thus early attaining to the zenith of the locomotive engineer's profession, which position is sought after and hoped for by thousands of young engineers when first entering the profession, but gained by a very few, and then usually after long, long years of hard toil and weary waiting, before which time the ardour and spirit with which they commenced their career has usually long since evaporated, and they enter into their new post, confirmed believers in the usual routine, as prepared for the occupiers of the position by their predecessors.

Mr Gooch's salary at first was £300 a year—a good start for a young man of twenty-one. This was increased to £550 upon the opening of the first section of the line, and to £700 in January 1841. In January 1846 it was raised to £1000, and to £1500 a year on 1st January 1851.

It cannot be said that Mr Gooch came to the Great Western Railway with preconceived views in favour of the Broad Gauge. On the contrary, the effect of his early surroundings must have, if anything at all, caused him to lean to the Narrow Gauge, since he was born and brought up among the ironworks and coal mines of Northumberland—the home of Stephenson's Waggon Gauge—while his experience of locomotive building was gained under the direction of Mr Robert Stephenson. But many great truths are in some way revealed to master minds; so was the superiority of the Broad Gauge to Daniel Gooch. He says,—'I was very glad to have to manage the Broad Gauge, which filled my mind as the great advance of the age, and in the soundness of which I was a firm believer.'

Before Mr Gooch was connected with the Great Western Railway Mr Brunel had ordered several locomotives—six from the Vulcan Foundry (where Mr Gooch had served under Robert Stephenson); four from Mather, Dixon and Company, Liverpool; two from Sharp, Roberts and Company, Manchester; two from Hawthorne and Company, Newcastle-on-Tyne; two from the Haigh Foundry Company; and, most curious to mention, two from R. Stephenson and Company, Newcastle-on-Tyne. These two were built from drawings by Mr Gooch himself, having been intended for a Russian railway with a 6 foot gauge, but the money not being forthcoming, the careful firm of Stephenson and Company did not part with them, so that they were afterwards altered to the 7 foot gauge and supplied to the Great Western Railway. They were the celebrated 'North Star'—the prototype of the modern passenger locomotive—and her sister engine the 'Evening Star.'

While the other railways and the locomotive builders were experimenting with engines constructed in every possible way, some with four and some with six wheels, outside and inside cylinders, with bores of from 6 inches to 22 inches, and strokes with longer variations. On some the cylinders were vertical, others would be inclined or horizontal, with bell cranks and all manner of curious contrivances to convey the motion; the driving wheel placed in the front,

E

middle or rear position, at times coupled, but often not. These and a hundred other methods were being tried on the Narrow Gauge at the time the Great Western Railway had practically settled its type of engine, which type even to-day would still pass as a good style of engine, exciting little comment as to its appearance among the ordinary travelling public. The 'Vulcan' built by the Vulcan Foundry Company, as already stated, was the first Broad Gauge locomotive delivered to Mr Gooch's care.

The following table gives the principal features of the earliest Broad Gauge's engines, that is, those ordered by Mr Brunel prior to Mr Gooch undertaking the production of the locomotive power of the Great Western Railway :—

Name.	Diameter of Driving Wheel.	Diameter of Cylinder.	Stroke.	Grate Area.	Heating Surface of Fire-box.	Total Heating Surface.	Builder.
	ft. in.	in.	in.	ft.	ft.	ft.	
Vulcan, .	8 0	14	16	9.58	55	589	Vulcan Foundry Company.
Æolus, .	8 0	14	18	...	57.15	587	Do.
Bacchus, .	8 0	14	18	...	57.15	587	Do.
Venus, ⎫							Do.
Neptune, ⎬	8 0	12	18	...	52.35	510	Do.
Apollo, ⎭							Do.
Ajax, .	10 0	14	20	10.22	57.3	474	Mather, Dixon and Company.
North Star,	7 0	16	16	13	70.10	724.8	R. Stephenson and Company.
Evening Star,	6 6	16	16	13	70.10	705.4	Do.
Premier, .	6 0	14	14	...	51.71	377	Sharp, Roberts and Company.
Lion, .	7 0	14	18	...	51.17	478	Do.

The gross weights of the above engines with tenders (loaded) varied from 23½ tons ('Lion') to 29 tons ('North Star').

The two engines built by the Haigh Foundry Company had driving wheels 6 feet in diameter, but geared up to 12 feet, with but small cylinders. Of these Mr Gooch says,—'I felt very uneasy about the working of these machines, feeling they would have enough to do to drive *themselves* along the road.'

Those made by Hawthorne and Company were designed by Mr Thomas Harrison, and were most curious examples of steam locomotives. Of these the

THE 'PREMIER.'
6 ft. driving wheels, 3 ft. 6 in. leading and trailing wheels, cylinders, 14 in. by 14 in.

'Hurricane' had driving wheels 10 feet in diameter, and the 'Thunderer' had wheels 6 feet in diameter, but driven by a gear of 3 to 1, so that they were equal to wheels of 18 feet diameter. The fire-box of both these engines was divided into two parts by a partition, and the boiler, fire-box, etc., was on one truck, while the motion was on a separate truck. The following are the other principal dimensions of these remarkable engines :—

Name.	Cylinders.	BOILERS.					FIRE-BOX.			HEATING SURFACE.			Weight. (empty.)
		Diameter.	Length.	No. of Tubes.	Length of Tubes.	Diameter of Tubes.	Length.	Width.	Height above Fire Bars.	Fire-box.	Fire Grate.	Total including Tubes.	
	in.	in. ft. in.	ft.		ft. in.	in.	ft. in.	ft in.	ft.	ft.	ft.		
Hurricane,	16 by 20	3 8	8.7	135	8.7	1¾	3 8½	5	4 1	108.26	17.12	516.37	11 tons.
Thunderer,	16 by 20					Si mila r			to	above,			12 tons.

In the geared engine the wheels were coupled.

The steam to the cylinders, and the exhaust to the funnel, were conveyed from one vehicle to another by a novel 'universal steam joint.' Mr Harrison adopted a plan to tighten the cog-wheels should they become loose by being worn. The water tank was placed beneath the frame of the boiler carriage.

The fault with these early engines was the extremely limited amount of heating surface, thus the 'Ajax,' with 10 feet driving wheels, only had 474 feet of heating surface, while the 'North Star,' with 7 feet wheels, had 724.8 feet, and a modern engine has some 1500 feet, and works with a steam pressure three times as great. No wonder that engines built on such lines proved failures. Had those with the 10 feet wheels and the geared ones been equipped with sufficient boiler power the result of their performances would have been very different.

The Great Western Railway stock at the end of 1838 consisted of fourteen locomotives, costing £1980 each; forty-two first-class carriages, costing £544 each; forty second-class carriages, costing £351 each; one hundred and eighteen trucks and waggons, costing £106 each, or a total value of £90,976 for the rolling stock then possessed by the Company.

In later years the 10 feet wheels of the 'Ajax' and 'Hurricane' were put to a novel use, being lent by the Great Western Railway Company to convey the bronze statue of the Duke of Wellington to Hyde Park Corner. Some of these early engines were provided with a projection in front, extending from the smoke box to the buffer beam, and shaped like the bow of a ship, the designer being under the impression that such a contrivance would offer less resistance to the air, and that, consequently, the train would be able to travel at an increased speed ; but from experiments that were made, it was found that no advantage was obtained by using this prow in front of the engine, and it was discarded ; yet such is the truth of the Wise Man's words, ' Nothing new under the sun,'. that a French railway is at this moment building loco-motives fitted with a similar prow, under the impression that so fitted they will offer less resistance to the air.

De Pambour (a Frenchman who came to England, to make experiments on railways), on 3d August 1839, attained a speed of 55.4 miles for over 2 miles, with the ' Evening Star ' ? on a trip to Maidenhead, with the engine, tender, and eight people. A higher speed could have been attained had the pumps for supplying the boiler been larger, but at this speed the engine evaporated the water quicker than the pumps supplied it, so that speed had to be reduced. He covered 14 consecutive miles as follows :—8 at the rate of 45 miles an hour, 4 at 48, and 2 at 55.4. Pambour mentions that this engine had 7 feet driving wheels, while the table we give on a previous page gives the ' Evening Star ' with driving wheels 6 feet 6 inches in diameter only. It was therefore probably the ' North Star ' that he used.

The first engines Mr Gooch designed were of two classes known as the ' Firefly ' and ' Fury,' and both of them were exceptionally good. Their dimensions were :—

	Driving Wheels.	Cylinders.	Heating Surface.
Firefly,	7 ft.	15 by 18 in. stroke.	700 ft.
Fury,	6 ft.	14 by 18 in. stroke.	608 ft.

Mr Gooch had the engines of these classes fitted with steel tyres, for which he had taken out a patent, as, although the tyres only contained a fifth part of sheer steel, that commodity fifty years ago was a very expensive item, and the price prevented the general introduction of these improved tyres to any other wheels than the engines and tenders.   The results obtained were very good, many of the locomotives fitted with these patent tyres running between 200,000 and 300,000 miles before they required to be re-tyred.   So that, in the long run, the result was certainly a considerable economy.

These engines were built by various makers, the most satisfactory by the Leeds firm of Fenton, Murray and Jackson.

Mr Gooch thus writes of these engines—his first venture in locomotive designing :—' I may with confidence, after these engines have been working for twenty-eight years, say that no better engines for their weight have since been constructed either by myself or others.   They have done, and continue to do, admirable duty ; advantage has been taken of new cylinders being required to give them an extra inch in diameter * and 4 inches more in stroke, and expansion gear has been added ; in other respects the engines are the same.'   The ' Witch' had driving wheels 7 feet 6 inches in diameter, and was the only Broad Gauge engine of its class.   We will conclude this chapter with a description of the early Broad Gauge passenger coaches, each of which ran on six wheels, while the Narrow Gauge vehicles had but four wheels, so that at first the Great Western Railway introduced one of the very best protections for the safety of its passengers. The Narrow Gauge carriage designers have long since copied the example set by Mr Brunel.   They now one and all declare that there is great risk in running four-wheel vehicles, for, should an axle break or a wheel come off, nothing can save a carriage having but four

* Thanks to the margin allowed by the Broad Gauge.

wheels, while a six or eight wheel one is, comparatively speaking, safe, in the event of such a mishap.

Mr Brunel's original idea, and one that influenced to a considerable degree the width of gauge chosen by him, was to hang the railway carriages between the wheels, after the manner of road vehicles. Only one coach, however, appears to have been so constructed, although much larger wheels were always used on the Broad Gauge than on the Narrow. The Broad Gauge allowing the centre of gravity to be raised with perfect safety, the wheels were made to enter the floors of the carriages, being, of course, boxed over. This latter method was rather awkward to passengers, when the wheel happened to be just under the door of a compartment, as unwary passengers were likely to fall over the projecting box. While the Narrow Gauge lines could only use wheels of 3 feet diameter for their rolling stock, the Broad Gauge were able to construct theirs with wheels of 3 feet 6 inches, 4 feet, and even 4 feet 6 inches diameter, thus causing the vehicles to travel with less noise and vibration, and considerable ease and extreme smoothness at the highest velocity.

The first-class carriages had four compartments, each with accommodation for eight passengers, and weighed 7 tons 8 cwt. The second-class had six compartments of twelve passengers, and weighed 7 tons 5 cwt. So that with the additional security of six wheels to each vehicle, the dead weight to be carried for each first-class passenger was only 588 lbs., and for each second-class passenger 225 lbs., while on the Narrow Gauge lines the second-class passenger required 238 lbs. of dead weight to be conveyed per person. The dead weight for each first-class passenger on the Narrow Gauge was 631 lbs, and these in unsafe four-wheel carriages.

The first Broad Gauge carriages were built by Davis of Wigmore Street, London, and were 21 feet long, with four compartments, or 18 feet long with only three.   They were 8 feet wide and about 6 feet 6 inches high, these dimensions being very considerably larger than those of the Narrow Gauge vehicles; and they were fitted with the 'clerestory' roof, and copper gauze wire panels for ventilation, covered with wooden slides.   Some of the first-class compartments had a door in the centre, thus being divided into two small rooms, each for four persons.   The Great Western Railway has continued the use of the 'clerestory' roofs for its passenger rolling stock, and is justly famed for the improvement, the Midland Railway has copied the Broad Gauge in this respect, many of its best carriages having the raised roofs and ventilators.   The public was not long before it found out the great superiority of the Great Western Railway carriages.   A writer in 1838 thus describes them :—' Those upon the Liverpool and Manchester Railway possess many advantages both of beauty and convenience, but still they are far sur passed by those placed upon the Great Western Railway by Brunel, which are complete with every convenience and luxury, being almost gorgeously fitted up.   They are particularly spacious and complete, with sofas and all the appliances for the agreeable occupation of time.

CHAPTER V.

THE EARLY DEVELOPMENT OF THE RAILWAY.

BEFORE we commence to narrate the greatest epoch in the history of the Great Western Railway, it will be as well to shortly describe the general position of the railway at the commencement of 1845—on the eve of the ' Battle of the Gauges.' Having already in previous chapters dealt with the main line of the Great Western Railway, we will turn our attention to the branches, etc., of this railway. At this time the Great Western system consisted of—

G.W.R. London to Bristol, .	118½ miles	
Branch, Didcot to Oxford, .	10	,,
Bristol and Exeter Railway, .	72	,,
Do. do., branch to Weston-Super-Mare, . .	2	,,
G.W. and Cheltenham Union, Swindon to Cirencester. .	18	,,
Total, . .	220½ miles.	

At this early period of its history the Great Western Railway was considerably the largest of the sixty-six railways then open for traffic, the Midland standing second with a length of 179 miles. The Oxford branch was opened on 12th June 1844, and, as is very rarely the case, was constructed for less than the estimated amount, and was opened before the date originally fixed for its completion.

The Bristol and Exeter line had been opened in

sections, the entire length being opened on 1st May 1844; it was a very level line to construct, and with one exception had no great engineering works. Leaving Bristol, it rises 1 in 436 for 4¾ miles, then falls 1 in 355 for 5¼ miles; for the next 28 miles it is practically level, the fall being but 1 in 3745; the gradient next rises 1 in 875 for 8½ miles, then 1 in 355 for 6½, then to the summit through the Whiteball Tunnel the rise is 1 in 127 for 4 miles, level for 1 mile, falls for 5 miles 1 in 227, and then right the way to Exeter, 17 miles, it falls 1 in 463. These were the ruling gradients, but some short pieces are as bad as 1 in 90.

The exception alluded to above is the Whiteball Tunnel, on an incline of 1 in 127. So great was the progress made in the art of tunnelling that this tunnel only cost £53 a yard to construct, while the Box Tunnel, built two or three years earlier, cost £100 a yard, and the Cheltenham Tunnel, a year or so later, but £34 a yard, although originally estimated to cost £136 a yard, while in October 1844 Mr Brunel had received tenders to construct tunnels at the low price of £28 a yard.

The Weston branch was worked by horse power. The 18 miles of the Great Western and Cheltenham Union line that was first opened consisted of 14 miles of the main line, Swindon to Kemble, and a branch from the latter to Cirencester, 4 miles in length.

The Bristol and Gloucester Railway was opened in July 1844. The line from Stonehouse to Gloucester was part of the Great Western and Cheltenham Union Railway, this portion used by the Bristol and Gloucester Railway Company having been completed before the connecting part from Kemble to Gloucester to enable the Bristol and Gloucester Company to open their line throughout without delay.

Upon the opening of the Bristol and Exeter Railway the up night mail left Exeter at 9.35 P.M., and arrived at Paddington at 3.40 A.M.

The present times are, depart 10.34 P.M., arrive 4 A.M., or an acceleration of only 35 minutes in fifty years. This of itself is very good evidence of the superior speed attained by the Broad Gauge at its inception, the mail from Liverpool to London on the Narrow Gauge at that time taking nearly as long again on the journey as it does at the present time, leaving Liverpool at 8 P.M. and arriving at Euston at 5.32 A.M., while the mail from Chester took 8 hours 10 minutes against 4 hours 12 minutes at the present time.

Two sensational mail robberies on one occasion happened to the up and down Exeter mails in 1849. The up mail leaving Plymouth at 6.35 P.M., and Exeter at 9 P.M., arrived at Bridgewater at 10.30 P.M. At this station various bags of letters, which had accumulated in the post-office van during the trip, were, in accordance with the usual custom of the guard, placed in a tender immediately at the rear of the post-office van, and securely locked up. The train, in addition to the post-office tender, consisted of six or seven first and second-class carriages, and left Bridgewater in due course and proceeded on its journey to Bristol, the run between these two places being timed to occupy 1 hour 10 minutes without stoppage at any station. On the arrival of the train at Bristol shortly before midnight, the guard went to the tender in the rear of the post-office, in order to deliver the Bristol bags, when he found that all the bags had more or less been tampered with, some being cut open and others left with the seals broken and strings untied. He then found that all the money or registered letters, as well as the bankers' parcels, had been abstracted. Without a moment's loss of time he communicated, first with the two travelling post-office clerks accompanying the mail, and subsequently with the post-office authorities at Bristol. The guard was quite positive the bags were safe when the train left Bridgewater, and as no stoppage had taken place between that town and the City of Bristol, it was evident that the robbery must have been effected by some parties travelling by the train, and while it was in motion.

After a few moments' consultation, it was resolved to send the Metropolitan bags on to London in the state in which the guard had discovered them, and, accordingly, the train left Bristol on its upward journey after a very short delay. On reaching town at an early hour the next morning, the guard proceeded direct to the post-office in St Martin-le-Grand, and made a full report. The various bags were immediately examined, when it was found that not only were the whole of the registered letters and bankers' parcels abstracted, but in some cases the bills on which all registered letters and valuable parcels are entered were also missing, so that it was impossible to say how far the plunder had extended. Information was then forwarded by the post-office authorities to the various city banking-houses, so that a check might be put upon the disposal of the contents of the stolen letters.

Later in the afternoon information reached town of a second robbery, precisely similar in character, perpetrated on the down mail which left London at 8.55 P.M. on the previous evening. In this case the bags deposited in the tender were perfectly safe on the arrival of the train at Bristol at 1.15 A.M. On the tender being opened at Bridgewater, a scene similar to that previously observed at Bristol presented itself, all the bags were more or less mutilated or disturbed, and the more valuable contents abstracted therefrom. The suspected thieves were this time luckily arrested. The parties alluded to were two men of respectable appearance, both of whom travelled in a first-class carriage, occupying the next compartment to the post-office tender. Their implication in the affair was placed beyond doubt by the discovery of several registered letters and money parcels in the carriage in which they rode. Immediately upon their apprehension they were conveyed to Exeter, where, upon investigation, it was ascertained their names were Poole and Nightingale. It appeared that the men did not enter the train at Exeter, but proceeded by private conveyance to Laira, the extremity of the South Devon Railway. They did this in order the more effectually to enable them to conceal their disguises, and also to prevent the recognition of Poole by the railway clerks and porters at the Exeter Station. On leaving Bridgewater, one of the men, if not both, left the compartment of the carriage in which they had been seated, and having taken about three steps (a feat of no great difficulty as appears from the peculiar construction of the Great Western carriages) were enabled to reach the door of the post-office tender, which they opened and entered. Having selected their booty, they left the tender on its slackening towards Bristol, and quitted the train. Having secreted the stolen property in Bristol, they returned to the station to take the down train. Here they arrived at what was called the 'Exeter shed' of the Bristol Station some minutes before the arrival of the down train and before the door of the booking-office was opened; Mr Lee, a retired tradesman of Clifton, was waiting at the door when the two men came up. Nightingale advanced first, and Poole, on seeing the stranger, receded a few yards, taking up his position under an arch. Mr Lee made some common-place observations about the non-arrival of the train, which, however, Nightingale did not answer but turned away and joined Poole under the arch. Here they carried on a conversation for some time in a low whisper, and on the bell ringing announcing the arrival of the train the two men made towards the booking-office. Poole passed through the office, and, observing Mr Lee looking at him, turned away his head. The manner in which Poole passed through the station, coupled with the circumstances which took place outside, excited that gentleman's suspicions. Mr Lee determined to watch their proceedings, and having received his ticket, proceeded to the end of the Exeter shed, in order that he might see their movements, while he remained unobserved. He was, however, disappointed in his expectation, for although he could distinctly hear two persons talking one to another in a subdued voice he could not see them, nor could he tell precisely from what point the sounds proceeded. On the ringing of the bell for the departure of the train the two men suddenly rushed forward, one from either side of the train, where they had probably been watching the post-office tender to ascertain whether or not anyone was placed there. They went forward to the first-class carriages, and the door of one of them was opened for them. Nightingale exclaimed, 'No, that won't do; we must have a compartment to ourselves.' The guard then showed them to another carriage in which they took their seats. It is supposed that immediately on the starting of the train the thieves commenced their operations.

Here are some more robberies.

At the end of 1844 the messenger who was dispatched from Paddington Station to a bank in the city with the takings of one day, amounting to £1287, 1s. 4d., alleged that the money disappeared in transit between the two places, while on another occasion the booking-offices at Paddington were broken into and considerable sums of money stolen. Then there were the notorious luggage robberies on the Great Western Railway, and the subsequent conviction of the thieves, who were railway officials, and systematically carried out the most audacious robberies of passengers' luggage. To Mr Nash, a solicitor who brought the miscreants to justice, at the expense of his own fortune, the travelling public of fifty years ago owed an unrequited debt of gratitude. Not only did the thieves send letters threatening to murder Mr Nash if he proceeded with the cases against them, but when on one count one of them was discharged for want of conclusive evidence, he started an action against Mr Nash for false imprisonment, in which he was backed up by a Great Western Director; but this aggressive thief did not succeed, for before the case came on for trial he was convicted on another charge of luggage robbery; the heavy expenses incurred in the various proceedings, however, resulted in the bankruptcy of Mr Nash, and the Great Western Railway ungenerously refused to help him, and discharged him their service—a good reward for zealousness in the discharge of his duties, surely!

At the present time railway managers pride themselves on their carefulness and economical working, if they can succeed in keeping the expenses somewhere about 52 per cent. of the receipts. We can therefore well imagine what exuberation would be theirs (and the shareholders also) if they could manage the line so that the working expenses were only $34\frac{1}{4}$ per cent. of the revenue. This was the proportion on the Great Western Railway for the second half of 1843; but, alas! undoubtedly these halcyon days of 10 per cent. railway dividends have gone like many more of the pleasing things of 'the good old times' never to return.

In these early days railways did not have the time-table books as now issued, nor did they post up time bills on the station walls, but time-table bills could generally be obtained on application to the booking clerk. This was anything but a satisfactory method of dispensing the necessary information as to the running of the trains, and caused intending passengers a great deal of inconvenience and loss of time and general delay to all concerned. The Great Western Railway, however, was more generous than the other lines, and obviated this cause of annoyance by hanging up the 'train bills' at all their stations in the same way as they do excursion handbills now, so that a traveller could obtain a time table at any time, and not be dependent on the booking clerk for the particulars of the running of the trains.

If anyone were weather hardened enough to travel third class, and time was no object—or at least not such an important object as money—he could travel third class in an open carriage attached to the goods trains, which left Paddington at 4.30 A.M. and 9.30 P.M., and in sixteen hours (if nothing occurred to delay the train) he would be landed at Taunton, a distance of 163 miles; but Mr Gladstone's parliamentary train act of 1844 improved the lot of the third-class passengers, giving them the, at that time, luxury of a covered carriage and a seat, and a minimum speed of 12 miles an hour including stoppages.   On 1st November 1844, the Great Western started its parliamentary trains, and took care to take the full time allowed, for the journey between Bristol and London took 9½ hours—the train left at 7 A.M. and stopped at all stations; the up train left Bristol at half-past nine each morning.   The passengers to stations beyond Bristol had to spend the night there, as the Company took advantage of the Bristol and Exeter Railway being a semi-independent company to arrange for the parliamentary trains on that line not to run in connection with the Great Western Railway trains.   After this date, third-class passengers had still the option of travelling by the 9.30 P.M. goods, but not by the 4.30 A.M. goods train.   On 1st January 1846, the third-class passengers between London and Bristol had another train each way daily put on for their convenience, and on the same date the Great Western Railway discarded the old-fashioned paper tickets as used by the stage coaches, and adopted Edmondson's invention of cardboard,—now universal.   Up to 5th August 1844, first and second-class passengers had enjoyed the *privilege* of being conveyed by goods trains on the Bristol and Exeter Railway, but on that date they had this *great* advantage taken from them.

In these exclusive days of fifty years ago, not only

was each class provided with distinct booking *offices,* (not pigeon holes), which still remain at some stations on the South Devon and Cornwall lines, but the platforms were divided by barriers into first, second and third-class portions.

On Monday, 2d September 1844, the Great Western Railway ran their first excursion. The train left London at 7 A.M. for Bath and Bristol, from which city it was continued on the Tuesday morning to Taunton and Exeter. The return train left Exeter at 4 P.M. on the same day, the night again being spent at Bristol or Bath, and passengers reaching London on Wednesday afternoon. The fares were :—

London to Bath and back, 28s. first class, 19s. second ; London to Bristol, 30s. first, 20s. second ; London to Exeter, 48s. first, 31s. second ; and if one person purchased seventy tickets or over, a discount of 1s. on each ticket was allowed. Some 500 persons left Paddington by this maiden excursion of the Great Western Railway, and the number was doubled by those who joined the train at Slough, Reading and other stations. This was the foundation of the famous Broad Gauge excursions to the West of England that have ever since been growing in popularity.

The following statistics relating to the Great Western Railway in the 'early forties' are of interest. In 1846, nineteen trains left Paddington daily, to-day the number is over one hundred. The number of passengers conveyed from the opening to 31st December 1845 were :—

1838 (from the 4th of June),	264,644
1839,	606,396
1840,	1,024,217
1841,	1,541,656

Carry forward,	3,436,913

F

	Brought forward,	3,436,913
1842, .	. . . . .	1,606,015
1843, .	. . . . .	1,629,150
1844, .	. . . . .	1,791,272
1845, .	. . . . .	2,441,255
		10,904,605

The following figures relate to the second half of 1845 :—

Miles open, .	. . . .	245
Train miles run, .	. . . .	1,090,612
Number of passengers,	. .	1,411,504
Miles travelled .	. .	47,938,473
Tons of goods, .	. . .	151,212

In 1846 the House of Lords ordered the Board of Trade to make a return of the railway rolling stock owned by the various railways. The Broad Gauge at that time possessed the following :—

G. W. R. 121 engines, 232 carriages, 919 waggons, trucks, etc.
B. & E. R. 11   „   20   „   213   „   „   „

The Great Western Railway had the largest number of locomotives. The London and Birmingham coming next with 117. While the Newtyle and Coupar Angus came last with 1 engine 2 carriages and 48 trucks. The South Eastern Railway in this first return had the most carriages (409), while the Pontop and South Shields had the largest number of trucks (2649), but had no passenger vehicles, hiring these latter from the Newcastle and Darlington Railway.

The cloakroom for passengers' left luggage was another great public convenience originally introduced by the Great Western Railway. The experiment was first tried at the Bath Station in July 1846, and the practice appears to have been exactly similiar to that now prevailing. 'A man appointed for that purpose has a room in which the articles are kept separate and locked up. A printed receipt is given to the passenger who deposits luggage, and in order to meet the responsibility and additional expense, a charge of 2d. upon each article is made by the Company. As far as it has yet gone, the plan is stated to work well, and likely to prove a great accommodation,' which it certainly has.

CHAPTER VI.

THE BATTLE OF THE GAUGES—THE BROAD GAUGE LEADERS.

THE great success of the existing railways having amply proved the lucrativeness of railway undertakings as investments, it was but natural that speculators and capitalists should turn their attention to promoting new railway companies.

The directors and officials of existing lines recognising that 'self-preservation is the first law of nature,' immediately took steps to defend their territories, but in this eagerness to protect their property, they made the mistake of taking offensive action, when defensive measures would have sufficed.

The Directors of the Great Western Railway in common with those of other railways fell into this error by giving support and encouragement to projected lines that were directly hostile to their neighbours, the London and South-Western on one side, and the London and Birmingham on the other.

To enable this, the most momentous and exciting period in the whole history of English railway enterprise, to be properly understood, we purpose treating the 'Battle of the Gauges' under three heads, viz. :—

The Commercial Battle;
The Parliamentary Battle; and
The Engineering Battle.

But before doing so, it will not be out of place to give some particulars of the careers of the Broad Gauge champions, all of whom were connected with the Great Western Railway.

ISAMBARD KINGDOM BRUNEL.

Born 9th April 1806.   Died 15th September 1859.

These were :—
Isambard Kingdom Brunel, the Engineer ;
Daniel Gooch, the Locomotive Superintendent ; and
Charles Alexander Saunders, the Secretary.

ISAMBARD KINGDOM BRUNEL.

Isambard Kingdom Brunel was born at Portsmouth on 9th April 1806. He was the only son of Mr (afterwards Sir) Marc Isambard Brunel, who occupied an important position in the Royal Dockyard at Portsmouth.

No wonder that the young Isambard should early develop a taste for engineering, being brought up amongst scientific instruments and books, while the dockyard afforded scope to his budding genius in examining the various machines, many of which his father, who was a celebrated engineer, had designed. The elder Brunel was born in Normandy, but being an ardent Royalist, when the Revolution broke out he was compelled to flee to America, where he was appointed Engineer to the State of New York; afterwards coming to England, he obtained an appointment in the Portsmouth Dockyard.

His son Kingdom early developed a taste for drawing, and when only four years old he had executed some, for such a child, remarkably clever sketches. When he was eight years old the family moved to Chelsea, and his father spent much of his spare time in teaching Kingdom mathematics, in which science he proved a most apt scholar. Shortly after he was sent to a school at Hove, near Brighton, where his talent for engineering soon showed itself, as the following extract from a letter written in 1820, when but fourteen years old, and addressed to his mother, shows,—' I have been making half a dozen boats lately, till I have worn my hands to pieces. I have also taken a plan of Hove, which is a very amusing job. I should be much obliged if you will ask papa whether he would lend me his long measure ; it is a long, soft tape ; he will know what I mean. I will take care of it, for I want to make a more exact plan, though this is pretty exact, I think.' That he was a most observing lad, is demonstrated by the following :—A range of buildings were being erected opposite the school at Hove, and one evening young Brunel startled his schoolfellows by offering to bet that the new buildings would collapse in the night ; the bet was speedily accepted, and the next morning, much to the surprise of the other boys, the buildings were found to have been blown down. They naturally wondered how Brunel could have known that such an event would happen, and his simple explanation ' that he had watched them building, and seen of what bad material and with what unskilful workmanship they were constructed, then judging from the state of the atmosphere that a violent storm would come on in the night, he concluded that the building was not strong enough to withstand it,' which opinion was duly verified.   In October 1820, he was sent to Paris to the College Henri Quatre, where he remained till August 1822.   During the time he was in Paris he made careful surveys of the various bridges and the public buildings of the city ; these he sent home to his father, together with his critical observations of the design and construction of the various edifices.

Early in 1823, he entered his father's office. At this time Mr Brunel, senior, was busily engaged in preparing plans and estimates for the construction of the Thames Tunnel, the necessity for which was at that time agitating the public mind, and although the younger Isambard was, of course, not responsible for that work, yet he offered much valuable advice, and was for many years engaged in the details of its construction.   After many almost insurmountable obstacles the tunnel was publicly opened on 25th March 1843. Upon one occasion the construction was abandoned for seven years.

In 1829, it was proposed to build a suspension

bridge to connect Bristol and Clifton, and plans were invited. Kingdom Brunel's plans were accepted out of a number sent in ; but Telford, who was consulting engineer to the Bridge Company, thought Brunel's proposed span too long, in his opinion the Menai Bridge, with a span of 660 feet, being the ultimatum for a suspension bridge. Consequently, new plans were advertised for, and Brunel set hard to work to convince the Bridge Company that his plans were practicable ; he, however, modified them somewhat, and finally they were accepted, and he was appointed engineer to the venture.

The work was commenced in 1836, little progress was made for want of funds, and in 1853 the building of the bridge was abandoned. After Brunel's death the work was taken over by a new company, and completed in 1864.

In 1831, the future founder of the Broad Gauge prepared the plans and designs for the Monkswearmouth docks, while the Bristol, Plymouth, Brentford, Milford Haven and Briton Ferry (Neath) docks were also designed by him and constructed under his supervision.

From 1841-45, he was engaged upon the Hungerford Suspension Bridge, constructed across the Thames for pedestrian traffic. This bridge was removed in 1861, as the site was required for the Charing Cross railway bridge, when, strange irony of fate, the materials were used to complete the Clifton Bridge, so that, although Brunel did not himself complete the latter bridge, yet it was finished with the materials provided by him for another work.

Without doubt, his *chef d'œuvre* was the construction of the Great Western Railway, with its magnificent 7 feet gauge, the particulars of which are contained in this volume. Besides the Great Western Railway and its Broad Gauge allies, Brunel constructed other railways in South Wales. And he looked upon Milford Haven as a harbour specially adapted for his monster steamship, the 'Great Eastern.' He was also engineer to an Irish railway, two others in Italy, and the Eastern Bengal Railway.

With regard to steam navigation, Brunel was the originator of the idea for a line of steamships between England and America, and he constructed the 'Great Western'—the first ship of a regular service across the 'herring pond.' This vessel was launched on 19th July 1837, and was at that time the largest vessel ever constructed; she was a paddle ship, and performed the journey from Bristol to New York in fifteen days. Shortly after he constructed a much larger one for the same line; this was christened the 'Great Britain.' When, in 1851, it was proposed to have a line of steamships from the Mother Country to Australia, Brunel proposed his idea of the colossal steamer, the 'Great Eastern.' The proposal was well received, and the ship was immediately commenced. This boat was propelled by both paddles and screws, improvements in the latter having then been recently developed.

After many disappointments and untoward accidents, the leviathian was successfully launched on 5th January 1858. She started on her first voyage on 7th September 1858, but her designer did not live to see the success of the ship, upon the construction of which he had devoted so much of his time, talent and money.

Among his minor works were the two towers at the Crystal Palace, and various improvements in artillery and gun carriages.

He was on the committee of the first great Exhibition (1851), and was the principal witness examined before the Select Committee of the House of Lords on the Patent Laws in 1851.

He married in July 1836, and his family consisted of two sons and a daughter. In his home life he was most generous and universally liked, but, like so many really clever men, he was somewhat reserved, which gave those not intimately acquainted with him the impression that he was cold and unfeeling. If possible, he never made enemies, remarking that 'spite and ill nature were the most expensive luxuries.'

Mr I. K. Brunel was a great lover of real art, and his drawings were much admired for accuracy of proportion, taste and form, while his residence in Duke Street, Westminster, was noted for its rare furniture, bronzes and china.

The public were very proud of him as a great engineer; this was shown in a remarkable manner. Once while performing a conjuring trick to amuse some children, he inadvertently swallowed a half-crown piece, which caused his life to be in danger; the newspapers published daily bulletins of his condition, which were read anxiously by everyone, and when at last the joyful news was made public that the coin was recovered, a feeling of thankfulness pervaded the whole nation.

But his end came sooner than would have been expected. He had been unwell in the winter of 1858-59, and had travelled in Egypt, hoping to recruit his strength. The interest he took in the 'Great Eastern,' then nearing completion, would not allow him to completely rest, as he should have done, and he returned to England to superintend the fitting out of his monster vessel on the 5th September 1859. Whilst so engaged, he became very unwell and went to his home, where he was immediately seized by an attack of paralysis from which he never recovered, dying on 15th September. He was buried at Kensal Green Cemetery. A memorial window has been placed in Westminster Abbey as a slight national tribute to the remarkable genius of Isambard Kingdom Brunel.

The characteristics of Brunel's French nationality are strongly developed in his works, all of them being either on a gigantic scale or on theoretical bases. He refused to follow other engineers. Many of his innovations were, without doubt, great improvements, as instanced by the 7 feet gauge for railways, and the various improvements in locomotives and railway rolling stock, the 'Great Eastern' steamship, etc.

But like many other clever people, he lived before the public were prepared for his great works. If he were starting his career in this year of grace, he would soon be to the front. He somewhat lost reputation over the South Devon Atmospheric Railway, but doubtless the principle is correct, but it has not been sufficiently developed for working on a large scale, and now engineers are too busily engaged with electricity to give their time to this simple method of propulsion. Brunel looked upon things from an engineer's point of view, and any bold idea, if it could possibly be carried out, he worked at energetically, never troubling to inquire if the venture would be financially successful; but although he did not inquire into the monetary condition of undertakings he was engaged in, yet he freely invested his money in them, thus showing that he believed in their ultimate success. The original Great Western proprietors were more than satisfied with him, and, on 17th January 1845, presented him with a service of plate costing 2000 guineas, the subscriptions to which were limited to 10 guineas. On the centre piece was the following inscription :—

PRESENTED TO

ISAMBARD KINGDOM BRUNEL, Esq.,

THE ENGINEER-IN-CHIEF OF THE GREAT WESTERN,
THE BRISTOL AND EXETER, THE CHELTENHAM
AND GREAT WESTERN UNION, AND THE
BRISTOL AND GLOUCESTER RAILWAYS,
BY 257 SUBSCRIBERS,
TO COMMEMORATE
THE COMPLETION OF THOSE
GREAT NATIONAL WORKS, AND TO
RECORD THEIR ADMIRATION OF THE
SCIENCE, SKILL AND ENERGY MANIFESTED
IN THE DESIGN AND EXECUTION OF THEM, THEIR
GRATITUDE FOR THE ADVANTAGES CONFERRED
ON THEMSELVES AND THE PUBLIC; AND
THEIR ESTEEM FOR THE INTEGRITY
AND WORTH OF HIS PERSONAL
CHARACTER.
A.D. 1845.

Mr Brunel rarely gave professional evidence for or against any scheme he was not interested in as an engineer, and was a most careful and useful witness, always making it appear most clearly that what he advocated was both highly necessary and easy of accomplishment. He was, however, always careful to personally prepare the proof of his own evidence, and to state the way in which the questions should be asked him in examination. Had Brunel lived for twenty or even ten years longer, there can be but little doubt that the Broad Gauge would still be flourishing and increasing in our midst, and all deep-thinking people would have long since come to the conclusion that it was unmistakably a better gauge for a railway than the 4 feet 8½ inches one. Under Brunel's able leadership they would have seen the Broad Gauge System managed and developed in a manner commensurate with the importance of the principles at stake in the issue between the rival gauges; but it was not to be.

Sir Daniel Gooch.

We hardly know whether to bestow the greatest praise upon the founder of the Broad Gauge, or upon his pupil—Sir Daniel Gooch. At any rate Mr Gooch lived longer and worked longer for the Broad Gauge than did Mr Brunel, and is therefore better known to the present generation.

He was born at Bedlington, Northumberland, on 24th August 1816, at 3 A.M., during a very violent thunderstorm. His father was engaged at the ironworks at Bedlington, which were owned by young Gooch's second cousins. At four years of age, the infant Daniel was sent to a school kept by two maiden ladies. Some few years later he was sent to a school kept by a clergyman at Condhall, 4 miles from Bedlington. His school life was a very happy one, full of youthful pranks and practical jokes, and Gooch was always found at the fore in these. Except on Sunday and during school hours, Daniel was allowed to spend his spare time as he pleased, and he says,—'I often used to be out of the house on a Saturday morning before any one was up. I remember eating my breakfast before going to bed to save time in the morning.' When Daniel was about twelve years old, it was evident to his parents that he had a decided talent for mechanical pursuits, and his father bought him a little box of tools. His first introduction to locomotives we give in his own words :—'Before I left Bedlington—I do not know in what year it was —I went to Morpeth to see a steam engine working on the common road. It was built by Messrs Hawthorn, of Newcastle, and drew a threshing machine after it. I believe it was for the Duke of Northumberland. It was on its way from Newcastle to Alnwick. I found it at a stand, owing to some defect, on a hill a little before reaching Morpeth, but I waited to see it repaired, and went on with the driver, making the turnings of the streets capitally. It made a strong impression on me. I knew all about the iron horses as they were then called on the waggon way. George Stephenson was often at my father's house, and used to take a great deal of notice of me by taking me on his knee and talking to me about pits, etc. At that time he was much engaged in advising on colliery matters, and had just commenced his glorious career. My eldest brother Tom went to his works at Newcastle as a pupil.' In February 1831, the Gooch family moved to Tredegar, in Monmouth, and Daniel, at the age of fifteen, commenced working in Humphrey's Ironworks there. In June 1831 occurred the Merthyr riots, and the rioters compelled the men employed at the Tredegar Works to go with them to Rhymney, where the 'Riot Act' was read, and the crowd was dispersed. While here Daniel had two narrow escapes. 'There were three large blowing

SIR DANIEL GOOCH.
Born 24th August 1816.   Died 15th October 1889.

engines at Tredegar at that time, and they were all connected by the blowing pipes, so that in case of accident to one engine the others could blow the furnaces. Each engine had a large regulator or sort of iron balloon to equalise the blast from the varying strength of the cylinders. To make their regulators tight, it was the practice to put powdered lime in them. A young fellow, a little older than myself, of the name of Jenkins, and I were inside the blowing cylinders putting on a new valve, when one of the firemen near lifted the valve between our engine and the next one, when the blast came through the regulator upon us, bringing with it the lime powder ; and we could not get out, for the pressure shut the valves where we were ; but as one was off in another place, the engine-house was also soon filled with lime, and the engineer, knowing where we were and what had been done, ran as hard as he could to shut off the valve again, and returned to find us nearly dead from suffocation. A very little more and it would have been all over with us. Another occasion, I believe it was quite accidental, but the result of carelessness, although the engineer was a great friend of mine and a good fellow. We were in the bottom of the cylinder, and had just finished the work, one of the men had gone out, and we were just about to follow, when we were much astonished to see the engine start. The piston at the time was about half stroke, so that we could stand nearly upright. Fortunately it made its first stroke upwards or we would have been flattened like a cake between it and the bottom of the cylinder. Before it had time to make the up-stroke and return, we were able to crouch down into the square valve box at the bottom (these tubes being about 2 feet square and the same depth, just enough to crouch into) when down came the piston again within an inch or so of our heads. Fortunately the man who had left us was in the engine-house, and shouted to the engineer, who stopped the engine at once before she could make another up-stroke, or I fear the valves would have given us a hard squeeze.'

Of the first wages Gooch earned he thus speaks :—
' Those first few sovereigns gave me more pleasure than millions could do now. When I first went to work the important question of my wages took some time to settle, and it was nearly four months before finally an arrangement was made. I had sixteen weeks pay due to me, and the amount per week being 9s., I was indeed a proud boy as I walked away from the pay table with upwards of £6 in my hand. I did not think there was so rich a person in the world. Oh, those first feelings of life once passed never to return with equal force or earnestness!' On 28th August 1833, Daniel had the great misfortune to lose his father. After Mr Gooch, senior, died, the family left Tredegar and went to Coventry, but Daniel stayed till 24th January 1834, when he went to the Vulcan Engine Foundry, near Warrington, the property of Messrs R. Stephenson and Mr Tayleur of Liverpool. This was the first time he had left home. He here got his first impressions of railway riding on the engines of the Liverpool and Manchester Railway, by permission of the locomotive superintendent. Daniel was not long at Warrington before his health gave way, and he went home to Coventry. His brother Thomas was at this time engineer on the Coventry section of the London and Birmingham Railway, then being constructed, and Daniel spent most of his time on the line. Early in 1835 he left home again, going to the Dundee Foundry at Dundee as a draughtsman, arriving there on 17th February. Mr James Stirling was the manager of these works. Here Daniel's salary was £1 a week, on which he kept himself. He left the Dundee Foundry on 31st December 1835, and on 27th January 1836 he commenced duty at Robert Stephenson's locomotive works at Newcastle-on-Tyne. On 8th October 1836, Mr Gooch left Stephenson's works and joined Mr R. Hawkes at

Gateshead, their intention being to go into partnership with a Mr Thompson as locomotive builders. He then went to order the tools for his new firm, and visited Tredegar and Bristol, where he called upon Mr Brunel to try to obtain an order for some of the Great Western engines. Brunel was not there, however, but, being Board meeting day, he saw the Directors of the Great Western Railway. In July 1837, he heard that Mr Brunel required a locomotive engineer for the Great Western Railway, and accordingly applied for the post, calling on Mr Brunel on 20th July.

Mr Brunel visited Manchester, where Mr Gooch was at that time residing, and on 9th August it was arranged that Daniel Gooch was to have the post he so much coveted, and so ably filled. He went to London and commenced his duties on 18th August 1837. In the chapters dealing with the Broad Gauge engines, we have an account of his future career for some years.

The small band of enthusiastic pioneers who had so valiantly fought for the noble Broad Gauge from its inception had year by year grown smaller, until, in 1864, all had left the Great Western Railway save Mr Gooch, and in September of that year he sent in his resignation. But his men at Swindon were so attached to him that they determined to have him as their parliamentary representative, and although at the time he was at sea on the 'Great Eastern,' he was returned by a considerable majority; this was on 13th July 1865. On 10th November 1866, Mr Daniel Gooch was created a baronet by Her Majesty. We have just alluded to the loss the Great Western Railway had undergone by the fact that all the energetic, far-seeing men who had raised the line to the first place in the railway world had by this time left; the Company having no capable men in authority it soon fell into a most deplorable position, and its dividends declined, and, of course, with them the market value of the shares, which had fallen to the very low price of

£90. Luckily at this critical juncture the shareholders thought of Sir D. Gooch, and he was unanimously invited to become the Chairman of the Company. No vacancy would have happened on the Board till 1867, but Sir Watkin Wynn, who had a seat by Act of Parliament, resigned it to make room for Mr Gooch, and on 2d March 1866, for the first time, he presided as Chairman of Directors at a general meeting of the shareholders of the Great Western Railway. Within three years he had the extreme satisfaction of being able to declare a dividend of 3¾ per cent., the highest that had been earned for eighteen years. In April 1872, the effects of his wise management was further exemplified by the payment being at the rate of 5⅜ per cent., and the value of the shares had risen to £120. For these splendid services the shareholders voted him an honorarium of £5000. He devoted his attention to his beloved Great Western Railway until 1889, when, in February, he presided for the last time at the general meeting of shareholders, and declared a dividend of 7¼ per cent. On 13th January 1881, Sir D. Gooch was appointed Chairman of the Railway Association. On 15th October 1889, Sir D. Gooch breathed his last. The event was not un- expected, as for many months previously his health had been very indifferent. The affection of his friends did all that was possible to lighten his illness, but both he and they recognised that the end was near, and, therefore, were not unprepared for it. He was buried in Clewer churchyard, and so ended the long and useful life of one of the greatest men ever connected with railways. It is possible that we may have other men who will do as much for railways, but it will not be possible for any man to do more to advance the progress and efficiency of the iron horse. Sir D. Gooch's splendid achievements will live in history long after the works of contemporary engineers are buried in oblivion. *Clarum et venerabile nomen.* Sir D. Gooch married twice, first on 22d March 1838, to Miss

Margaret Tanner, who died on 23d May 1868; and second on 17th September 1870, to Miss Emily Barder, who survived his decease.

CHARLES ALEXANDER SAUNDERS.

When, in 1833, the Great Western Railway was first projected and governed by two Boards of Directors—one in London and the other at Bristol —Mr Charles Alexander Saunders was appointed secretary to the former one, and, after the line had been constructed, the two Boards were amalgamated and Mr Saunders was appointed secretary and general superintendent of the railway, as a reward for the very marked ability, tact and general utility he had evinced in the development of the scheme.   Nor could it have been possible for the Directors to have chosen a better man in any way to fulfil this most important position, so ably discharged by Mr Saunders.   The interests of the Broad Gauge could not have been better looked after, more jealously guarded, nor its system more zealously developed than was the case under Mr Saunders's able guidance.   It is true that, in later years, he rather pushed his ideas to the front, and so caused somewhat strained relations between himself and the Board; not that the Directors were led to do exactly as Mr Saunders advised, for, had his advice been followed on more subjects than one, future events proved that the Great Western Railway would have amply benefited thereby.   So entirely had he given his sole attention to the progress of the Great Western Railway that, in the railway world, it was a common event to hear the observation that 'Mr Saunders *is* the Great Western Railway.'   In 1845 the shareholders were so gratified with the masterly way in which he had fought their parliamentary battles that they subscribed for and presented him with 300 reserved fifths shares in the Great Western Railway,

while, some years later, they voted him an honorarium
of £5000. It was over the extensions northward
from Oxford that Mr Saunders made enemies. We
shall elsewhere detail how some of the shareholders
in the Birmingham and Wolverhampton ventures were
bought over by the London and North Western Railway, and the long legal fight that resulted from the
treachery of these men; but Mr Saunders took and
maintained a determined position on behalf of the
Broad Gauge, and it was doubtless through his indomit-
able pertinacity of purpose and steadfast resolve to
conquer, that the Broad Gauge gained the triumph,
and was enabled to extend its system north of
Oxford. The Narrow Gauge clique above referred
to, seeing how determined Mr Saunders was to safe-
guard the interests of the Broad Gauge, sent one of
their leading men, who offered to give Mr Saunders
£25,000 to purchase an estate if he would retire from
the Great Western Railway's service. This person
had to beat a hasty and undignified retreat from the
presence of the irate Great Western secretary; had he
not done so, Mr Saunders threatened to throw him out
of the window for daring to make such an offer; but
the visitor, knowing Mr Saunders determination,
wisely decided that discretion was the better part of
valour, and showed his heels without further parley.
From this time the London and North Western party
became greatly embittered against Mr Saunders, and
in every way made his position as uncomfortable as
possible. Mr Brunel could not have had or desired a
more zealous partisan than he found in Mr Saunders,
for the latter was always ready to second every fresh
development of the Broad Gauge that Mr Brunel suggested. The death of Mr Brunel was the first real
blow the Broad Gauge received, and it never recovered
from the shock; while his death considerably weak-
ened Mr Saunders's position, and caused his enemies
to redouble their efforts to dislodge him from his position. He wore out his life in the many hard struggles

he made for the Great Western Railway, and, early in
1863, he wished to retire in consequence of failing health.
At that time the Great Western Railway Directors had
a most important Bill in Parliament for the amalgamating of the West Midland with their own system,
and so impressed were they with Mr Saunders's great
knowledge of railway parliamentary business that they
begged of him to stay and help them through with
the measure. Although the Bill was one galling to
the fine susceptibilities of Mr Saunders, in that it was
a compromise with Narrow Gauge lines, and pledged
the Great Western Railway to lay down the mixed
gauge over a large part of their system, he loyally
stayed to fight the battle on behalf of the Great
Western Railway, and was successful in so doing.
Mr Saunders resigned his position in September
1863, thereby effectually showing his disapproval
of the new policy. At the half-yearly meeting of
shareholders, held on 18th September 1863, the
Directors proposed to make him a retiring allowance
of £1200 a year; this led to a most heated and acri-
monious discussion among the shareholders, which
lasted for five hours. His enemies mustered in full
force, and some went so far as to say that, instead of
paying him a pension of £1200 a year, he ought to
be made to pay the shareholders a large sum yearly
for the loss he had caused them. The Directors' proposition was, however, carried. Unfortunately, Mr
Saunders lived but a short time after his retirement, for
on 19th September 1864, he passed away, when sixty-
seven years old. In retirement he missed the
bustle of his previous busy life, as is often the case
with an energetic person, who, so long as he remains in harness, defies ill health, but as soon as
the ceaseless exertion is relaxed, disease enters the
system already enfeebled by overwork, and carries
off another victim to join the great majority. Not
only does the Great Western Railway owe a
great deal to the life work of Mr Saunders, but

every other railway as well; for when, in 1844,
Mr Gladstone introduced the 'Railway Confiscation
Bill,' that gentleman, now known as the 'Grand
Old Man,' but then as a 'very Jesuit with railways,' said,—'If this Bill is thrown out, I shall
regard Mr Saunders as the man who has done it.'
Had this measure passed, the position of railway
shareholders to-day would have been worse than
that of Irish landlords; but, thanks to Mr Saunders,
it did not pass. A Great Western shareholder thus
summed up the character of Mr C. A. Saunders:—
'That gentleman had given them not only the
best years of his life, but the energies also of his
active and capacious mind, and his practical knowledge
of railway matters, in which he was unsurpassed. He
had given them not only the labour they had a right
to expect from a secretary, but his days and nights
also. He had no object nearer his heart than the pro-
sperity and success of their great undertaking. More
hearty or emphatic eulogy was never bestowed, and
the modesty with which it was received confirmed its
justice.'

CHAPTER VII.

BATTLE OF THE GAUGES—SOCIAL AND COMMERCIAL.

THE Great Western Railway is usually credited with being responsible for the evils attending a break of gauge, against which the trading community, strongly supported by the Narrow Gauge railways, were always murmuring, yet, in reality, the Narrow Gauge was entirely responsible for the delays that occurred. It was at Gloucester that difficulties first arose as to transferring goods from one gauge to another. A Narrow Gauge line—the Birmingham and Gloucester—was opened between those towns on 24th January 1840, while the Bristol and Gloucester, a Broad Gauge line, was opened for passenger traffic on 6th July 1844. This latter line was 37½ miles long, and Mr Brunel was the engineer. The line, although an independent one, was considered by the Great Western Railway as a dependent of theirs, the Great Western having subscribed £50,000 of its capital, while the Bristol and Gloucester line proper ended at Stonehouse, the 9 miles from thence to Gloucester being leased from the Great Western Railway, the Bristol and Gloucester trains also used the Temple Meads Station of the Great Western at Bristol. In passing, we mention that on this line London time was observed at all the stations from the first, although other railways were then and for some years after running their trains according to local time. The first time table of this line states that London time is eleven minutes before Bristol time. Goods traffic was commenced on Monday, 2d September 1840, and in less than three months after a series of strong leading articles appeared in the *Railway Chronicle* on the ' Grevious mismanagement in the goods traffic from Bristol through Gloucester and Birmingham.'   These articles show clearly that the Birmingham and Gloucester Company was entirely to blame, for we read, ' the evil lies chiefly at the Birmingham end of the line, where, according to all accounts, the goods traffic is in a lamentable state.' The management of the Birmingham and Gloucester Company is just now in a state of anarchy, and the article goes on to say,—' Now, what are the interruptions in the passage of the traffic by railway ?   They arise from the existence of two gauges (the Birmingham and Gloucester being the Narrow Gauge, and the Bristol and Gloucester being the wide gauge) and two managements.   The difference of gauge is now to be regarded as a physical difficulty to be overcome as it can best be done (just as if it were a steep incline); and the greatest care should be taken that the frequent recurrence to it as a *pretext for delay* do not render it as a bugbear in the eyes of the public ; if it does so a great injury will be inflicted on both railways.   With two managements such a result will be sure to ensue. We all know that somehow or other, with the most virtuous intentions, the management on two contiguous lines of railway never acts as one—there is always a little cross pulling, a little difficulty as to dividing receipts and expenses, a little jealousy of each other. A very slight knowledge of human nature will tell us why this is and must be, and that it is so there is no doubt.   This is the case with the wisest and best of managements, much more so with the worst ; and we fear that the Birmingham and Gloucester (the Narrow Gauge line) is to be placed in the latter category.' This article ends by suggesting the amalgamation of the Great Western, Bristol and Gloucester, and Birmingham and Gloucester.

    But a very different arrangement was made, for, in May 1844, the North Midland, Midland Counties, and the Birmingham and Rugby Junction Railways amalgamated under the title of the Midlands—now the Midland Railway, and as is usual the amalgamation spirit increased, and the Midlands looked with longing eyes towards the Birmingham and Gloucester line. In those days the practice was, when one railway wanted to influence the policy of another, to purchase shares as private individuals, and then, under the guise of being shareholders, to endeavour to get the policy of the purchasing company carried out by the Board of the line in which the shares had been purchased. We readily understand, then, that when the Midland had in this way obtained an influence in the Birmingham and Gloucester Company, their Narrow Gauge connections, together with the Narrow Gauge prejudices of George Hudson and Robert Stephenson, and also having in view the amalgamation of the two lines from Birmingham to Bristol with their own company, that this new influence was not used to make the working of the change of gauge at Gloucester any smoother. So that from this time the complaints as to the evils of the break of gauge were more numerous, and were for the reasons we have already mentioned being continually forced into public notice. The Great Western Railway is in a measure to blame in not obtaining the Bristol and Gloucester line themselves, but they appear to have been under the impression that it was virtually their line, and, therefore, perhaps, did not pay sufficient attention as to how matters were developing with regard to it ; so that while the Broad Gauge champions were busy in other districts, the Midland Railway had quickly and quietly obtained the Birmingham and Gloucester Railway, and the Bristol and Gloucester line, by giving 6 per cent. guaranteed shares of their own in exchange for the ordinary shares of the Bristol line, which was an extremely good bargain for the shareholders of the latter company. Matters now stood like this—a determined Narrow Gauge railway was owner of a through route from Bristol to Birmingham, on which occurred a break of gauge. The owning company, anxious to have the whole line Narrow Gauge, and so to gain this end it naturally made as much fuss as possible about the break of gauge, while the trouble might have been reduced to an insignificant minimum had it been to the Midland Company's interest so to do. No one could fail to acknowledge that to the goods traffic a break of gauge was an evil, causing loss of time and possible damage to the goods in transhipping from one truck to another, besides being an additional expense. It was therefore proposed to have trucks with moveable bodies so that these bodies could be removed by a crane from Broad to Narrow Gauge frames, and *vice versâ;* but various objections were raised to this system. The real reason, however, why this practical remedy was not carried out being that none of the companies interested would go to the expense of constructing the rolling stock necessary for this purpose. This question of expenditure is also answerable for another, but less practical method, not being inaugurated, viz., the introduction of vehicles with telescopic axles—a misleading description, as the axles were not to be telescopic at all, they really being axles long enough for the Broad Gauge, but on which the wheels were not immovably fixed, but could be slid along the axles and fixed at widths suitable for the Broad or Narrow Gauge. Then a species of crocodile Broad Gauge trucks was suggested. These were to have low bodies, on the surface of which were rails of the Narrow Gauge so that Narrow Gauge trucks could be run on to them, and so complete their journey to Broad Gauge stations. Had this method been employed only the Great Western Railway would have had to provide the suitable vehicles, and we consider it was the most feasible of all the propositions, being exactly similar to the present method of conveying pantechnicon and other road vans on railway trucks. The Gauge Commissioners, in the wisdom of their report, rejected this proposal 'as entirely inapplicable to the traffic of railways.' Another proposal was to pack through goods in immense cases, and tranship these from Broad Gauge to Narrow Gauge trucks, and *vice versâ.* The Gauge Commissioners reported this method as 'totally inapplicable,' yet the registered baggage between London and Paris *viâ* Boulogne is daily conveyed in this way, and undergoes two transhipments in each journey, while but one would have been necessary with the break of gauge.

Although fifty years ago all the Narrow Gauge railways said it was impossible to convey·Broad Gauge vehicles over their lines, yet, 'truth being stranger than (Narrow Gauge) fiction,' the 'impossible' is done every day in Germany at the present time. The Standard Gauge waggons, measuring 24 feet 4 inches long by 9 feet in width, are conveyed on the .75 metre gauge (2 feet 5½ inches) of the Wurtemberg Railway, a Narrow Gauge truck being fixed under each axle of the larger waggon, which thus becomes a bogie vehicle on the .75 metre line, and travels at high speed, and round curves of short radii without accident; the whole alteration from one gauge to another not occupying 5 minutes per waggon.

With regard to the actual conveyance of goods both the Broad and Narrow Gauge systems were about equal, as we do not know of the partisans of either claiming any special advantage in this respect for one system or the other, save that a glass merchant at Worcester found that the Narrow Gauge broke 1½ per cent. more in transit than the Broad Gauge, while the Broad Gauge had the undoubted advantage of greater speed and a greater carrying capacity per truck.

The disadvantages of a break of gauge with regard to the passenger traffic were, of course, no worse than the ordinary changing at junctions to and from branch trains, about which no one complained; in fact, on a long journey, travellers are glad to change for the sake of variety, yet a great outcry was raised about the inconvenience of changing; and since the Broad Gauge brought passengers through to Gloucester, the drawback of the Cheltenham passengers was the one usually commented upon. The Great Western line to Gloucester was opened for passenger traffic on 12th May 1845. It was necessary for London passengers for Cheltenham to change from the Great Western to the Birmingham and Gloucester train at Gloucester, so the Narrow Gauge company, to aggravate the presumed inconvenience, arranged their time table accordingly. The Narrow Gauge trains from Cheltenham arrived at Gloucester just after the Great Western trains had left for London, and the Narrow Gauge trains to Cheltenham left Gloucester shortly before the Broad Gauge trains from London were due. While travellers arriving by the last Great Western train at Gloucester had either to proceed to Cheltenham by 'bus, if there were room, or stay the night at Gloucester. The table shows how the Narrow Gauge unnecessarily inconvenienced travellers.

Cheltenham,	depart	8.25. A.M.	10.18 A.M.	1.25 P.M.	Narrow Gauge.
Gloucester,	arrive	9.5 ,,	10.55 ,,	2.5 ,,	
,,	depart	10.50 A.M.		4.0 ,,	Broad Gauge.
,,	arrive from London	9.25 P.M.			
,,	depart for Cheltenham,	8.50 ,,	(*last train*)		Narrow Gauge.

The reasons urged against the break of gauge in regard to the passenger traffic are certainly amusing. Thus one person complained that owing to the break of gauge he exchanged 'the companionship of a pretty young lady for that of an ugly old one with her parrot and pet cat.' A clergyman at Banbury said, ' He did not want the little hair he had on his head rubbed off by riding in the London and Birmingham Company's low carriages. He would vastly prefer travelling the whole distance in one of the splendid carriages of the Great Western Company than being transferred to one of the little pig boxes on the London and Birmingham line.' 'Jeames,' in *Punch*, very cleverly takes off the alleged inconveniences in his account of a journey to Cheltenham. 'I never thought that I should have been injuiced to write anything but a bill again, much less to edress you on railway subjix, which with all my sole I abaw. But as a man an' 'usband, and a father and a freebon Brittn, my jewty compels me to come forwoods, and igspress my opinion upon that nashnal newsance—the break of gage. An interesting event in a noble family, with which I once very nearly had the honour of being kinected, acurd a few weex sins, when the Lady Angelina S——, daughter of the Earl of B——, presented the gallant capting, her husband, with a son and hair. Nothink would satisfy her ladyship but that her old and atacht *fam-dy-shamber*, my wife Mary Hann Plush, should be present upon this hospicious occasion. Capting S—— was not jellus of me on account of my former attachment to his lady. I cunsented that my wife Hann should attend her, and me and my wife, and our dear babby acawdingly set out for our noable friend's residence, Honeymoon Lodge, near Cheltenham. Sick of all railways myself, I wisht to poast it in a chay and four, but Mary Hann, with the hobstenacy of her sex, was bent upon railroad travelling, and I yealded like all husbinds. We set out by the Great Western in an eavle hour. We didn't take much luggitch—my wife's things in the ushal band-boxes, mine in a potmancho. We had, ingluding James Hangelo's (the baby before mentioned) rattle and my umbrellow, seventy-three packidges in all. We got on very well as far as Swindon, where, in the splendid refreshment room, there was a galaxy of lovely gals in cottn velvet spencers, who serves out the soop, and one of whom maid an impresshn upon this 'art which I shoodn't like Mary Hann to know— and here to our infanit disgust we changed carridges. I forgot to say that we were in the secknd class, having with us James Hangelo and twenty-three other light harticles. First inconvenience, and almost as bad as break of gage. I cast my hi upon the gal in cottn velvet, and wanted some soop of course; but seasing up James Hangelo (who was layin' his dear little pors on an 'am sangwidg) and seeing my igspresshn of hi, " James," says Mary Hann, "instead of looking at that young lady—and not so very young neither—be pleased to look to our packidges and place them in the other carridg." I did so with a 'evy 'art, I eranged them twenty-three articles in the opsit carridg, only missing my umbrellow and baby's rattle; and just as I came back for my baysn of soop, the beast of a bell rings, the whizzling injians proclayms the time of our departure—and farewell soop and cottn velvet. Mary Hann was sulky. She said it was my losing the umbrellow. If it had been a cottn velvet umbrella I could have understood. James Hangelo, sittin' on my knee, was evidently unwell without his coral, and for 20 miles that blessid babby kep' up a rawring, which caused all the passingers to simpithize with him igseedingly. We arrive at Gloster, and there, fancy my disgust at being ableeged to undergo another change of carridges. Fansy me holding up moughs, tippits, cloaks and baskits, and James Hangelo rawring still like mad, and pretending to shuperintend the carrying over of our luggitch from the Broad Gage to Narrow Gage. " Mary Hann," says I, rot to desperashn, " I shall throttle this darling if he goes on." " Do," says she, "and go into the refreshment room," says she, a-snatchin' the babby out of my arms. " Do go," says she, "you're not fit to look after luggitch," and she began lulling James Hangelo to sleep with one hi, while she looked after the packits with the other. " Now, sir, if you please, mind that packit—pretty darling—easy with that box, sir, it's glass—po-o-o-o-ty poppet—where's the deal case, marked arrowroot, No. 24?" she cried, reading out a list she had—and poor little James went to sleep. The porters were bundling and carting the various harticles with no more ceremony than if each packidg had been of cannon ball. At last—bang goes a packidg marked "glass," and containing the chayny bowel and Lady Bareacres' mixture, into a large white band-box, with a crash and a smash. " It's my lady's box from Crinolines!" cries Mary Hann, and she puts down the child on the bench, and rushes forward to inspect the damage. As James was asleep, and I was by this time uncommon hungry, I thought I *would* go into the refreshment room and just take a little soop ; so I wrapped him up in his cloak and laid him by his mamma and went off. There's not near such good attendance as at Swindon. We took our places in the carridg in the dark, both of us covered with a pile of packidges, and Mary Hann so sulky that she would not speak for some minutes. At last she spoke out, " Have you all the small parcels?' " Twenty-three in all," says I. " Then give me the babby." "What, haven't y-y-yo-o-o-o got him?" says I . . .. O Mussy! you should have heard her sreak. *We'd left him on the ledge at Gloster.* It all came of the break of gage.'

To show how severely the gauge controversy raged, we mention that at Gloucester the Great Western had the following placard posted up at their station and about the city.

'Observe — Petition !!! Petition !!! 50 miles an hour *versus* 25. Coaches before waggons. No change of carriage. The blessings of the Broad Gauge for the northern districts. Safety and speed before cramp and delay. Advancement before retreat. The petition will be ready in a day or two. Brunel for ever!! Hurrah !

'To the Right Honourable, the Commons in Parliament assembled,—

'The humble petition of the undersigned passengers, travelling between Birmingham and Bristol by railway on the ——— day of ——— ;

H

'Sheweth,—That your petitioners travelled between Birmingham and Bristol by railway, and that when they arrived at Gloucester they were compelled, owing to the change in the width of the rails (which your petitioners believe is called "break of guage") to remove from one carriage to another.

'That your petitioners were 1 hour and 45 minutes in performing the journey between Bristol and Gloucester, a distance of 37 miles, on what your petitioners believe is called the "Broad Gauge;" and that they were occupied 2 hours and 35 minutes in the remaining part of the journey, between Gloucester and Birmingham, in what your petitioners believe is termed the "Narrow Gauge," a distance of 33 miles. That your petitioners thereby consider that they were detained ——— hours ——— minutes, beyond what they consider a reasonable time for the performance thereof. That your petitioners were provided with a large and commodious carriage for their accommodation on what they believe is termed the Broad Gauge; and that your petitioners were cribbed, crowded, cramped and confined and nearly stifled in the small and inconvenient one provided by that portion which your petitioners believe is called the Narrow Gauge portion of their journey. That your petitioners observe with regret that the decision of certain narrow-minded and antiquated persons has been mistaken for the experience of men of wide experience, intelligent and enlightened. And therefore your petitioners implore your honourable House not to be biassed thereby, but to adapt to locomotion the same expansive and comprehensive principles that your honourable House has latterly applied to legislation.

'That your petitioners entreat your honourable House not to impede the advancement of science and improvement of locomotion, nor to confine it to the narrow limits of 4 feet 8½ inch gauge, and a speed of 25 miles an hour. That your petitioners would not be inconvenienced if an uniform gauge did not exist in the northern and southern districts of the country.

'That your petitioners therefore entreat your honourable House not to debar the northern and southern districts from the advantage of the superior accommodation of the Broad Gauge, but to remedy the existing evils, by extending it throughout to all the districts alike.—Your petitioners,' etc.

The books and pamphlets written on the subject would form quite a modest library if collected. Personally, we are acquainted with the titles of at least twenty-one of the interesting works on this momentous question.

The Midland did not alter the gauge of the Bristol and Gloucester Railway when it first obtained control of it, for at the time Slaughter & Company held a contract for ten years from the opening of the line to provide the rolling stock and work the railway. The engines provided had driving wheels 6 feet 6 inches diameter, the carriage wheels 3 feet 6 inches diameter, while the goods trucks were only four wheel ones instead of six wheel, as usually provided for the Broad Gauge.

CHAPTER VIII.

THE PARLIAMENTARY BATTLE.

In the Session of 1844 the London and South
Western Railway obtained powers for the construction of a railway to Salisbury. The Great Western
Railway considered this to be an invasion of their
territory. In the same Session a so-called independent company, but in reality the London and South
Western, also applied for powers to construct a railway
from Basingstoke to Newbury; the Great Western
Railway offered strenuous opposition to this line, and
although the Commons pronounced in favour of it by
166 votes to 73, the Lords' Committee threw the Bill
out. So that, as the Great Western Bill was thrown
out by the Commons, and the South Western by the
Lords, no railway was sanctioned to Newbury in 1844.
To the north of their line the Great Western Railway
had no Parliamentary battle to fight in 1844, but in
that year new lines were projected from Oxford to
Rugby, and another from Oxford to Worcester and
Wolverhampton, both these the London and Birmingham opposed, and projected rival schemes. The
London and South Western, or the so-called local
companies, promoted lines from Salisbury to Yeovil,
this being a continuation of the Basingstoke to Salisbury branch in course of construction, and a line from
Salisbury to Dorchester and Weymouth, also a railway from Basingstoke to Didcot, and another through
Newbury to Swindon. The Great Western lines in
opposition to these latter were from Reading to
Basingstoke, and to Hungerford *via* Newbury, while

another line was projected from Chippenham to
Yeovil, Dorchester and Weymouth, with a branch to
Salisbury. To show the magnitude of the Parliamentary struggle which was expected to take place
in the Session of 1845, we give the following list
of Bills to be fought over by the Great Western
Railway.

Narrow Gauge Lines opposed by Great Western Railway.	Broad Gauge Lines supported by Great Western Railway.
Cornwall and Devon Central.	Cornwall Railway.
Gloucester and Hereford.	Crediton and Barnstaple.
Staines and Windsor.	Exeter and Crediton.
Southampton and Dorchester.	Forest of Dean, Gloucester and Hereford.
Basingstoke and Didcot.	South Devon and Tavistock.
Basingstoke to Swindon.	Oxford, Worcester and Wolver-hampton.
London and Birmingham Rail-way.	Oxford and Rugby.
Worcester, Dudley and Wol-verhampton.	Berks and Hants Railway.
Salisbury and Weymouth.	South Wales Railway.
Salisbury and Yeovil.	Torquay and Newton Abbot.
	Monmouth and Hereford.
	Wilts, Somerset and Weymouth.
	Uxbridge and Staines.

But at the commencement of 1845 the Great
Western and London and South Western Railways entered into an arrangement by which it
was agreed, that upon consideration of the Great
Western Railway giving up to the South Western
the lease of the Southampton and Dorchester Railway, which line the Great Western had before agreed
to work, the London and South Western withdrew
the Bills they had promoted, so by this clever arrangement the Narrow Gauge Basingstoke, Didcot and
Swindon Junction Railway, the Salisbury and Yeovil
Railway, the Hook Pit Deviation to Salisbury, and
the Dorchester; and the Salisbury and Weymouth

Railway were not proceeded with, and the London and South Western also agreed to withdraw the support they were giving to the Cornwall and Devon Central Railway. The fight in Parliament between rival Broad and Narrow schemes was by this arrangement confined to the lines to the north of the Great Western main line, and to the competing Cornwall Railways.

On the 3d of March the Oxford and Rugby Bill first came before the Committee of the House of Commons; the next day the Committee reported that the standing orders had been complied with, and the Bill was read a first time on 5th March, and on the 10th it was read a second time, while the Oxford, Worcester and Wolverhampton Bill was read a first time on 19th March, and a second time on 8th April. The Select Committee ' F,' consisting of five members, before whom the Bills in the Oxford and Birmingham district were fought, commenced sitting on 5th May. The real fight was between the Worcester, Dudley and Wolverhampton Railway, promoted as a Narrow Gauge line by the London and Birmingham, and the Oxford, Worcester and Wolverhampton, and the Oxford and Rugby, which were Broad Gauge lines. The Board of Trade had already reported against the Broad Gauge, as Mr Austin, who conducted the case for the London and Birmingham Company, did not forget to continually remind the Committee ' that this question of gauge was the great one the Committee had to settle.' He admitted that on great lines the Broad Gauge was most advisable, but not on this one, it being in the nature of a branch, and he argued that the break of gauge ought to be located at Oxford and Bristol, as was then the case, and not at Birmingham and Rugby, as the Broad Gauge wished it to be. Mr M'Connell, the locomotive engineer then of the Bristol and Gloucester Railway, but afterwards of the London and North Western Railway, was a witness for the

Narrow Gauge, and he stated that the Broad Gauge had advantages in respect of speed and power, and must always continue to have, since they had more room for the boilers and machinery of the engines. All the chief Narrow Gauge railway engineers, including Robert Stephenson, were called in support of the London and Birmingham Company's line, and after having heard evidence for twelve days in favour of this line, the case for the Broad Gauge was begun. The inhabitants and merchants of Worcester were wholly in favour of the Great Western line. Mr Williams, engineer to the Severn Navigation, stated that the London and Birmingham wished him to give evidence, but when they heard his views of the schemes they said,—'We will have nothing to do with you, your evidence will sink us.' After the Committee had sat for three weeks, the Chairman stated that they had heard quite sufficient evidence proving the popularity of the Great Western Railway over the London and Birmingham line, and that part of the case closed. During the whole of 28th May Mr Brunel was giving his evidence. His principal points were, that this Great Western line had been projected as long ago as 1836, and that the gradients of this line were better than the Narrow Gauge ones, his steepest being 1 in 80, while the Narrow Gauge had 1 in 67, besides which his line was shorter by 15 miles, and the Broad Gauge line traversed a more densely populated district than that of the London and Birmingham. No difficulty would arise as to transhipping trucks from one gauge to another, as he had invented a simple contrivance to carry out this purpose, and it worked admirably. Nearly the whole of the next day was taken up with Mr Brunel's cross-examination. The Secretary of the Grand Junction Railway also gave evidence in favour of the Broad Gauge line. The opposition of the Grand Junction Railway was felt very much by the London and Birmingham Railway, and so fearful was the latter

that the former would amalgamate with the Great
Western Railway, and so give the Broad Gauge access
to Manchester and Liverpool and the north-western
district generally, that the fear of such a coalition was
the principal factor that caused the London and
Birmingham to be so desirous of amalgamating with
the Grand Junction Railway, and which was duly
carried into effect in 1846. The evidence was
finished on 2d June, and then Mr Cockburn addressed
the Committee on behalf of the Broad Gauge line.
Mr Austin replied in behalf of the London and
Birmingham project, and on 4th June, after deliber-
ating for three hours, the Committee decided that
the preamble of the Broad Gauge Bills had been
proved, and that the Narrow Gauge had not. The
Committee sat for five weeks hearing the evidence
for and against these rival proposals. This was
indeed a decided success for the Great Western, more
especially as their propositions had been reported
against by the Board of Trade. In the House of
Commons, on 20th June, Lord Ingestre moved the
consideration of the report on these Bills, and Mr
Cobden moved an amendment asking for a Select
Committee to inquire into the gauge question. After
a very long debate the original motion was carried by
a majority of 134 in a House of 360 members. On
24th June the third reading of the two Bills was
moved, and an amendment proposed 'that the Bill
should be read a third time that day six months.' On
this occasion the Worcester Bill was passed without
a division, and the Rugby one by 132 votes to 95.
The next day Mr Cobden moved—' That it having
been represented to this House by petitions from
various public bodies, as well as from merchants,
manufacturers and others, that serious impediments
to the internal traffic of the country are likely to arise
from the " breaks " that will occur in railway communications from the want of a uniform gauge ; and these
representations not having been fully inquired into by

any of the Committees of this House upon private Bills, and it being desirable that the subject should be further investigated, an humble address be presented to Her Majesty, praying Her Majesty to be graciously pleased to issue a Commission to inquire, whether, in future private Acts for the construction of railways, provision ought to be made for securing an uniform gauge, and whether it would be expedient and practicable to take measures to bring the railways already constructed, or in progress of construction, in Great Britain into uniformity of gauge ; and to inquire whether any other mode of obviating or mitigating the apprehended evil could be adopted, and to report the same to this House.' This after a long discussion was agreed to, and in the *London Gazette* of Tuesday, 5th July 1845, notice was given of the appointment of Sir John Mark Frederic Smith, Lieutenant-Colonel of the Royal Corps of Engineers, late Inspector-General of Railways ; George Biddell Airy, Esq., Astronomical Observertor in Her Majesty's Observatory at Greenwich ; and Peter Barlow, Esq., Professor of Mathematics in the Royal Military Academy at Woolwich, to act as Commissioners. The Worcester and Rugby Broad Gauge Bills came before the Lords' Committee on 8th July, and on the 24th, after spending fourteen days in hearing the evidence, the Committee declared the preamble proved. These Bills for the Broad Gauge lines from Oxford to Worcester and Rugby were passed on 28th July, and received the Royal assent on 4th August. The Rugby line was 50½ miles long, with a capital of £600,000, and the Wolverhampton had a mileage of 103¼, and a million and a half capital. The other Broad Gauge Bills that passed in this Session were—

Berks and Hants,	.	. 39 miles long,	£400,000	capital.
Exeter and Crediton,	.	5¾ „ „	£70,000	„
Monmouth and Hereford,	.	36¼ „ „	£550,000	„
South Wales,	.	. 182⅝ „ „	£2,800,000	„
Wilts, Somerset and				
Weymouth,	.	. 129¼ „ „	£1,500,000	„

Here, then, were a series of triumphs for the Broad Gauge. Victorious everywhere, yet by these very victories the cause of the Broad Gauge was in danger of annihilation, for the various Narrow Gauge companies, fearing the onward march of the Broad Gauge, amalgamated their railways and consolidated their forces for a renewed and more determined attack. The public generally were in favour of the Broad Gauge ; the larger vehicles, the more powerful engines, and the higher rate of speed, all appealed to the popular fancy, while much of the success of the Great Western Bills must be ascribed to the remarkable talent, skill and decision of Mr Brunel and Mr Saunders ; each in his own sphere designed, managed and carried through the various arrangements necessary for the great Parliamentary contests of this memorable year.

The next move in the battle was made by the Narrow Gauge parties, and we cannot but own that it reflects great discredit on those who were responsible for these dishonest and underhanded proceedings. The London and Birmingham, not being successful in obtaining their Worcester, Dudley and Wolverhampton Act, set to work to try and acquire the line sanctioned by Parliament, viz., the Broad Gauge Oxford, Worcester and Wolverhampton Railway. It must be remembered that although this line was promoted, and its Parliamentary battle fought by the Great Western Railway, it was nominally an independent company, although the Great Western Railway had subscribed half the capital. The first general meeting of shareholders of the Oxford, Worcester and Wolverhampton Company was held on 14th October 1845, and the question was raised by a person who turned out to be a nominee of the London and Birmingham Railway as to whether some better terms could not be obtained for their line than those provisionally agreed between their Company and the Great Western Railway. A discussion followed, but the arrangement with the Great Western Railway was confirmed.

The Directors, however, afterwards obtained a guarantee of 4 per cent. and a share of the profits from the Great Western Railway Company, and a lease of the line was granted to the Great Western Railway on these terms for 999 years. Matters progressed in a satisfactory manner till the half yearly meeting, held in August 1846, when Lord Redesdale (who up to that time had been a staunch supporter of the Great Western Railway) surprised the Oxford, Worcester and Wolverhampton shareholders by stating—' He was a holder of five shares, but he appeared on public grounds and on behalf of many individuals connected with the district in which he resided, and who thought with him that if the company allowed the Great Western to carry out the Oxford and Birmingham line they would be perpetrating a suicide on themselves. All that they got from the Great Western was 4 per cent. That amount and more they could get from the London and Birmingham to-morrow if they chose to go to them.' In answer to this, one of the largest shareholders stated that ' Reports of Gauge Commissioners and Acts of Parliament had been thrown in the way of the extension of the Broad Gauge, but they were to be treated as so many cobwebs. The Commissioners' report had been proved to be not worth a rush, and to be founded in the teeth of evidence and truth, and the Act of Parliament just passed was not worth much more. A Broad Gauge would bear up to Liverpool as well as to Birmingham before two or three years were over. The men of London were travelling to Exeter, 200 miles, in 4 hours, while to Liverpool, only 3 or 4 miles more, they were more than 6 hours ; and the best possible proof that this prediction would be realised was the fact that Mr G. Stephenson told him a month ago that they had got to the maximum of their speed on the Narrow Gauge, and could not go faster to Liverpool. Merchants in Liverpool also had told him that they would not rest till they got the Broad Gauge if they could save 2 hours between Liverpool and London.' However, the shareholders still remained loyal to the Broad Gauge, and at this meeting a dividend of 4 per cent. was declared payable by the Great Western Railway, although the Oxford, Worcester and Wolverhampton Railway was only then being constructed. Matters, to outward appearances, remained in a peaceful condition, and progress was made with the construction of the line, but the Narrow Gauge party was working in secret, and in March 1847 they called a meeting of the shareholders, at which a resolution was carried that a committee be formed to adopt steps to set aside the lease to the Great Western Railway Company. Meetings to agitate the same question were shortly after held in Leeds and Liverpool (towns far away from Broad Gauge railways). Leaving the Parliamentary struggle for the present we now propose to describe the exciting events of the engineering battle that raged at this time, including the experiments made by the Gauge Commissioners. In a future chapter we shall return to the Parliamentary struggles of subsequent years.

CHAPTER IX.

ENGINEERING BATTLE.

In a previous chapter we have given a somewhat detailed account of the early engines and vehicles in use on the Great Western Railway.

Our readers will also remember that on the day the line was opened to Exeter the train conveying the Great Western Directors returned to London in 4 hours 40 minutes; this was, of course, a special train, and made an exceptionally quick run. But the gauge contest put the Great Western Railway on their mettle, and from the 12th May 1845 it was arranged that the express trains to and from Exeter would perform the journey in 4½ hours—the down train left Paddington at 9.45 A.M. and arrived at Exeter at 2.15 P.M., and the up train left Exeter at 12 noon and arrived at Paddington at 4.30 P.M. At present the fastest down train (the 'Cornishman') starts at 10.15 A.M. and arrives at Exeter at 2.20 P.M., while an up express now leaves Exeter at 12.12 P.M. and arrives at 4.30 P.M. Not much improvement with regard to speed during half a century certainly! Then, as now, all trains had to stop at Swindon 10 minutes for refreshments, the Great Western Railway having covenanted to do this in the lease for ninety-nine years granted to the refreshment contractor, who pays them a rental of 1d. per annum in consideration of him building the refreshment room at his own cost. One writer, in describing these expresses, states, that 'This was before the Great Western Railway suffered from the incubus of the Swindon Refreshment Rooms.'

He is, however, in error, as the lease was then in existence, and no sooner had the new trains, which did not stop at Swindon, been put on the road, than the lessee commenced an action against the railway for breach of covenant.   The railway in their defence alleged that the plaintiff ought to have proved that there were passengers in these trains who wished to take refreshments at Swindon before he would be entitled to sue.   The Court, however, decided in favour of the refreshment contractor; but as the Long Vacation had interposed during the hearing of the action, this judgment was not delivered until 1st December 1845.   But although these fast trains did not for the first few days stop at Swindon, they had to contend with a far more serious hindrance at Bristol, which caused considerable delay, and which we have not found mentioned by other writers.   At Bristol the lines of the Great Western and the Bristol and Exeter met at right angles, so that the vehicles of all through trains had each to be uncoupled from another, and one by one placed upon a turn-table and turned round 90 degrees, and then the carriages had to be connected again before the train could proceed, and this was, of course, an effectual bar to any acceleration that might have been obtained by not stopping at Bristol.   These express trains had not been running long before the down one unfortunately met with an accident.   On 17th June the train, which consisted of an engine and tender, a four-wheeled luggage van, and two first and two second-class carriages, each with six wheels, left Paddington at the booked time, and travelled as usual until after passing under the Dog Kennel Bridge, 15 miles from Paddington, when the wheels of the van left the rails on the south side; but the longitudinal sleepers kept the wheels quite close to the rails, so that none of the officials or passengers were aware of the mishap.   After running for about a mile and a half with the van off the line, the train reached a place where the railway crossed over a road by means of a bridge. The rails being laid in trough-shaped girders here, the wheels of the van which were off the line ran foul of these girders. This threw all the vehicles off the line except the engine; the carriages were turned completely over, and thrown down an embankment. There were 130 passengers in the train, amongst whom were Mr Brunel and an assistant, and Mr Clarke, the superintendent of the line, and his wife. Fortunately none of the passengers sustained any more serious injuries than a few bruises and a severe shaking. The total weight of the train was as follows:—Engine, 16 tons; tender, 10 tons; van, $3\frac{1}{2}$ tons; two first-class carriages, each $7\frac{1}{2}$ tons; two second-class carriages, each 7 tons; total, $58\frac{1}{2}$ tons. The cause of the accident was the elasticity of the rails, combined with the light weight of the van, causing the latter to 'jump' off the line. The Narrow Gauge party immediately attributed this catastrophe to the speed and the gauge, but the Government Inspector in his report distinctly stated that it was due to the lightness of the van and rails, and recommended the use of a six-wheel van and heavier rails, which recommendation was immediately carried out; in fact, heavier rails were already being put down, and the work had been finished nearly up to the spot where the derailment took place. At the time the Gauge Commission was appointed there were open in Great Britain and Ireland 2264 miles of railway, of which

274	were	7	feet			(Broad Gauge),
25	,,	6	,,	2	inches	(Irish),
32	,,	5	,,	6	,,	(Scotch Gauge),
32	,,	5	,,	3	,,	(Irish Gauge),
1901	,,	4	,,	$8\frac{1}{2}$	,,	(Narrow Gauge),

including the Eastern Counties and Blackwall Railways which had recently altered their gauge from 5 feet. There were also a few miles of 4 feet 6 inch gauge in Scotland. Besides which $651\frac{3}{4}$ miles of additional Broad Gauge lines had received Parliamentary sanction, some portions of which were then under construction. At the same period the highest speeds were :—

Great Western,	.	.	48.2 miles per hour (B.G.),	
Northern and Eastern,	.	43.8	,,	(N.G.),
London and Birmingham,	43.7	,,	,,	
South-Western,	.	.	40.6	,,	,,
London and Brighton,	.	39.3	,,	,,
Grand Junction Railway,	.	36.9	,,	,,

The Great Western speed for the whole journey, London to Exeter (194 miles), was at the rate of 44 miles an hour, while the London and Birmingham average was but 23.6 miles per hour for its express trains.

We have already stated the names of the Gauge Commissioners; of these Sir F. Smith, a lieutenant-colonel of the Royal Engineers, had formerly, but not immediately prior to his appointment on the Commission, filled the office of Inspector General of Railways, so that he had some theoretical knowledge of railways; Professor Barlow, C.E., was a well known mathematician, and had undertaken many experiments in connection with railways—he was therefore well fitted to act as a Commissioner; but the appointment of Sir G. B. Airy, the astronomer royal, was certainly a questionable one. A newspaper, in an article dealing with Sir G. B. Airy's appointment, thus criticises it,—'What the third party, Professor Airy, the astronomer royal, can have been appointed for we find railway men rather puzzled to see, the connection between the satellites of Jupiter or the last comet and the motion of railway trains being rather obscure to unscientific eyes. The only paper of a practical nature we have ever seen from the pen of the astronomer royal went to prove that, in practice, a short connecting rod gave out as much power as a long one, and we fear such an investigation is not likely to impart great confidence in the practical wisdom of his decisions. With two such coadjutors, however, it is not likely that he will do much harm if he do no good; and, perhaps the public, who are much influenced by names, may think a decision stamped with the authority of an astronomer royal more valid than a better opinion with a more vulgar appendage. We think, however, that we may say that the railway world are well satisfied with the appoinment of Professor Barlow and Sir Frederick Smith, and if the ornament of the third name shall give their decision more weight with the Government, it will not impair its influence with the railways.' The Commissioners, whose office was in the House of Commons Committee Room, No. 16, soon got to work, and its first act was to issue a circular addressed to the various railways, asking them to tender evidence before the Commissioners, and also to forward copies of their last two half-years' reports for information on the following subjects :—' *Tunnels, etc.*—Length, breadth, height, distance from terminus.—*Embankments above* 100 *yards in length.*—Width, extreme height, distance from terminus. *Cuttings above* 100 *yards in length.*—Width, extreme depth, distance from terminus. *Viaducts.*—Length, width, height, distance from terminus. *Bridges.*—Number of passed under, passed over; width between the piers; width between the parapets; distance from terminus; point of junction with adjacent lines or branches, name of adjacent line or branch; breadth of gauge, principal line, branch.

'*Support for the Rails.*—Length of line on continuous bearing; length of line on blocks; length of line on transverse sleepers; average length of transverse sleepers. *Permanent Way.*—Cost of formation; cost of maintenance between the 1st of January and the 31st of December 1844.

'*Engines with Outside or Inside Cylinders.*—Number of engines having four or six wheels; diameter of driving wheels; diameter of cylinder; length of stroke; average weight when charged.

' *Carriages.*—Class of carriage, first class, second class, third class ; trucks, horse boxes, goods waggons, sheep cages ; number of carriages with four or six wheels ; diameter of wheels ; average weight.

' *Value of Locomotive and Carrying Stock.*—Value of locomotive engines ; value of carriages, trucks, horse boxes, goods waggons, etc.

' *Carrying expenses from 1st January to 31st December* 1844.—*Passenger trains.*—Average expense of locomotive department per train per mile ; heads of expense included in this return ; average number of passengers per train per mile ; average speed. *Goods trains.*—Average expense of locomotive department per train per mile ; heads of expense included in this return ; average load carried per train per mile ; average speed. *Express trains.*—Average speed of express trains from the 15th of June to the 15th of July ; average load ; description of engine used ; number of accidents from going off rails ; length and radius of curves.'

Not content with the answers to these exhaustive inquiries, a supplementary list was shortly after formulated. These questions, which dealt principally with the transhipment of goods at points where the two gauges met, were as follow :—1. In the delay it will occasion to express trains. 2. On passenger trains generally. 3. On merchandise traffic. 4. On mineral and agricultural traffic. 5. The Commissioners request the suggestions of the directors as to the best means of transhipment, or of otherwise diminishing any evil which may arise where different gauges meet.

In reference to the general questions of the relative superiority of the Broad and Narrow Gauge an opinion is requested :—1. As to the mechanical properties of either gauge as regards safety, speed, and passenger accommodation. 2. As to the economy of construction, working (referring separately to lines of large traffic and lines of moderate traffic). 3. As to commercial advantages and convenience having regard to merchandise, mineral traffic and agricultural traffic.

On 6th August 1845, the Commissioners met for the first time, for the purpose of hearing evidence; Mr Daniel Gooch, the locomotive superintendent of the Great Western Railway, was left to fight for the Broad Gauge before the Commissioners. Mr Brunel and Mr Saunders being at this time abroad on a holiday, and not giving their evidence till the end of November, when Mr Brunel proposed the famous experiments with passenger and goods trains, particulars of which are given in the next chapter. The Narrow Gauge party strongly opposed these practical tests, although in their evidence they had all affirmed that the Narrow Gauge engines were quite as capable with regard to speed, safety and hauling powers as the Broad Gauge. They had been building new and larger engines, hoping that these would be able to equal those in use on the Great Western Railway, who were content to use their ordinary engines in these trials. Had the Great Western Railway had the 'Great Britain' built in time for these experiments, Mr Gooch affirms that the whole character of the gauge report would have been entirely different. The new Broad Gauge engines were, however, not designed until after the experiments. Mr Gooch, writing of the new engines built for the experiments by the Narrow Gauge party, thus relates his experience of them :—'They constructed the boilers of great length without getting any more heating surface in the fire-box, and allowed this exceptional length to overhang the wheels at each end. 'The White Horse of Kent,' on which I had a number of experiments made, was so unsteady that it was necessary to be tied on to make experiments on the smoke-box temperature, and the tube surface was carried to so great an extent, that the heat in the smoke-box was less than the temperature of the steam used, so that one end of the engine was actually acting as a condenser.'

The Commission examined forty-six witnesses, and some of these more than once.   Thirty of these were in favour of the Narrow Gauge, four in favour of the Broad Gauge, and nine in favour of an intermediate gauge.   Of the remaining three, two generals in the army only gave evidence against the break of gauge, and the other, Major General Pasley, the Government Inspector of railways, was in favour of a 5 feet gauge; and in 1843, when the question of gauge began to attract general attention, Major General Pasley wrote to the various railway engineers the following letter :—
'Supposing that there were no railways in England, and that a system of new ones were proposed to embrace the most important communications all over the country, what would you with your present experience recommend as being the best uniform gauge to be adopted for the whole of them, so that they all might work together in such a manner that the locomotive engines and carriages of any one railway might travel on all the others?'   Of all these engineers, the two Stephensons were the only ones who replied that they were in favour of the 4 feet 8½ inch gauge, and George Stephenson admitted in the correspondence that 5 feet 2 inches would have been a better gauge. Mr Brunel was not asked as his answer was a foregone conclusion; but for the same reason the Stephensons should have been omitted from the list of those questioned.   Mr Gooch in his reply stated,—' That he was not inclined to recommend a greater gauge than 6 feet.'

The Broad Gauge witnesses were :—Mr Brunel, the engineer of the Great Western Railway ; Mr Gooch, locomotive engineer ; Mr Saunders, secretary ; Mr Clarke, superintendent of the line, while all the principal locomotive engineers were in favour of an intermediate gauge, none considering the Narrow Gauge suitable to the development of the locomotive.

Bury, William and Benjamin Cubitt, Gray and

Roberts were the locomotive engineers who gave evidence against the 4 feet 8½ inch gauge, while Vignoles was in favour of a 6 feet gauge, and Landmann (engineer to the Greenwich Railway) of a gauge between 5 feet and 6 feet.

CHAPTER X.

THE GAUGE EXPERIMENTS.

THE Great Western Railway proposed that the experiments should take place on the Broad Gauge between London and Bristol and back, and on the London and Birmingham Railway between those two places, both ways for the Narrow Gauge; but the latter party would not agree to this obviously fair proposal, the 4 feet 8½ inch champions preferring a short length of line, such as could be run without stopping for a fresh supply of water. The Narrow Gauge therefore chose a very straight and level length of line between York and Darlington, 45 miles long, while the Great Western chose the 53 miles from London to Didcot. The Great Western used cold feed-water for their locomotives, and started their experimental trains from a state of rest, while the Narrow Gauge used *warm water*, and attained a velocity of 10 miles an hour before the starting point was reached. The Broad Gauge experiments were carried out on the days arranged—in the middle of December—two of these days were very unfavourable, on one a high wind was blowing, and on the other a small drizzling rain was falling, both causing the speed to be considerably less than would have been the case under more favourable atmospheric conditions.

The Broad Gauge engine used for the passenger train experiments was the 'Ixion,' built by Fenton and Murray, a six-wheel engine with single drivers, 7 feet diameter, cylinders 15 inches diameter, 20 inch stroke, weight of engine loaded, about 22 tons. On 16th

December the experimental train consisted of eight carriages, each weighing 10 tons, the gross weight being 81 tons 13 cwt. (exclusive of the engine and tender). The following is the official timing of this trip up and down :—

No. of Miles.	Stations.	First Trip			
		Down, A.M.		Up, P.M.	
		hrs.	min.	hrs.	min.
	Started from Paddington,	9	58½		
	Reached first mile post, .	10	2½	1	4¾
	West London Crossing, .	10	6½	1	2½
5½	Ealing, ...	10	11	12	59
7¼	Hanwell, . . .	10	13	12	57
9	Southall, . . .	10	14¾	12	55½
13	West Drayton, . .	10	20	12	50¼
18	Slough, ...	10	25½	12	44¼
22½	Maidenhead, . . .	10	30½	12	40
30¾	Twyford, . . .	10	40	12	31
35¾	Reading, . . .	10	46	12	26
41¼	Pangbourne, . . .	10	52¼	12	20
44¾	Goring, ...	10	56½	12	16
47½	Wallingford Road, .	11	0	12	13
53	Didcot, ...	11	6½	12	4½
	Total time on road . (52 miles)	1	4	1	0¼

It will be well here to observe the gradients between London and Didcot on the down journey. They are as follows :—

	Miles.		Posts.	
From	¼	to	2¼	rise 3 feet per mile
,,	2¼	,,	9¾	,, 4 ,, ,,
,,	9¾	,,	10¼	level.
,,	10¼	,,	12¾	fall 4 ,, ,,
,,	12¾	,,	15½	level.
,,	15½	,,	17¼	fall 4 ,, ,,
,,	17¼	,,	20	rise 2 ,, ,,

	Miles.	Posts.	
From	20 to	23	rise 4 feet per mile.
,,	23 ,,	32¾	,, 4 ,, ,,
,,	32¾ ,,	36¼	fall 4 ,, ,,
,,	36¼ ,,	42	rise 4 ,, ,,
,,	42 ,,	43	level.
.,	43 ,,	44	rise 2.1 ,, ,.
,,	44 ,,	53	,, 4 ,, ,,

being a total rise of 122¾ feet in the 53 miles, or, deducting the 52 feet fall, we have a net rise of 70¾ feet,
against which the down train had to contend, which,
coupled with a head wind, accounts for the longer
time on the down journeys.

In the afternoon another trip was made with only
seven carriages of a total gross weight of 71 ton (exclusive of the engine and tender). The times on this
occasion were less, the train starting from Paddington
at 2.4½ P.M., and arriving at Didcot at 3.8 P.M., taking 1
hour 3½ minutes for the journey, and on the up journey
56½ minutes. We may mention that in the official
timing of this train on the up journey, with wind and
gradient in its favour, 1½ minutes is the time booked
as occupied in travelling the 3¼ miles from Wallingford
Road to Goring, or at the rate of 130 miles an hour ;
there must surely be some mistake in the timing on
this particular part of the journey. The train was
that evening got ready with six carriages of a gross
weight of 60 tons (without engine and tender), and left
at the platform in readiness for the trip on Wednesday morning. Before starting, Inspector Craig, one
of the Paddington Station officials, examined the train
to see if all were right, when, to his amazement, and to
the astonishment of the Broad Gauge party, it was
found that the grease had been removed from the
axle boxes of all the carriages in the night, and but
for Mr Craig's great carefulness, the trial would have
been spoilt, considerable damage done to the rolling
stock, and possibly even an accident to the train.

Let us hope, for the honour of British fairness, that the Narrow Gauge officials were not responsible for this underhand proceeding, although doubtless it was the work of some Narrow Gauge fanatic. Mr Craig only retired from active duty at Paddington Station at the end of 1893, after over fifty years' service.

The trips on the 17th were timed as follows (drizzling rain falling the whole time) starting from Paddington at 10.2½ A.M., and arriving at Didcot 11.5 A.M., thus taking 1 hour 2½ minutes to complete the journey; and on the return, starting at 12.4 P.M., and arriving at Paddington 1.3 P.M., 59 minutes in all.

This train consisted of six carriages, and weighed (without the engine and tender) 60 tons. Despite the unfavourable state of the weather, so successful had the Broad Gauge experiments been, that the Narrow Gauge engineers said that it was unnecessary for a trial to be made with the 50-ton train, as they well knew their engines would be unable to perform the feats already achieved on the Great Western Railway, and they did not want another defeat with a still lighter train. Although not in the official experiments, the 'Ixion' a few days later worked a train of twelve carriages, or 120 tons, from London to Didcot in 1 hour 7 minutes, being at the rate of 47 miles an hour, a very fine performance, seeing that in the official trials the same engine only took 80 tons at the rate of 50 miles an hour.

For the goods train experiment the Great Western Railway used the 'Sampson,' a six coupled engine with wheels of 5 feet diameter, cylinders 16 inches by 18 inches, and with a fire-box area of 97 square feet, and a tube area of 600 square feet.

This engine (not built for, nor being in any way especially qualified for the trial) easily drew a train of 400 tons from London to Didcot at an average speed of 24 miles per hour for the whole journey.

The first Narrow Gauge experiment was made on 30th December. The passenger engine was a six-

wheel one with four coupled 6 feet 6 inch wheels; outside cylinders, 15 inches by 21 inches; height of boiler
top from rails, 7 feet 4 inches.   The engine was a new
one built for the occasion by R. Stephenson and Company, and weighed with the tender 28 tons.

The weight of the train was 50 tons only.   It will
be recollected that the weights of the experimental
trains upon the Broad Gauge (exclusive of engine and
tender) were fixed at 80 tons, 70 tons and 60 tons, but
that the actual tonnages were 81 tons 13 cwt., 71 tons
12¾ cwt., and 61 tons 2 qrs.   It will be seen, therefore, that this experiment upon the Narrow Gauge
line has no parallel working upon the Broad Gauge.
The   Broad   Gauge   party   appeared   to   be   considerably surprised at the reduction of 10 tons below the lowest of the weights taken by the Broad
Gauge engine, and Mr Brunel, Mr Saunders and Mr
Gooch stated that the result of the working of such a
train, to the running of which, however, they said they
did not object, could not have the slightest reference
to any one of the experiments tried between Paddington
and Didcot.   The determination to take 50 tons was
come to without consulting the Commissioners.   Mr
Brunel's original proposition was, that the experimental trains should respectively weigh 90 tons, 80
tons, and 70 tons; but to gratify the desire of the
Narrow Gauge interests, he agreed to run trains of 80,
70 and 60 tons.   Professor Barlow said he thought it
not fair to run a 50-ton train when the lowest of the
tonnages taken by the Broad Gauge locomotive was
60 tons.   Mr Bidder said the object of the advocates
of the Narrow Gauge was to show the capacity of their
engines as well with a 50-ton as with 60, 70 or 80-
ton trains, and that they should most assuredly take
experimental trips with those tonnages.   At 9 hours
7 minutes 15 seconds the train started from the
station in order to proceed to the first mile post,
from which it had been understood the experiment
was to commence.   Upon the Great Western line, the

experimental trains left the Paddington Terminus and were brought to a stand-still at the first mile post. This, however, was not the case with the Narrow Gauge, the train passing the post at 9 hours 12 minutes 17 seconds.

The train stopped at the Darlington Station at 10 hours 27 minutes 20 seconds. It will here be seen that the 43 miles were performed in 1 hour 13 minutes and 53 seconds, or at the rate of nearly 35 miles per hour. The maximum speed (between the fifth and sixth mile posts) was nearly 53 miles per hour, and the minimum rate rather more than 25 miles an hour. The average speed of the 80-ton train (exclusive of the engine and tender) upon the Broad Gauge line was 47.5 miles per hour, and the maximum speed 55 miles per hour. There was, however, one thing greatly against the Narrow Gauge experiment of this morning, viz., the wind. When the train left the York Station the weather was not at all unfavourable ; the horizon promised rain, but very little wind was stirring. Up to the tenth mile post, the result promised to be very good.

The poorness of the result was attributed by the Narrow Gauge engineers to the oblique wind, blowing across the rails, first encountered about the tenth mile post from York. When Mr Brunel heard these excuses made for the slowness of the trip, he facetiously observed that it was caused by the presence of George Hudson, the ' Railway King,' who was at his usual practice of ' raising the wind.' After waiting at the Darlington Station about an hour, Mr Bidder proposed to return with four carriages only. Professor Barlow objected to return in a train of four carriages, and that number of carriages which had been detached from the train was again put on and the return trip commenced at 12 hours 8 minutes 15 seconds. The train reached the first mile post from the York Station at 1 hour 32 minutes 8 seconds, performing the 43 miles, therefore, in 1 hour 23 minutes and 53 seconds, or at a speed of about 30 miles an hour. The following day a further trial was made with the 50-ton train, when the 43 miles were covered in 53 minutes 28 seconds, or at the rate of 48 miles an hour; the wind being in favour of the train this time. The next trip was with an 80-ton train, which, however (contrary to the Broad Gauge practice), had attained a speed of 12 miles an hour when passing the first starting point, and this train also had the wind in its favour, while the Broad Gauge 80-ton train had a strong wind blowing against it. The train took 58 minutes 30 seconds to cover the 43 miles against 52 minutes 37 seconds on the first 43 miles of the Broad Gauge trip of 53 miles. The average speed on this occasion on the Narrow Gauge was 44 miles an hour. On the third day a serious accident happened ; another Narrow Gauge engine having been brought from Derby and four carriages being attached to it, it started on a trip from York to Darlington. The Commissioners were not in the train, but most of the rival engineers were, five people being on the engine itself. The train had travelled 22 miles in 27 minutes, when the engine ran off the line and pitched into a ditch 60 yards further on; only the stoker being seriously injured. In consequence of this accident no formal experiment took place on this day, nor were any further experiments made with passenger trains on the Narrow Gauge. On the next day (Friday) the goods train experiments took place. The engine chosen was the ' Hercules,' with six coupled wheels 4 feet 6 inches diameter, cylinders 15 inches by 24 inches, fire-box area 60 square feet, tube area 900 feet, or a total heating surface of 263 feet in excess of the Broad Gauge goods engine. The train of 200 tons was taken from York to Darlington in 2 hours 14 minute 20 seconds. The return trip with forty-seven loaded trucks weighing 400 tons and over 300 yards long, was performed in 2 hours 16 minutes and 41 seconds, or at the rate of 19 miles an hour. The results of the experiments were in every case greatly in favour of the

Broad Gauge. Not only were the speeds higher and the journeys performed for a longer distance and under conditions less favourable as regards the weather, together with the locomotives employed starting from a state of rest, and the use of cold feed water, but in all issues, and especially in those where the weights of the trains were equal, the results attained by the Broad Gauge stand out far superior to the Narrow Gauge efforts.

Well might the Broad Gauge party have looked forward to a favourable report, extolling the greater excellence of their system in every particular, and for a clear and unreserved commendation of the 7 feet gauge by the Commissioners, together with full leave for the extension of the Broad Gauge lines in all directions, where public support of the fully demonstrated and undoubted superiority of Mr Brunel's railways and vehicles, required such lines to be constructed. But alas! this justly-expected and completely-warranted expectation on the part of the 'Sesquipedalians' was unhappily doomed to disappointment, for, soon after the experiments were completed, rumour (who for once lied *not*) said the report would be in favour of the Narrow Gauge, and so it was; for, in the middle of February 1846, the Commissioners presented their report.

CHAPTER XI.

THE GAUGE COMMISSIONERS' REPORT.

THE report was delivered by the Commissioners in
the middle of February (and will be found in detail in
the Appendix at the end of this volume). It was
divided into three sections, with a general conclusion.
Each of these sections was again subdivided under
several heads.

Section 1, on the break of gauge, was subdivided. Fast or express trains.—The report
under this heading may be considered in favour
of the Broad Gauge, the conclusion arrived at by the
Commissioners being that they did not 'consider the
break of gauge in this instance as being an inconvenience of so grave a nature as to call for any legislative measures, either for its removal or for its
mitigation.'

Section 2. Ordinary or mixed trains.—The evil of
a break of gauge (although then only existing at
Gloucester) was considered in this section 'to be an
inconvenience of a very serious nature . . . legislative
interference is called for to remove or mitigate such an
evil.' What a conclusion! And if this evil were
present then, when the break of gauge occurred at
the junction of two distinct and independent companies at Gloucester, how much more frequently does
the necessity for changing carriages happen in travelling to and from branch lines, which are owned,
managed and worked by the same company as the
main line. To be logical, the Commissioners should
have 'called for legislative interference, requiring the

companies to run through carriages to and from each branch and the main line by every train.' Nor could they, with a sense of justice under similar circumstances, refuse a through carriage to any passenger who had booked to a station on a 'foreign line,' which makes this conclusion of the Commissioners a veritable *reductio ad absurdum*.

Section 3. Goods trains.—Considering that at the time the experiments were made, and the report presented, most of the goods traffic was in the hands of railway *agents*, who did all the work, and in many cases provided the waggons, the *railway companies* then only hauling the trains of waggons from place to place, which (or the still more simple purpose of providing a railway only for others to use) was the original intention for which railway companies were incorporated. But the whole method of dealing with goods traffic now being long since changed, the railway companies now doing the whole of the work themselves, so that under these entirely changed conditions the report upon this sub-section has really but little application at the present time.

Section 4. Conveyance of troops.—' This is another use of railways which *we have deemed it necessary to consider.*' The lieutenant-colonel, who was one of the Commissioners, evidently wished to show he had a *practical* knowledge of *something*, and so deemed it necessary to consider 'something' they were never appointed to consider ; and after this Commissioner had made this occasion to drag in his personal experience, and having heard the expert evidence of such important authorities as the Quarter-Master General of the Forces, and the Inspector-General of Fortifications, they found that in time of peace the inconvenience of a ' break of gauge' would not amount to 'an evil of great importance,' but in time of war the case would be different. For a break of gauge, when it would be necessary for the troops to travel with their artillery, the delay caused by the break of gauge 'might expose the country to a serious danger.' But the artillery of to-day does not consist of pocket pistols, and is not usually carried about with the troops, 100-ton guns being a bit too heavy for the Narrow Gauge. Our coast defences would certainly be in a bad condition if they were waiting for the artillery to be delivered by the local railways when required for use.

Dealing with Section 2, *remedies for the evils of a break of gauge*, the following methods were reported upon :—'*First*. What may be termed telescopic axles? An arrangement of the wheels and axles of carriages permitting the wheels to slide on the axle, so as to contract or extend the interval between them in such a manner that they may be adapted to either of the gauges. *Secondly*. A form of truck adapted to the Broad Gauge, but carrying upon its upper surface pieces of rail 4 feet 8½ inches asunder, so that a Narrow Gauge carriage may be run upon these rails without any disturbance of its wheels. *Thirdly*. A method of shifting the bodies of the carriages from a platform and set of wheels adapted for one gauge to a different platform and set of wheels adapted to the other gauge. *Fourthly*. A proposal to carry merchandise and minerals in loose boxes, which may be shifted from one truck to another, and of which one only would probably be carried upon a Narrow Gauge truck, while two would be conveyed on a Broad Gauge truck.'

On telescopic axles they reported :—' In respect to the shifting axles, the attendant would have to adjust a great many carriages in succession (as there are sometimes a hundred waggons in a goods train). The adjustment must be made hurriedly and often in the night; and the attendant's thoughts would probably have been partly occupied with the loading of goods and other station arrangements. On the score of danger, therefore, we think that this construction might be at once abandoned.

With regard to the second proposed remedy, the Commissioners prefaced their answer with this sage remark,—'The plan of placing a Narrow Gauge carriage upon the top of a Broad Gauge truck has, on the face of it, this obvious difficulty, that a Broad Gauge carriage cannot be placed in the same manner upon a Narrow Gauge truck.' Surely less highly intelligent men than an astronomer royal, a lieutenant-colonel, and a professor of mathematics could have found this out, without being specially appointed as a Royal Commission.

Third, shifting bodies. This the Commissioners allowed to be practical, since they could not do otherwise, as the Broad Gauge had taken pains to investigate the plan which was in daily use in France, and to bring the same before the Commissioners, who reported :—'The system of shifting the bodies of carriages from road wheels to railway wheels is practised successfully in France, where the diligences from Paris to distant towns, proceeding on road wheels from the Messagerie of Paris to the railway station, are carried on a peculiar railway truck as far as Rouen and Orleans, and are then again placed on road wheels to continue their journey.

The use of loose boxes for goods was the last method considered, and 'the result of this experience is, that in one instance of a temporary character, where the whole operation was under the control of one engineer, it succeeded.' The result of the conclusions under this head was, 'That no method has been proposed to us which is calculated to remedy, in any important degree, the inconveniences attending a break of gauge.'

Section 3, on uniformity of gauge, sub-divided under headings—(1) for safety ; (2) public accommodation and convenience; (3) comparative speeds on the gauges ; (4) comparative economy.

For safety.—No preference was given to either

K

gauge, except for trains running at high speed, when the Broad Gauge was considered to be the safer.

Public accommodation and convenience.—This section of the report was generally in favour of the Broad Gauge, the Broad Gauge carriages being stated to be more commodious and the travelling smoother, especially at high speeds. The Narrow Gauge was reported on as more convenient for goods traffic.

Comparative speed on the gauges.—Here again the Broad Gauge was considered decidedly superior. 'We are fully satisfied that the average speed on the Great Western, both by the express trains, and by the ordinary trains, exceeds the highest speed of similiar trains on any of the Narrow Gauge lines.' A high tribute was paid to the fairness of the methods used in the trials by the Broad Gauge engineers. 'We must observe, however, that while the Great Western Company have not altered in any degree the plan of their engines, the higher velocities of the Narrow Gauge lines have been attained by the introduction of a more powerful kind of engine than was employed at an earlier period, and probably the new engines now used on the Narrow Gauge lines are as powerful as they can well be made, within the limits of their gauge, whereas the Broad Gauge lines have still a means of obtaining an increase in the power of their engines and of increasing their speed.' How far Mr Gooch at this time was ahead of all other locomotive engineers is clearly shown in this section of the report, for we read,—'In proceeding to compare the locomotive engines, we remark, in the first place, that the fire-boxes, boilers, etc., of the Narrow Gauge engines still possess a smaller evaporating power than those of the Broad Gauge engines, although recent attempts have been made to raise the former to the level of the latter; but those attempts have not succeeded; and it is indisputable that, whatever can be done for the Narrow Gauge in this respect, can be surpassed on the Broad Gauge.'

The report on this section concluded with this paragraph :—'*Impediments* to maintaining the present express speed. The chief of these are :—*First.* The difficulty of arranging the trains where the traffic is frequent, so that the fast trains shall be entirely protected from the chance of interfering with, or coming into collision with, the slower trains, or those that stop at numerous stations. *Second.* The difficulty of seeing signals, especially in foggy weather, in time to enable the engine-driver to stop the fast trains. We feel it a duty to observe here that the public are mainly indebted for the present rate of speed, and the increased accommodation of the railway carriages, to the genius of Mr Brunel and the liberality of the Great Western Railway Company.' But the invention of the block system of signalling and continuous brakes have entirely done away with these impediments. The engineering improvements and scientific developments of later years have completely removed all the objections of the Commissioners. The various obstructions which they considered fatal to farther advancement, or precluding of amelioration, have been swept aside and entirely overcome by the forward march of applied science.

Had the Commission taken place thirty or even twenty years later, one half of the report would not have been written, for the deductions and conclusions drawn by the Commissioners on the results that would accrue from the various suppositional premises would at this later period have been found to be entirely incorrect, or else the conditions under which the conclusions were arrived at would have been so completely changed that such speculations would have been unnecessary in the face of various improvements which had in the meantime been developed, and which were at this later period in daily use on railways.

Comparative economy.—The conclusion under this head of the report was meant to be entirely in favour of the Narrow Gauge, and although it was proved that the Great Western Railway worked their locomotives more economically than the London and Birmingham, yet the Commissioners, by a superficial but ingenious method of calculating what it would cost the Great Western Railway as a Narrow Gauge line, concluded that the Narrow Gauge was more economical. The Broad and Narrow Gauge locomotive power is compared thus :—' The London and Birmingham Company have from the commencement persevered in the use of light four-wheeled engines, while the Great Western, availing themselves of the facilities their gauge affords, have adopted large and powerful engines, which are worked at nearly the same cost per mile as the former ; and if such engines as those on the London and Birmingham line 'were essential to the Narrow Gauge, the question as to the economy of working might be at once decided in favour of the Broad Gauge.'

The general conclusions of the Commissioners were —'*First.* That as regards the safety, accommodation and convenience of the passengers, no decided preference is due to either gauge, but that on the Broad Gauge the motion is generally more easy at high velocities. *Secondly.* That, in respect of speed, we consider the advantages are with the Broad Gauge ; but we think the public safety would be endangered in employing the greater capabilities of the Broad Gauge much beyond their present use, except on roads more consolidated and more substantially and perfectly formed than those of the existing lines. *Thirdly.* That in the commercial case of the transport of goods, we believe the Narrow Gauge to possess the greater convenience and to be the more suited to the general traffic of the country. *Fourthly.* That the Broad Gauge involves the greater outlay, and that we have not been able to discover either in the maintenance of way, in the cost of locomotive power, or in the other annual expenses, any adequate reduction to compensate for the additional first cost.'

In some further remarks the Commissioners state,—
'We are desirous, however, of guarding ourselves from
being supposed to express an opinion that the dimension of 4 feet 8½ inches is in all respects the most
suited for the general objects of the country. Some
of the engineers who have been examined by us have
given it as their opinion that 5 feet would be the best
dimension for a railway gauge ; others have suggested
5 feet 3 inches, 5 feet 6 inches, and even 6 feet.' The
report concluded with the following recommendations :
—'*First.* That the gauge of 4 feet 8½ inches be declared by the legislature to be the gauge to be used in
all public railways now under construction, or hereafter to be constructed in Great Britain. *Second.*
That, unless by the consent of the legislature, it should
not be permitted to the directors of any railway company to alter the gauge of such railway. *Third.* That
in order to complete the general chain of Narrow
Gauge communication from the North of England to
the Southern Coast, any suitable measure should be
promoted to form a Narrow Gauge link from Oxford
to Reading, and thence to Basingstoke, or by any
shorter route connecting the proposed Rugby
and Oxford line with the South Western Railway.
Fourth. That as any junction to be formed with a Broad
Gauge line would involve a break of gauge, provided
our first recommendation be adopted, great commercial
convenience would be obtained by reducing the gauge
of the present Broad Gauge lines to the Narrow Gauge
of 4 feet 8½ inches ; and we therefore think it desirable that some equitable means should be found of
producing such entire uniformity of gauge, or of
adopting such other course as would admit of the
Narrow Gauge carriages passing without interruption
or danger along the Broad Gauge lines.'
    The cost of the Gauge Commissioners to the
country was £571, 10s., and the result, like that of
most other Royal Commissions, was a long report,
with various recommendations, which, as usual, were,

or were not, acted upon by those concerned as was the more convenient upon certain occasions.

The Broad Gauge party were greatly surprised at the text of the report, as we have already stated that they considered that the whole of the events and evidence had tended directly and indirectly in their favour, and therefore the unexpected rebuff thus administered to the Great Western Railway was the more severely felt. But never was a presumably defeated side so cleverly and fearlessly led and defended as was the Broad Gauge party by the 'Dauntless three.' For with all the other railways, as well as those indirectly connected with the railway world, against them, and these strengthened by the report of a Government Commission; they had against this solid phalanx, for the time being, fickle popular opinion on their side, for the public had witnessed the plucky combat, and partly because the Broad Gauge was fighting against such tremendous odds, partly because of the superior accommodation provided by the Great Western Railway in the matter of commodious and comfortable carriages, quick trains and smooth travelling, but chiefly because many of the public had studied the question from an impartial standpoint and had arrived at the definite conclusion that the Broad Gauge was immensely superior to the Narrow in very many respects.

So the Broad Gauge leaders, undismayed by the tenor of the report, continued the fight. The first thing Messrs Brunel, Saunders and Gooch did, was to prepare a reply to the report of the Commissioners, which was published in the middle of March—a most expeditious literary production considering the voluminousness of the work and the necessity for accuracy of detail, dealing as it did with all phases of the gauge controversy. The book was entitled, '*Observations on the Report of the Gauge Commissioners presented to Parliament,*' by the promoters of the Broad Gauge. It was a folio publication, consisting of fifty closely printed pages, illustrated with plans and maps, the price being 1s. It appeared to be compiled in a half-humorous spirit, the compilers hoping by flippancy to cast opprobrium on the report. Mr Gooch thus describes its preparation :—'We had some good fun over it. We met at Mr Saunders's house for a few hours each day until it was complete, and we of course proved that the Commissioners had come to quite a wrong conclusion.'

In the conclusion of the *Observations* the writers give a summary of the points they considered to have been proved in the controversy, viz. :—

'That the question of "break of gauge" originated as a cloak to a monopoly.'

'That even if the gauge were uniform, through trains would be impracticable.'

'That the transfer would be of little inconvenience. That any advantage of small waggons was applicable to the Broad Gauge, but that the advantage of large waggons was not applicable to the Narrow.'

'That the competition between the two systems was advantageous.'

'That the final recommendations of the Commissioners were at variance with their separate conclusions.'

'That it would be unjust to refuse to allow the Broad Gauge to be laid down on lines for which it was already sanctioned by Parliament.'

'That the inquiry before the Commissioners was not properly conducted, and that consequently no legislation ought to be founded on it.'

'That the data published by the Commissioners were often wrong, and in some cases led to the reverse of their conclusions.'

'That greater economy was proved on the Broad Gauge.'

'That the Broad Gauge was superior in the points of safety, speed and conveyance of troops.'

'That the experiments made in the presence of the

Commissioners had demonstrated beyond all controversy the complete success of the Broad Gauge
system.'

For these and other reasons, a strong protest
was made against any legislative interference with
the Broad Gauge system. A reply was published
to these arguments, and during the controversy a
large number of pamphlets, articles and other publica-
tions appeared on both sides.

Mr Brunel's views on the whole question about
this time are concisely expressed in the following
letter, written to a friend in France, who asked for
information on the subject of the Broad Grauge :—

'*August* 1845.

'I am just off for Italy, but write a few hasty
lines in reply to Mons. ——'s queries, and which
you must scold him for not addressing direct to me.
Nobody can answer such questions but myself, and
I am compelled to be very brief.

'In answer to the first I send a drawing. Secondly,
I see no reason why the ordinary construction of
rails, chairs and sleepers should not be equally
applicable to the wide gauge as to the narrow. I
have used them occasionally. I should think 75 lbs.
per yard heavy enough for any purposes. Thirdly,
within all ordinary limits, certainly in curves of more
than 250 metres (12½ chains) radius, the gauge does
not affect the question of curves. The effect of a
curve of larger radius than this appears, both as from
much observation as from theory, to arise merely
from two causes, the one centrifugal force, which is
easily neutralised, and is independent of gauge ; the
other from the axles not being able to travel in the
direction of the radius, and consequently the wheels
not running in a tangent to the curve. This also
is unaffected by the width of gauge. Practically I
believe the conditions are not altered. Fourthly,
the expenses of construction are not dependent on

the breadth of gauge unless the total width allowed for the loads or carriages is thereby, or for other reasons, increased, which is not a necessary consequence of a 7 foot gauge. The wide gauge could be laid upon the London and Birmingham Railway without altering any of the works; but in constructing the Great Western Railway I thought it desirable to provide for carrying larger bodies, and I placed the centres of the two railways 13 feet apart instead of 11 feet, and therefore my railway became 4 feet wider in total width. The increased cost of this, including the cost of land, will vary from £300 to £500 per mile. Fifthly, the increase of width will not increase the weight of an engine (of the same power) 500 lbs., but I avail myself of the larger width to get more powerful engines, and they weigh, with water in the boiler, 18 to 21 tons. I send a drawing of one; the stroke is 18 inches. Sixthly, the passenger carriages are all on six wheels, and excessively strong; at present the frame-work of carriages and the whole of the waggons are made of iron. The first-class carriages weigh, with wheels, etc., 7 tons 16 cwt. (17,472 lbs.), and carry thirty-two passengers. Second-class about the same weight, and hold seventy-two. Seventhly and eighthly, the comparison being on different railways, under different managements, and totally different circumstances, no strictly correct comparative results can be given; and, of course, the most opposite opinions are entertained and expressed. I believe we travel much quicker at the same cost, and with more ease, and certainly the wear and tear of engines and carriages is *very much less* with us than with the other lines; but for the reasons above stated it cannot be made matter of exact proof, but remains " matter of opinion." '

The Great Western Railway Board prepared another document, entitled *Additional Observations*, and also sent a letter to the Lords of the Committee of Privy Council for Trade, suggesting that certain districts should be marked out for the 7 feet gauge, and that railways on that gauge should not be constructed in any other part.

On 6th June 1846, the Lords Committee presented their report, which was in favour of the South Wales Railway being constructed on the Broad Gauge, as sanctioned by its Act, so that the through route to and from London to Milford Haven for the South of Ireland traffic might not suffer from a break of gauge. The Lords concluded their report by the following suggestions :—' 1. That no line shall hereafter be formed on any other than the 4 feet 8½ inch gauge, excepting lines to the south of the existing line from London to Bristol, and excepting small branches of a few miles in length in immediate connection with the Great Western Railway, but that no such lines, as above excepted, shall be sanctioned by Parliament unless a special report shall have been made by the Committee on the Bill setting forth the reasons which have led the Committee to advise that such line should be formed on any other than the 4 feet 8½ inch gauge. 2. That, unless by the consent of the legislature, it shall not be permitted to the directors of any railway company to alter the gauge of such railway. 3. That, in order to complete the general chain of Narrow Gauge communication from the North of England to the Southern Coasts, and to the port of Bristol, any suitable measures should be promoted to form a Narrow Gauge link from Gloucester to Bristol, and also from Oxford to Basingstoke, or by any shorter route connecting the proposed Rugby and Oxford line with the South-Western Railway. 4. That the South Wales line and its branches to Monmouth and Hereford should be permitted to be formed on the Broad Guage, as sanctioned by their Act. 5. That the Rugby and Oxford line, and the Oxford, Worcester and Wolverhampton line, should be permitted to be formed on the Broad Gauge, as sanctioned by their

Acts; that the Lords of the Committee of Privy Council for Trade shall exercise the powers conferred upon them by the several Acts, and shall require that additional Narrow Gauge rails shall forthwith be laid down from Rugby to Oxford, and from Wolverhampton to the junction with the Birmingham and Gloucester line; and that if it should hereafter appear that there is a traffic requiring accommodation on the Narrow Gauge from the Staffordshire districts to the Southern Coast any suitable measure shall be promoted by Parliament to form a Narrow Gauge link from Oxford to the line of the Birmingham and Gloucester Railway.

The result of this report was the 'Guage Regulation Bill,' which was introduced in the House of Lords and duly passed; it was then sent down to the Commons, where it was read a third time on 12th August 1846, and duly received the royal assent. The preamble sets forth that 'it is expedient to define the gauge on which railways shall be constructed.' Clause 1 commences as follows :—'That after the passing of this Act, it shall not be lawful (except as hereinafter excepted) to construct any railway for the conveyance of passengers on any other gauge than 4 feet 8½ inches in Great Britain, and 5 feet 3 inches in Ireland.' Clause 2 excepts certain railways, viz., 'those constructed under Acts in which the gauge is specially defined, railways then in course of construction in Cornwall, Devon, Dorset and Somerset, the Uxbridge branch of the Great Western, the Maidenhead and High Wycombe branch, and any railway which is in its whole length southward of the Great Western Railway.' Clause 3 authorises 'the South Wales Railway, its extensions, branches and connections, and also a railway for making a communication between the city of Bristol and the South Wales Railway, and a branch therefrom to be constructed on the 7 foot gauge.' Clause 4 states 'that it shall not be lawful after the passing of this Act to alter the gauge of any railway used for the conveyance of passengers.' Clause 5 excludes the Oxford and Rugby, and the Oxford, Rugby and Wolver-hampton Railway from the provisions of this Act. Clause 6 'that if any railway used for the conveyance of passengers shall be constructed and altered contrary to the provision of this Act, the company authorised to construct the railway, or in the case of any demise or lease of such railway, the company for the time being having the control of the works of such railway shall forfeit £10 for every mile of such railway which shall be so unlawfully constructed or altered during every day that the same shall continue so unlawfully con-structed or altered; and in estimating the amount of any such penalty, any distance less than 1 mile shall be estimated as a mile.'   Clause 7 declares that rail-ways constructed contrary to the Act may be abated. Clause 8 enacts 'that all penalties under this Act, and the amount of cost and charges of abating any such railway, and restoring the site thereof, as aforesaid, may be recovered from the company liable to pay and make good the same,' etc.

But the Great Western Railway obtained Par-liamentary sanction to alter the gauge of their line as long ago as 1866, so that there is no chance of an 'informer' recovering the penalty of £10 per mile per day.

CHAPTER XII.

In 1846 the Birmingham and Oxford Junction Railway obtained an Act to construct a line from Fenny Compton (on the Oxford and Rugby line—the Act for which was obtained in the previous Session) to Birmingham, 42¾ miles in length. By the passing of this Act, not only did the Broad Gauge obtain an entrance into Birmingham, but an alternate route was provided between that town and London as well. This line had been proposed a few years previously by the Grand Junction Railway, when they were at war with the London and Birmingham; but at the time this Act was obtained these two Narrow Gauge lines were in process of amalgamation, and therefore, under the peculiar circumstances, no very strenuous opposition could be offered by either of these companies, although the London and Birmingham opposed the measure by every indirect way possible. By this Act, incorporating the Birmingham and Oxford Junction Railway, the shareholders were empowered to lease their line to the Great Western Railway if three-fifths of the shareholders were in favour of doing so. This clause presented an opportunity to the newly-formed London and North Western Railway to endeavour to obtain possession of this competing line, and, if successful in so doing, to prevent the competition and loss of traffic that would take place by the opening of a rival line. The Directors of the London and North Western Railway lost no time, but commenced to purchase as many of the shares of the

Birmingham and Oxford Junction Railway as they could possibly obtain.

Besides the Birmingham and Oxford Junction Railway, with a capital of £1,000,000, there was the Birmingham, Wolverhampton and Dudley Railway, 14½ miles long (which also obtained its Act in 1846), with a capital of £700,000, thus making the total capital of the undertakings £1,700,000. Both of these the Great Western Railway agreed to purchase at a premium of 51¼ per cent.; but to prevent this arrangement being carried out, those shareholders who held shares on behalf of the London and North Western Railway presented a petition to that company asking it to purchase the undertaking, which the London and North Western Railway agreed to do at a premium of 75 per cent. This better offer made some of the genuine shareholders waver, but since they had already ratified the agreement entered into by their Directors to sell to the Great Western Railway, there was no pretext for their vacillation, except the hope of obtaining the better price offered by the London and North Western Railway for the Birmingham and Oxford line.

We now come to one of the most extraordinary proceedings ever enacted in the annals of railway meetings. There were twelve Directors of the Birmingham and Oxford Junction Railway, and the London and North Western portion of the shareholders had a special meeting called to raise the number of Directors to eighteen. This proposition was duly carried out—the six new ones being in favour of selling to the London and North Western; and, at the general meeting, held on 13th March 1847, four of the old Directors should have resigned, and the London and North Western party had four more ready to take their place. By this means a majority on the Board would have been obtained who were favourable to rescinding the sale to the Great Western Railway, and accepting the offer of the London and

North Western Railway; but the Broad Gauge Directors refused to withdraw, and the case was brought before Parliament, where it was discovered that the London and North Western Railway held 40,000 of the 50,000 shares constituting the capital of the company. The House of Lords appointed a Committee of five to inquire into the whole facts of the case; but, after a number of sittings, the House agreed to defer acting on the report of the Committee until judgment had been given in the various legal proceedings then being fought out in the Law Courts.

In February 1848, the Great Western Railway obtained a final judgment in their favour, confirming the original lease to them, and declaring the six extra Directors elected by the London and North Western nominees on 13th March 1847 to have been illegally elected. But, in the meantime, the Narrow Gauge had gained a great concession by obtaining Parliamentary powers to have the Narrow Gauge as well as Broad Gauge laid down on the Birmingham and Oxford Junction Railway. This part of the Gauge contest is dealt with in the next chapter (Mixed Gauge). The Great Western Railway, having been successful in the law suit, immediately proceeded with a Bill authorising them to purchase the Birmingham and Oxford Junction Railway at £30, 5s. for each £20 share. This Bill was duly passed; when first before the House, a meeting of the shareholders of the Birmingham and Oxford Junction Railway was called, and the shareholders continued to meet almost daily for several months, until the final result was known.

Having thus chronicled the fight between the gauges in the north, we now proceed to narrate the perhaps more outrageous and underhand conduct of the Narrow Gauge party in the West of England, in connection with the Exeter and Crediton Railway, with which, despite the shameful and dishonourable tactics of the

Narrow Gauge, the Broad Gauge for a time was again victorious. The Exeter and Crediton Railway Company was incorporated in 1845 for the construction of a line from Cowley Bridge (Exeter), on the Bristol and Exeter Railway, to Crediton, a length of 6 miles. The line was to be worked by the Bristol and Exeter Railway for a percentage of the receipts; but the London and South Western Railway had their eyes on the line, and saw it might become useful to them in after years as part of a through route to North Devon, so they commenced buying up the shares in the approved Narrow Gauge style, and, on 17th February 1847, a special meeting was called to 'consider a proposition made by the Taw Vale to lease the Exeter and Crediton in perpetuity on the following terms :— 5 per cent. to be paid by the Taw Vale on amount of paid-up capital, the profits exceeding 5 per cent. up to a ½ per cent., and when exceeding 5½ per cent., the surplus to be divided equally; the profits to be estimated after deducting one-third for the working expenses, and the lease to be guaranteed by the South Western Company.

This proposition was a great surprise to those original shareholders who remained in the Company, and who naturally considered their line as a *protégé* of the Bristol and Exeter Railway. No decision could be come to, and the meeting was adjourned. This meeting was held on 12th April, but in the interim every exertion was made to get the line opened, and Mr Buller, with the sanction of the majority of the Directors, entered into an agreement with the contractor to supply the plant and work the traffic on the intended opening. The line was not, however, opened; for, when all was ready, the Taw Vale party obtained an injunction from the Vice-Chancellor to restrain the Directors from opening the line, from completing the junction with the Bristol and Exeter line at Cowley Bridge, or from entering into any agreement to work or lease it on the Broad

Gauge to the prejudice of the proposed agreement with the Taw Vale Company.

We will give an account of the extraordinary proceedings of this meeting, extracted from the columns of a newspaper of that time. 'Mr Thorne (one of the Directors appointed by the Taw Vale shareholders) moved that the Directors should be reduced to six, and that the four to be turned out should be Messrs Buller, Brown (Deputy-Chairman of the Bristol and Exeter Company), Fripp and Bastard. Mr Younge seconded the motion. The Chairman replied very fully to the charges made against him. He reverted to the change in the proprietary, and remarked that if it had not been for the tempting offers of money which had been made to the original shareholders to part with their shares, he was convinced they would have felt it imperative to confirm the lease to the Bristol and Exeter Company; and, unless different principles than those of honour —which regulated individuals—were to regulate companies, the agreement with that company was as binding as any agreement ever framed between parties able to contract. The question of law became the subject of discussion. Mr Wilkinson (solicitor to the Taw Vale) read the opinions of Mr Sergeant Wrangham, and Mr Rowe and the Attorney - General and the Hon. Mr Talbot, conjointly, in favour of the shareholders having power to remove the Directors down to six, and to elect who should be removed; and Mr Pring (the solicitor to the Crediton Company) read the opinion of Mr Sergeant Kinglake in support of the Directors' view, that it was illegal to diminish the number of Directors except at the ordinary half-yearly meeting, and that the parties to retire were subject for ballot at the Board.

The Chairman then refused to put a resolution which he was deliberately advised was illegal.

Mr Thorne (the mover) then said he must take the liberty of putting it himself. (Confusion.)

The Chairman would not allow any other person to put the resolution until he had left the chair. (Great disorder.)   Mr Thorne put the resolution.

A number of hands were held up amid the utmost confusion, above which were heard the voices of the shareholders, "You have no right to call for a show of hands." "We didn't hold up our hands, because we wouldn't recognise the thing."

The Chairman said he had never witnessed anything so disorderly, and called on any gentleman to propose a resolution.

Mr Wilkinson.—"Having taken the vote of the meeting, you are no longer a Director, and therefore I tell you you have no right to hold that chair." (Uproar.)

The Chairman.—" I shall not leave the chair until the meeting is over; I shall dissolve the meeting first." (Great disorder.)

Mr Wilkinson.—"You not being in the chair, I beg to move that Mr Thorne take the chair."

Mr E. Cooper (Chairman of the Taw Vale) seconded it.

Mr Wilkinson put his motion in the same way as Mr Thorne had, and the same uproar ensued. It was carried unanimously.

Mr Thorne asked the Chairman if he would give up his seat.

Mr Buller.—"Certainly not."

Mr Cooper said they would consider Mr Thorne in the chair.

Mr Buller.—"If any gentleman has any motion to put, I am ready to hear him. There being no further business, I dissolve the meeting."

The Chairman left the chair.

Mr Brown sprang forward and caught up the minute-book which was lying on the table. Mr Thorne immediately collared and grappled with Mr Brown, and Mr Bastard clung to the skirts of Mr Thorne's coat. At this time a rush was made by the

Directors' party, and the book was thrown by Mr Brown on the floor and passed to the Secretary (Mr Hartnoll). Surrounded by the whole body of shareholders and Directors composing the minority, the Secretary was escorted from the room, with the book, amid a scene of unparalleled disorder.

Mr Thorne then took the chair, and a motion for affixing the Corporate Seal of the Company to the agreement for a lease to the Taw Vale Company was unanimously carried; but here arose another difficulty, they had not possession of the seal.

Mr Cooper and Mr Woolmer (two Directors) went to the private office of the Secretary to demand it, but the door was locked and no one there. Another resolution to restrain the Directors from carrying on the works on the Broad Gauge, or opening the line, or incurring any further expense in completing the junction with the Bristol and Exeter at Cowley Bridge was also carried. A resolution, calling on the Secretary to lend his assistance in carrying the foregoing resolutions into effect was passed.'

The result of this quarrel was that the Narrow Gauge party obtained an injunction restraining the opening of the line on the Broad Gauge, although it was quite ready for working. After being left unused for a year or so, the Broad Gauge was taken up and the Narrow Gauge laid down in its place. The line now consisted of a length of 6 miles of Narrow Gauge, joining a Broad Gauge line 2 miles from Exeter; therefore, if the line had been opened, it would have been useless. A proposal was made to continue the railway by an independent Narrow Gauge line into Exeter, but as more money had already been spent on the line than the amount authorised by the Act, it was found impossible to raise the funds necessary to complete this extension. Never had a railway been in a more awkward predicament, nor has often a clearer example been seen of a too clever party over-reaching itself; but in this case,

the Narrow Gauge met with an unexpected obstacle
to their further dishonourable proceedings. The Railway Commissioners refused to sanction the opening
of the line on the Narrow Gauge, as the Act was
obtained for a Broad Gauge railway, and the Commissioners insisted upon the Exeter and Crediton
Railway complying with this Act and being a Broad
Gauge line. For many years the line remained un-
worked, the sole income being derived from the hay
crop that was regularly gathered from the grass that
grew on the unused railway. But after these years of
inaction, Parliamentary power was obtained to raise
further capital with which the line was re-converted to
the Broad Gauge, and finally opened and worked by
the Bristol and Exeter Railway on the same terms
as contained in the original lease entered into in 1846.
Besides these years absolutely wasted by the disgrace-
ful action of the London and South Western Railway,
which prevented the opening of the line, the capital
of the company was increased by the extra expenses
incurred in consequence of these proceedings of the
Narrow Gauge party from £70,000, the original
amount, to £119,999, so that besides the great inconvenience the public suffered from the shameful
tactics of those who were interested in forcing the
Narrow Gauge into Devonshire, the shareholders in
this luckless company had to divide any profit that
might accrue from the line over a capital of two-thirds
larger than would have been necessary if the railway
had been opened at first as originally intended. All
the extra capital consisted of debenture and preference
shares, so the fight between the gauges on this occasion took away all hope of the original proprietors
obtaining any reasonable return on the £70,000 they
had invested in the concern. No wonder that with
proceedings such as these fresh in the minds of the
west countrymen, the Narrow Gauge was not looked
upon with favour in Devonshire and Cornwall.

This line ultimately was merged in the London

and South Western Railway system, and was again altered to the Narrow Gauge, and forms the first part of the North Devon Railway beyond Exeter. It is not generally known that the Great Western Railway still assert their right to work over this line, by running two goods trains each way daily, between Exeter and Crediton.

In 1846 Parliament sanctioned the following Broad Gauge lines, all of which were connected with the Great Western Railway :—

Ashburton, Newton and South Devon.

Birmingham, Wolverhampton and Dudley.

Birmingham and Oxford Junction (with branches to Stratford, etc.) extension into Birmingham.

Bristol and South Wales Junction and Ferry from the Great Western at Bristol to Aust, and New Passage on the Severn to be continued by means of a ferry and extension line to the South Wales Railway.

Bristol and Exeter (Crewkerne branch).

Cornwall—Broad Gauge line from Plymouth to Falmouth in continuation of the South Devon. Promoted and assisted by the Great Western Railway.

Exeter and Exmouth.

Oxford, Worcester and Wolverhampton (branches to Witney, Stratford-on-Avon and Droitwich) line with two gauges. Leased to the Great Western.

Portbury Pier and Railway.

South Wales, No. 2. (Broad Gauge branches to Haloe, Swansea, Haverford West, etc.). Leased to the Great Western, and ultimately to be amalgamated.

South Devon, No. 2. (Broad Gauge branches to Torquay, etc.), atmospheric line. Assisted and worked by the Great Western Railway.

Tenby, Saundersfoot and South Wales — Broad Gauge line in connection with South Wales Railway, and purchase of Saundersfoot Railway and Harbour.

Vale of Neath Railway.

West Cornwall—Broad Gauge line from Falmouth

to Penzance, with branch to Truro.   Promoted and assisted by the Great Western Railway.

Wilts, Somerset and Weymouth—Extensions and branches to Devizes, Bathampton, etc.   Leased to the Great Western Railway.

The Exeter and Exmouth and the West Cornwall from Truro to Penzance were afterwards constructed on the Narrow Gauge, and, upon the opening of the Cornwall Broad Gauge Railway to Truro, the West Cornwall added a third rail to their line, and so became a Mixed Gauge.

In 1847, the principal gauge battle was in connection with a more direct line between London and Exeter, the fight being between three companies, or rather the Great Western Railway had to fight the London and South Western Railway on one side and the Bristol and Exeter on the other.   The Great Western proposed a new line from Hungerford, through Westbury and Devizes, then along the Wilts and Somerset to Yeovil, thence to Exeter by a proposed line parallel with the present London and South Western Railway from Yeovil to Exeter.   The Bristol and Exeter Railway proposed a Broad Gauge line from Taunton to Bruton, and thence by the proposed Great Western line to Hungerford, from which place to London the Great Western line would be used.   At the present time the Great Western Railway is constructing two short lengths of line which, when completed, will form a line between London and Exeter substantially similar to the one proposed by the Bristol and Exeter Railway in 1847.

The London and South Western Railway's Narrow Gauge lines were, an extension of the line (then in course of construction from Basingstoke to Salisbury) from the latter city through Yeovil to Exeter.   Beyond Exeter the South Western proposed to construct Narrow Gauge lines through Okehampton and Tavistock to Plymouth, and from Okehampton, through Launceston and Camelford, through the middle of

Cornwall, to Truro; and now we find that after many years of waiting and many rebuffs the South Western has, piece by piece, and year by year, added to its system, so that it has within the last few years completed its Narrow Gauge line over the whole of this district to Plymouth, and is fast completing its line in Cornwall, which, however, does not take quite the course originally proposed, as, instead of striking inland at Camelford, the line at present under construction keeps to the North Coast to Newquay, from which town Parliamentary powers are being sought to construct a railway to Truro. But this is a digression, treating of lines that were not constructed for very many years after the period of which we are now writing; we will therefore return to the Parliamentary battle of the gauges as fought in 1847. The result of the triangular duel in the Commons was the passing of the South Western Railway Bills, thus authorising, so far as the Lower House was concerned, a Narrow Gauge line to Exeter. This triumph of the London and South Western Railway was due to the fact that Mr Cockburn conducted their case. In previous years Mr Cockburn had been briefed by the Great Western Railway, and was, in consequence, fully acquainted with their arguments, and upon this occasion he used them against his old clients the Broad Gauge. His speech lasted for three days, and was remarkable for the merciless way he treated Brunel, Russell and Saunders, bringing out and taking advantage of all the information and suggestions they had given him, when he was fighting for the Broad Gauge interest in previous years. He again and again made use of the expression—'Out of your own mouth I judge you.' Altogether during these three days the Broad Gauge officials had *une mauvaise quatre d'heure* of a very lengthened description. These Bills were then suspended, with leave to come before the House of Lords in the 1848 Sessions, and they duly received the Royal assent in that year.   The Great Western Railway unsuccessfully endeavoured to get a clause inserted for the lines to be Double Gauge ones, so that it could run Broad Gauge trains on these railways. Although the London and South Western Railway had obtained powers for these extensions, nothing was done towards constructing the lines for several years, the company's finances being in a very bad state. The new London and South Western Railway extensions opened in 1848, consisting of 139 miles of additional line, only produced an increased revenue of £72,000 in 1849, so that the dividends fell from 8 per cent. to 3 per cent.   We can therefore well understand the shareholders not being in favour of constructing any further extensions.   At this time the London and South Western Railway had locked up in the various lines proposed to be constructed, in opposition to the Broad Gauge, the following sums :— Exeter and Exmouth, £3871, 10s. ; Exeter, Yeovil and Dorchester, £90,240, 1s. 10d. ; Exeter and Crediton, £2000 ; Western lines, £217,162, 9s. 3d. ; Cornwall and Devon, £3000 ; Sutton Harbour, £9426 ; Bodmin and Wadebridge, £33,096, 9s. 8d.

The Acts obtained in 1848 having lapsed, the Salisbury and Yeovil Railway was constructed by an independent company, which obtained its Act in 1854, and was opened throughout on 1st June 1861.   In 1856, the London and South Western Railway obtained new powers to construct a line from Yeovil to Exeter, which was opened on 19th July 1860, or twelve years after the threatened invasion.   In 1860 the South Western obtained an Act 'to extend the Exeter line, and to connect it with the Bristol and Exeter ; also to make alterations in the St David's Station of that line, and to lay down and work over Narrow Gauge rails from Exeter to Cowley Bridge Junction on the Bristol and Exeter Railway, and thence to lay down Narrow Gauge lines on the Exeter and Crediton, the North Devon and Bideford Extension,' all of which lines had been constructed on the Broad Gauge, despite the various tricks of the London and South Western Railway to get them made as Narrow Gauge railways. The construction of these Narrow Gauge lines in Wilts and Dorset caused the Broad Gauge Companies to proceed with the construction of their authorised lines, the completing of which had remained many years in abeyance. The railway to Salisbury was opened in 1856, and to Weymouth in 1857.

The Broad Gauge gained one notable triumph, by obtaining powers to construct a line from Oxford to Cheltenham, the London and North Western Railway's proposition for a somewhat similar line being defeated. Although from a financial point this line could never of itself be a success, yet as a strategetic line it was most useful, as by it the Narrow Gauge was completely shut out of the district between London, Gloucester and South Wales. The contests we have described virtually decided the ' Battle of the Gauges,' as although in other years the Broad and Narrow lines came into collision, the struggles were only over minor branch lines of but local importance. Being thus victorious the Broad Gauge rested from strife for several years, gradually extending the mileage of its lines in the West and North West of England, and in South Wales, but the change came *sponte sua*, when the Great Western Railway found the Narrow Gauge obtaining the principal share of the mineral and goods traffic, and to conserve as much as possible of this traffic to itself the Great Western Railway one evil day commenced to alter a part of its system from Broad to Narrow Gauge. The ' powers that be ' forgot the truism *obsta principiis*, and the suitability of the alteration once admitted, the Narrow in place of the Broad increased year by year, until at last the Broad Gauge became a thing of the past.

CHAPTER XIII.

THE MIXED GAUGE.

THE Gauge Act in a measure prevented the Great Western Railway from extending its lines to the north and north-west of the main line; but as the Great Western Railway and the allied companies required to make further extensions in these directions on the Broad Gauge, their opponents immediately brought forward the Gauge Act to bar the further progress of the Broad Gauge lines. To meet this opposition the Great Western Railway proposed to put down lines suitable for both gauges on these new branches.

Two methods were suggested as practical, the Double Gauge, consisting of four parallel lines for both the up and the down trains, or eight metals in all. The outside lines of each group were 7 feet apart, and on these Broad Gauge vehicles were to run; the two inner lines were 4 feet $8\frac{1}{2}$ inches for Narrow Gauge stock. By this means it was proposed to run trains composed of both Broad and Narrow Gauge vehicles; not only was this project strenuously opposed by the Narrow Gauge companies, whose opposition was outwardly based on the danger, expense and impracticability of such means of working railways; but the real cause of their objection was the desire to retain the monopoly of these important districts themselves; and the leading Narrow Gauge engineers were retained by them to give scientific evidence as to the dangers and inutility of such an arrangement of lines. It is certainly to be deplored to find men, high in the engineering profession, giving such evidence as was adduced on behalf of the Narrow Gauge.

These engineers, including Robert Stephenson, seemed to forget that it was their experience and their opinion as engineers that were required, and that they were not employed to back up certain parties at all costs, such methods of fighting being left to counsel. Yet one and all of the Narrow Gauge engineers were so unmindful of their status as to declare the impossibility of so laying the metals and working two gauges. It is humiliating to find these positive assurances of men, who, above all, should be capable of judging as to the practicability or non-practicability of a certain method, completely disproved in actual working, and what they said was '*impossible*' being daily successfully carried out. Such evidence only detracts from the weight usually given to the statements of those who are supposed to be qualified to give opinions on certain subjects, and leads the public to think that the opinion and evidence of scientific witnesses follow the fees, and are therefore of little value.

The other proposal of the Broad Gauge was to lay down three rails, the outside ones for the Broad Gauge, and one of the outer to be common to both gauges, and the middle one to be used by the Narrow Gauge trains. This was called the *Mixed Gauge*, and was the system usually adopted. But this proposal was as distasteful to the Narrow Gauge party as was the Double Gauge, and the same evidence was brought forward to prove the utter inutility and the great danger that would arise from such a mixture. How completely false the predictions of the Narrow Gauge engineers have proved we have good means of judging by the fact that the Mixed Gauge was in daily use on hundreds of miles of railway on the Great Western Railway for forty years or more, and yet without accident. So much for the opinions of Robert Stephenson and his Narrow Gauge brother engineers.

On 1st June 1847, the Commons passed the following resolution :—'On consideration of the report of the Coventry, Banbury and Oxford Junction Bill to move that the Bill be re-committed for the purpose of enabling the Committee to report their reasons for recommending, in their twelfth resolution, that such line should be formed on any other than the 4 feet 8½ inch gauge.' The House of Lords, on 25th June 1847, ordered the Railway Commissioners of the Board of Trade to examine the question for laying a Mixed Gauge on the Birmingham and Oxford Junction Railway.

This report was in favour of the Mixed Gauge, which was accordingly laid down to Birmingham. On 7th July 1847, Mr Robert Stephenson made a long report to Mr Creed, the Secretary of the London and North Western Railway, in which he strongly inveighed against the Double Gauge. His conclusions were as follow :—*First.* Permanent way.—That the four-rail system increases the complication so much as to be inadmissible, except where absolutely necessary, as at turn-plates, etc. That notwithstanding the exercise of the utmost care in construction and maintenance of way, the mixture of gauges, either by means of three or four rails, introduces in the road itself a greatly increased risk of accident, entirely incapable of remedy, and scarcely justifiable by any considerations of mere convenience. *Second.* Station arrangements.—' That collisions on a three-rail Mixed Gauge line between trains of different gauges would necessarily be even more disastrous in their consequences than under the present system ; the blows would be oblique, and would therefore tend to twist and double up the train, and so to bring the carriages into a position in which they would be least able to resist the crushing force. The four-rail system for sidings has already been shown to involve a greatly increased number of dangerous points of intersections. It would also be inconvenient at the platforms. The only alternative, then, is to lay separate sidings for the two gauges, or, in other words, completely to duplicate station arrangements.' *Third.* Traffic arrangements.— Mr Robert Stephenson reported that if the traffic was conducted in a fair way double the number of trains would have to be run, viz., the usual complement of each gauge—'By the Mixed Gauge system, the evils hitherto confined to one district will be repeated in new and distant parts of the country. The break of gauge, in short, cannot be remedied by the mixture of gauges until such mixture becomes co-extensive with railways themselves, and thus, after enormous expense, we should arrive at last at uniformity, but without the simplicity of construction and arrangement which can alone insure the economy, safety and efficiency of the railway system.' When we read that Mr Stephenson, before the Commissioners, in answer to a question, gravely and emphatically said that 'the rejection of the Mixed, is, I think, beyond all question. I do not know a single practical man in this country who has not felt that as strongly as myself.' Certainly illogical enough to make one smile! but his reply to the (next) question, 'You think the Narrow better, yet you are of opinion that whatever may be the decision with respect to the Narrow or Broad, that the effect of experiment will be the absolute rejection of all the Mixed?' 'Certainly!' makes us laugh outright, so completely has his prediction on this score been falsified. So much for the expert evidence of this celebrated Narrow Gauge engineer. Mr Locke corroborated this evidence. He stated, in most distinct terms, 'that having turned his attention to the question of mixing the gauge of railways, he was not disposed to recommend or sanction it anywhere; that he thought it would be liable to cause great interruption of traffic; would be attended with vast expense, far greater than was at all contemplated; that it would be absolutely necessary to have separate stations; that danger would be produced by the multiplication of points and crossings, and by the consequent diminution of the solidity of the road. Points and crossings are not good things at high speeds, and so long as the speed on a railway is very small the inconvenience of a point or crossing is not very great, but when you have a station with a number of points and crossings, and express trains passing through at 50 or 60 miles an hour, then it becomes rather serious.'

Mr Locke also addressed a long letter on the evils of the Mixed Gauge to Lord John Russell, who was then Premier. In this epistle he tried to prove that the remedy of a Mixed Gauge was a far greater evil than the break of gauge itself, and ended up by submitting to his Lordship, 'that it is clearly the duty of the Government to see that the evils of the complexities of gauge are not inflicted upon the railway system, and to put an effectual stop to the accumulating evils which private legislation is every day causing in further extending the untried system of Mixed Gauge.'

Soon after the publication of Mr Locke's fallacious letter, a caustic article appeared in the *Morning Herald*, which completely proved the utter want of soundness in the theories and views expounded by Mr Locke; and the subsequent general extension of the Mixed Gauge has completely verified the opinion expressed by the *Morning Herald*.

In connection with the evidence given before the Commissioners with regard to the Mixed Gauge on the Birmingham and Oxford line, Mr Gooch made his world-famous experiments as to the resistance of trains at various speeds. Mr Gooch thus writes of those experiments :—'I felt a complete series of experiments was required, and having the authority of the Board to spend what was necessary, I designed and constructed an indicator to measure and accurately record the speed at which the train was moving, and also on the same paper to record the traction power used by the engine measured by a spring; also on the same paper the force and direction of the wind. To check the traction I also at the same time took indicator cards from the cylinder of the engine so as accurately to measure the power exerted there. It also gave me the power expended in moving the engines. I made a great number of experiments over a level piece of line on the Bristol and Exeter line at various rates of speed and loads. They gave me results very different from those obtained by the Narrow Gauge, which, however, were done more by calculation than by actual experiment. They cost me a vast amount of labour, both in calculations and in making the experiments. It was rather a difficult task to sit on the buffer beam of the engine and take indicator cards at speeds of 60 miles an hour.'

These experiments were considered at the meeting of the Institution of Civil Engineers on 18th April and 2d May 1848, and led to considerable discussion, as the results arrived at were very dissimilar to those obtained on the Narrow Gauge a year or so previously, the trains performing which had not been propelled but had descended various banks by gravity. Mr Gooch for his experiments constructed a dynamometer carriage at Swindon in which all the results required were registered upon a large scale on the same roll of paper, thus exhibiting at one view, and in the same period of time, the tractive power exerted upon the train, and the force and direction of the wind ; the registration of the results was made upon the paper at every sixteenth part of a mile, and the time was registered in correspondence with the distance traversed during every fifth part of a second. The dynamometer spring used was 7 feet 6 inches long, and very carefully arranged. It was only necessary to count the number of seconds or fractions of a second in one or more of the distance divisions and the speed was accurately ascertained. The force and direction of the wind was ascertained by a wind gauge, placed 5 feet above the top of the carriage, with the connections brought down to pencils, which indicated on the same sheet all the results. Indicator cards were also taken simultaneously from the steam cylinders as frequently as was practicable, but not continuously, as it was a service of some danger, the experimenter being obliged to sit on the buffer beam of the engine at a velocity of 60 miles an hour, and in that windy position to take off four sets of cards in three-quarters of a minute. The spot selected for performing the experiments was one mile of railway, perfectly straight and level, and nearly on the surface of the ground; in the plan the height of the trees, hedges, and every intervening object which could affect the influence of the wind is clearly marked. The experimental train consisted of first and second-class carriages, each on six wheels, 4 feet diameter, taken indiscriminately from the working stock and loaded with iron to represent a fair load of passengers, giving a gross weight to each of 10 tons. The experiments were tried with various weights and speeds up to 100 tons and to 62 miles per hour, and the results were classified and arranged in a tabular form with copious explanatory headings so as to render reference to them exceedingly easy. After the discussion at the Institution the Broad Gauge made some more experiments, letting the trains travel by gravity down the Wooton Bassett and White Ball Tunnel inclines with varying loads, the engines hauling the trains to the summits and then shutting off steam. The following engines were employed, 'Milo,' 'Firebrand,' 'Saturn,' 'Load Star,' 'Bellona,' 'Ariel,' 'Orion,' and 'Mars.' A writer who chronicles these experiments thus concludes :—'We perfectly well recollect that Mr Brunel was laughed at when he stated, some years ago, that he could get 60 miles per hour out of a locomotive. We now get 75 miles per hour with heavy trains. His opinion that he could obtain a uniform velocity of from 50 to 55 miles per hour by gravity down 1 in 100 was treated with scarce less courtesy. These practically demonstrated and demonstrative affirmatives of things declared to be "impossible" should teach some of our extremely clever paper calculators and ingenious theorisers the insecurity — for their own fame—of laying down "general" rules upon incomplete or one-sided data. They are too positive and too clever—genius is modest, and usually doubts in these matters.'

The Narrow Gauge engineers had made such an outcry as to the unsafeness of the Mixed Gauge, especially at the junctions, that to allay the fear that might naturally arise in the minds of timid travellers, a very ingenious means to obviate the use of points was employed on the Cheltenham and Gloucester line, which was the first line opened on the Mixed Gauge. This mixed line had been laid down some time, but was not used as a Broad Gauge line till 23d October 1847. The first through train covered the 121 miles, Paddington to Cheltenham, in 2 hours 45 minutes, including several stoppages. A Narrow Gauge engineer thus describes a journey on this the first Mixed Gauge line, and the method of working same :—' From Gloucester, southward to Standish, a distance of about 7 miles, there is a Broad Gauge railway used in common by the Great Western Railway Company for the traffic between Gloucester and Cheltenham, *viâ* Swindon to London, and by the Bristol and Birmingham section of the Midland Company's lines for their traffic from Gloucester to Bristol, the Bristol and Swindon lines (both on the Broad Gauge) diverging at Standish.

From Gloucester northwards the Narrow Gauge of the Midland Company proceeds to Birmingham, and between Gloucester and Cheltenham, in addition to the Narrow Gauge rails, the Great Western have laid a third rail on each track, to allow of Broad Gauge trains running to Cheltenham, where they have a separate station from the Midland Company. Be-

M

tween Gloucester and Cheltenham there is thus the first example of a Mixed Gauge railway.   On arriving at about three-quarters of a mile from the Gloucester Station, by an express train from London, I found that our train was turned by a switch (meeting the train) across the up line of the Bristol and Gloucester Railway.   When we had gone about 200 yards further we crossed a turn-table on the main line, and pulled up.   As we crossed this turn-table I perceived with some dismay an engine and two carriages approaching us at a distance of about 50 yards upon a line of railway which crossed the turn-table, which we had just crossed over, at right angles to the line on which we were running.   This engine and train having stopped (fortunately in time, or of course it would have cut our train in two), several passengers got out of their carriages and made for our train, one or two with luggage in their hands.   Two carriages of our train were then detached by means of the turn-table, and were taken back by the engine on the ' spur ' line, as it may be termed, to Gloucester, while we proceeded to Cheltenham.   All passengers from Gloucester to Cheltenham, a distance of 7 miles, by any of the through Broad Gauge trains have thus to change on an exposed platform a mile from Gloucester.

' This mode of working the Gloucester traffic as a branch traffic, with a separate engine and train for the branch, such branch being less than a mile long, and cutting the main line at right angles, is the result of the lines of two different gauges.   Having parted with our Gloucester carriages, and picked up the Gloucester branch traffic as described, we proceeded to the point where the Broad and Narrow Gauges become mingled, which is at a place called Barnwood. In order to get on to the down track of the Bristol and Birmingham Narrow Gauge line, we here crossed the up line of that railway again.   We were now on the Mixed Gauge.   On getting on to it, we got a sharp shake, and the road itself between this and the point where the Broad Gauge rails turn off to the Cheltenham Station was somewhat rough, but not particularly so. The road is adapted to the Broad Gauge by the laying of an additional rail on each track fastened to the sleepers, which are new and longer than the ordinary sleepers for a Narrow Gauge track. These additional rails are put on the outside of the Narrow Gauge outside rails, so that the common rail is the *inside* rail of each line, and not the outside rail as suggested by Mr Brunel in his report on the Oxford and Rugby line. On approaching Cheltenham we were "slowed" and turned off to the Broad Gauge Cheltenham station, which is distinct from the Narrow Gauge station, crossing here again, and for the third time in a distance of 7 miles, the up line of the Bristol and Birmingham Railway.

'The turn off is effected not by means of a switch in the usual form, but by cutting a notch in the common rail, and so making a fixed point (meeting all the trains of both gauges), and then by raising the level of the Broad Gauge outer rail 5 inches above the level of such fixed point, while the level of the Narrow Gauge outer rail is kept 3 inches below such fixed point. The Broad Gauge carriages are thus canted over so as to run on one side of the fixed point, while the Narrow Gauge carriages are canted over in the opposite direction so as to take the other side of the fixed point.'

This it will be seen is merely substituting a 'fixed point meeting the trains for a half switch.' He ends up by stating, 'The necessary result of these fearful complexities is, that the speed has to be reduced to a walking pace three times in a distance of 7 miles, and that the last mile into Gloucester has to be performed at little above a walking pace. A complexity of signals is also requisite, altogether exceeding belief, which complexity is increased by two systems of signalling obtaining on the two gauges. Strange as it may seem, I actually stood in one spot near Gloucester and counted ten different signal posts of several forms. The general conclusion to which I came, from my visit, was that the mixture of gauges resulted in a form of railway so unsafe, so intricate and broken up, and so extravagant in point of expense, as to render it altogether inadmissible as a practical arrangement, and ruinous to that simplicity on which the utility and safety of railways depend.'   His conclusions thus show that he had the usual Narrow Gauge prejudices against the Mixed Gauge.   But despite these impractical croakers the Mixed Gauge continued to increase, and after the Oxford and Birmingham and Wolverhampton Mixed Gauge line was opened, the third rail was gradually laid down over the Great Western line from Oxford to London.

It was on 1st October 1852 that the first Broad Gauge train was run from Paddington to Birmingham ; and looking back by the light of subsequent events, the fact that this train, which was drawn by the famous ' Lord of the Isles,' came into collision at Aynho with a preceding slow train from Oxford, this accident might almost be taken as an omen of the ill fate awaiting this section of the Broad Gauge system, for it was on 1st October 1861, exactly nine years later, that Paddington Station first suffered the ignominy of a Narrow Gauge train being despatched from that stronghold of the wide gauge ; but the enemy once having obtained an entrance there, held on tenaciously, and certainly came to stay. Before thirty-one years had expired all traces of Brunel's grand gauge had disappeared from the Great Western Railway headquarters.   On that eventful morning how well we can picture the sad look on the faces of the station officials as they made preparations to send away the first Narrow Gauge passenger train.   How humiliated Nicolas Graiff must have felt as he opened the regulator of the cramped locomotive he had been deputed to drive, while the late start must have filled his mind with grief, and caused him to think ' that with the Narrow Gauge they could not even get the trains away

to time,' nor could the station staff help admitting
that the inauguration of the Narrow Gauge service
had not been a success, and if any were given to pre-
judging events by the result of the first attempt, their
conclusions as to the Narrow Gauge must have been
of a dismal kind. The following official timing of the
train is of interest:—

The first Narrow Gauge train which left Paddington
on 1st October 1861.

BOOKED TIME.

STATIONS.	Arr. A.M.	Dep. A.M.	REMARKS.
Paddington,		9.35	
Reading, .	10.27	10.30	
Oxford, .	11.10	11.15	
Leamington,	12.20	12.23	Collect tickets.
Birmingham,	12.55		Time allowed, 3 hrs. 20 min.

ACTUAL TIME.

Paddington,		9.37	2 min. late,	13 on.	
Reading, .	10.29	10.34	2 ,,		
Oxford, .	11.15	11.20	5 ,,	4 off.	
Leamington,	12.17	12.29	3 ,,	1 off hot box.	
Birmingham,	12.58		3 ,,	8 on.	

Engine No. 75.—Paddington to Oxford.
Engineman.—Nicolas Graiff.
Engine No. 76.—Oxford to Birmingham.
Engineman.—Ralph Eliott.

Weather fine, but hazy on approaching Birmingham.

SUMMARY OF TIME AND TRAINS.

From	To	Running Time. Min.	Stops. Min.	Miles.
Paddington	Reading	52	3	36
Reading	Oxford •	40	5	27½
Oxford	Leamington	65	3	42⅞
Leamington	Birmingham	32		23¼
		189 11 stops		
	Total,	200 mins. = 3 hrs. 20 min.		

The Mixed Gauge was early in the conflict laid down from Oxford to Basingstoke, so as to form a Narrow Gauge connection between the London and South Western Railway and the North. The laying of the third rail for this 42 miles cost the Great Western Railway over £138,000, which was solely for the accommodation of other railways. In 1857, £13,341 was expended at Reading to provide for through accommodation of Narrow Gauge traffic from the north to the South Eastern Railway. From this time the Mixed Gauge was gradually laid down over various parts of the Great Western system. Exeter being the place farthest west reached by the continuous Mixed Gauge, which was in 1874, it being here where for many years goods traffic from Narrow Gauge stations to places on the South Devon and Cornwall lines was transhipped, until the final conversion in May 1892 rendered it unnecessary. At one time there was 272 miles of Mixed Gauge railways in operation.

CHAPTER XIV.

BROAD GAUGE LOCOMOTIVES.

THE various Narrow Gauge companies having constructed new engines much larger in size, and extremely powerful in every way, the Great Western Railway took measures to improve their locomotives early in 1846, and Mr Gooch was instructed to build a colossal engine without delay, and to have it in work before the Parliamentary Session commenced. The result was, by working day and night for thirteen weeks, the 'Great Western' was produced, and was first tried in April 1846. As originally constructed she was a six-wheel engine, but it was soon found that there was too much weight on the leading wheels, so Mr Gooch added another pair of small wheels before the 'drivers,' and so was inaugurated that world famous type of Broad Gauge express engines. Every writer on locomotives—including the most red hot partisan of the cramped 4 feet 8½ inch gauge—has nothing but unqualified praise for these splendid examples of engineering skill, which have done more than anything else to place England at the head of locomotive constructors, and which position has been held for so many years by this country, but which, alas! with the extinction of the Broad Gauge, appears to be passing away from us. One writer, in describing these unequalled engines, only a few years ago, says, —'No engines in the world have so long and as famous a history as these old engines of Sir Daniel

Gooch. They look to-day, with their great 8 feet driving wheels, and their old-world brass dome and brass wheels covers, just as they must have looked forty years ago, when our fathers gaped open mouthed at the tale of their achievements, and indeed their achievements were, in sober earnest, remarkable enough.'

Mr Bowen Cooke in *British Locomotives* thus speaks of these engines, ' And magnificent engines they were ; but unfortunately there is no longer any track on which they can display their powers. There must be but few railway men who can help regretting that such a step has had to be taken.'

Even Mr C. Stretton, who has most extreme views on the gauge question, and appears to consider that the Narrow Gauge is without question the best possible one in every respect that could have been chosen, acknowledges that ' This splendid locomotive (" The Great Western ") was highly successful, and was found capable of evaporating 300 cubic feet of water per hour, and it is a noteworthy fact that engines of this class appear to be among the most economical ever run, the consumption of coal being as low as $2\frac{1}{4}$ lbs. per horse power per hour.'

The fame of the ' Great Western ' engine was soon being talked about everywhere ; but at first the Narrow Gauge engineers would not believe the remarkable tales told of its power, nor the more wonderful records of the speed attained by it which appeared in the newspapers ; but personal observation soon proved the entire truth of these statements to the most sceptical opponents of the Broad Gauge. One of its first remarkable trips was from Paddington to Swindon and back with a train of fourteen carriages, weighing 140 tons, the entire journey performed at an average travelling speed of 57 miles an hour. On another occasion she took the 9.45 A.M. express from Paddington to Exeter, $193\frac{3}{4}$ miles, in 3 hours 28 minutes (travelling time), or at the rate of 53 miles an hour for the whole journey. On

Saturday, 13th June 1846, a sensational trip was made, which Mr Russell justly called a 'great fact,' and there is no doubt better results would have been attained had not one of the pumps supplying the boiler broken down at Slough (this was before the days of injectors.) This accident necessitated reducing the speed, as the remaining pump could not supply water to the boiler as quickly as it could have been evaporated had the engine been driven at full speed. 'The train (the "Great Western") weighed 100 tons, and consisted of ten first-class carriages, seven of which were ballasted with iron, the other three being occupied by the Directors and those interested in the experiment. The train started from Paddington at 11 hours 47 minutes 52 seconds; at Didcot a stop of 5¼ minutes was made; Swindon was reached in 78 minutes. After staying there 4 minutes 27 seconds the journey was continued to Bristol, the whole distance of 118½ miles being covered in 2 hours 12 minutes, or at the rate of 54 miles an hour, or, excluding the 9¾ minutes spent in the two stoppages, at about 59 miles an hour for the complete journey, including the slowing down and getting up speed again on three occasions. The maximum speed was obtained between the eighty-third and ninety-second mile posts (from the eightieth to the eighty-fifth mile there is a falling gradient of 8 feet per mile, and from the eighty-fifth and a half to about the eighty-sixth and a half mile there is a falling gradient of about 1 in 100, and a fall of 8 feet per mile then reaches to about the ninetieth and a half mile post; a rising gradient of 8 feet per mile then succeeds and extends beyond the ninety-second mile post) performing the 10 miles in 9 minutes and 8 seconds, or at an average speed of nearly 66 miles an hour. The eighty-seventh and eighty-eighth miles, on a falling gradient of 8 feet per mile, were run over at a rate of 69 miles per hour.'

After a luncheon the party returned again to London by the special train, Mr Brunel driving the engine on both occasions. A speed of 78 miles an hour has been attained by this engine on many trips. The splendid engines of this class continued to work the famous Broad Gauge express trains until that gauge was no more.

One of the most famous of these locomotives was the ' Lord of the Isles,' which was exhibited at the first International Exhibition in Hyde Park in 1851, at Edinburgh in 1890, and again at the Chicago Exhibition in 1893. This engine was the usual one given as a type of locomotives described in works on the steam engine for many years. The following are the principal dimensions of the 'Great Western' as first built :—'Cylinders, 18 inches diameter and 2 feet stroke ; driving wheels, 8 feet diameter ; supporting wheels, 4 feet 6 inches diameter ; 278 tubes, 9 feet long 2 inches diameter ; fire box, outside, 5 feet 6 inches by 6 feet—inside, 4 feet 10 inches by 5 feet 4 inches, with partition through the middle, giving 160 feet of heating surface and 20 feet of fire grate area ; total heating surface, 1751 square feet ; height from level of rail to top of boiler, 9 feet 6 inches, and from level of rail to top of chimney, 14 feet 8 inches ; length of engine, 24 feet ; weight of engine, 30 tons ; tender, 15 tons. Later the tubes were increased to 300, making the total heating surface 1767 square feet, and, as already explained, an extra pair of supporting wheels were added between the driving and leading wheels. The average coal consumption of these engines was extremely low, only about 27 lbs. per mile.

The following is a list of the thirty engines of the ' Great Western ' class, giving also the distance run by each before being rebuilt :—

BROAD GAUGE ENGINES—GREAT WESTERN CLASS.*

Name of Engine.	Builder.	Built.		Rebuilt or Condemned.		Total Mileage before Renewal.
Great Western, .	G.W.R.	April	1846	Dec.	1870	370,687
Iron Duke, . .	,,	April	1847	Oct.	1871	607,412
Lightning, . .	,,	April	1847	April	1878	816,601
Great Britain, .	,,	July	1847	Oct.	1880	403,644
Emperor, . .	,,	Sept:	1847	June	1873	690,225
Pasha, . . .	,,	Nov.	1847	June	1876	613,038
Sultan, . . .	,,	Nov.	1847	Aug.	1876	727,300
Courier, . .	,,	June	1848	Nov.	1877	746,120
Tartar, . . .	,,	July	1848	Aug.	1876	731,817
Dragon, . .	,,	Aug.	1848	Dec.	1872	670,757
Warlock, . .	,,	Aug.	1848	June	1874	639,410
Wizard, . .	,,	Sept.	1848	Nov.	1875	711,908
Rougemont, .	,,	Oct.	1848	Aug.	1879	772,401
Hirondelle, . .	,,	Dec.	1848	May	1873	605,010
Tornado, . .	,,	Mar.	1849	Mar.	1881	688,000
Swallow, . .	,,	June	1849	Aug.	1871	569,232
Timour, . .	,,	Aug.	1849	Nov.	1871	569,893
Prometheus, . .	,,	Mar.	1850	June	1870	538,025
Perseus, . .	,,	June	1850	Dec.	1880	722,458
Estafette, . .	,,	Sept.	1850	June	1870	504,544
Rover, . . .	,,	Sept.	1850	June	1871	461,344
Amazon, . .	,,	Mar.	1851	July	1877	729,840
Lord of the Isles (Built 1850, commenced work 1852),	,,	July	1852	July	1881	789,300
Alma, . . .	Rothwell	Nov.	1854	June	1872	444,600
Balaclava, . .	,,	Dec.	1854	Nov.	1871	406,425
Inkerman, . .	,,	Mar.	1855	Oct.	1877	650,220
Kertch, . .	,,	April	1855	Dec.	1872	326,246
Crimea, . .	,,	May	1855	Sept.	1878	605,701
Eupatoria, . .	:,	May	1855	Oct.	1878	618,275
Sebastopol, . .	,,	July	1855	Oct.	1880	707,148

When the Great Western Railway first started it had, with other improvements, introduced brake vans

* *The Locomotive Engine and its Development.*

for the guards to travel by, instead of these officials being perched at the top of the carriages, to get half frozen by the cold of winter, wet through in the rainy weather, or baked by summer heat, and at all times to run the risk of being blinded by the sparks and pieces of coke emitted by the engine. But in October 1847, in consequence of the great speed of the Broad Gauge express trains, the Directors considered an additional precaution necessary for the protection of the passengers, so an iron box was provided at the end of the tender for a 'travelling carriage porter,' whose duty was to see that the train was attached to the engine, and to report to the driver any signal made by the guards or passengers in the train. The following circular, which was issued by the superintendent of the Great Western Railway, sets forth in full the duties of this new train attendant.

'On and after the 4th day of October 1847, a man, to be called the "travelling carriage porter," will accompany every express train in each direction. The business of this man will be to ride on the seat placed for him on the tenders, and to keep a steady and vigilant look out on both sides and along the top of the trains, so that in case of any accident to any of the carriages of the train, or of any signal from the guard, or any apparently sufficient cause that may come to his observation, he may at once communicate with the engine man, and, if necessary, stop the train. Further, it will be his business, generally, to have charge of the carriages forming the train, to see that in every respect they are in good condition and properly coupled up, the axles greased and the lamps (at night) burning properly, and he will alight immediately the train stops, and go to the axle boxes of the carriages and grease and examine them, and see that they are all in proper order for travelling. And in case at any one station he may have noticed any one or more boxes getting hot, he must turn his first attention to these.

He will in a like manner examine the couplings and the lamps, and call the attention of the lamp-man at the station to any deficiencies. He will report to the principal guard every circumstance connected with the train which may require notice. He will be required to observe carefully the running of the different carriages, and to take note of the number of any one that may appear to run unsteady, or have any other defect, and to enter a note of this and of any other circumstance, such as hot axles, etc., requiring to be remedied, in a report book to be made up for each journey. The travelling carriage porter will be furnished with a pilot coat, etc., in addition to his present suit, with grease box, grease knife, picker, lamps, etc. Their pay will be 25s. per week, and the men will be selected from the body of porters, and the appointment will be considered a reward for good and steady conduct, general intelligence and acquaintance with the management of the carriages.

' SEYMOUR CLARKE, *Superintendent.*

'PADDINGTON, 26*th September* 1847.'

So bigoted were the Narrow Gauge enthusiasts that they claimed this new departure of the Great Western Railway as a further proof of the superiority of the Narrow Gauge, having the audacity to state that the Broad Gauge had to go back to the original Narrow Gauge method of having a man outside the train to see that all was right, and yet they would not own that the person in the sentry box, ' or iron coffin ' as they called it, on the tender, was better protected than the guard perched on the top of the carriage on the Narrow Gauge trains. Here are the views of one of the enlightened Narrow Gauge officials as expressed by him at the time the Great Western introduced these travelling porters :—' The placing a guard outside the train has always been the practice on the Narrow Gauge railways, and the not doing so, but, on the contrary, placing both the guards inside the carriages, where they might duly go to sleep among their parcels, was one of the peculiarities of the Broad Gauge on which they particularly piqued themselves. It now seems that the Broad Gauge authorities have relinquished their peculiar arrangement and adopted the much more sensible practice of the Narrow Gauge companies. They are quite right in doing this, although one does not exactly see that the discontinuance of an absurd practice requires to be puffed in the *Times.* The position of the guard on the tender (as the Great Western authorities propose to place him) instead of on the last carriage (as he is generally placed on Narrow Gauge trains) appears to me to be no improvement, for, in the first place, the fireman, who is already on the tender, if he obeyed his printed instructions, should keep an eye on the train. The arrangement, therefore, now at length, in deference to common sense, adopted on the Great Western is still, as it seems, a very imperfect application of the practice which has always been pursued on the Narrow Gauge system of railways.'

Later on, when an efficient system of communication between the guards and the men on the engine had been established, the 'travelling porters' were withdrawn.

Besides the engines of the 'Great Western' class, the Great Western Railway had built other powerful engines at Swindon, twenty-four being turned out beween April 1846 and September 1847. Among these were the 'Queen,' a six-wheel passenger locomotive with single driving wheels, 7 feet diameter; cylinder, 16 inches diameter; 24 inch stroke; boiler and fire-box, 14 feet long; weight of engine, 25 tons; tender, 9 tons. The 'Premier,' a goods engine with six coupled wheels of 5 feet diameter, the other dimensions being similar to those of the 'Great Western'; when tried, this engine drew a train weighing 483 tons at about 30 miles an hour. Another passenger engine, designed by Mr Brunel and built by Mr Gooch, was the 'Elk,' a six-wheel engine with 7 feet single

drivers; cylinder, 16 inches; stroke, 18 inches; boiler
and fire-box, 14 feet long; weight of engine, 25 tons;
tender (empty), 9 tons. This engine drew trains of
six carriages from Swindon to Paddington, 77½ miles,
in 80 minutes.

We think we have now given a sufficient account
of the Broad Gauge engines of this period; but while
on the subject it will be as well to mention the
equally famous Broad Gauge engines constructed by
the Bristol and Exeter Railway in 1853.

It will be remembered that the Great Western
Railway worked the Bristol and Exeter under a lease
at a rental of £71,957 a year, and a toll of a ¼d. a

BRISTOL AND EXETER TANK ENGINE.
9 ft. driving wheels, leading and trailing bogies; wheels, 4 ft. diameter.

mile on every passenger carried, and also the same
amount per mile for every ton of goods conveyed
over the line. This lease expired on 30th April 1849,
so that from that date the Bristol and Exeter Company had their own locomotives and rolling stock.
These at first were built by private firms, but afterwards
the company had works of its own at Bridgewater.
Mr Pearson was the engineer of the Bristol and
Exeter Railway, and his patriotism for the Broad
Gauge brought forth the renowned 9 feet single tank
engines, which were built from his design by Rothwell
and Company, Union Foundry, Bolton. These engines

soon gained fame among railway engineers for their low coke consumption (only $21\frac{3}{4}$ lbs. per mile), and were still more famous to the public at large by the high speed they attained ; in fact, one of these engines was credited with the highest authenticated speed until very recently, and now it is only the Americans who claim to have exceeded it ; and since the Yankee claim to 'lick creation' in so many things we cannot be surprised that they have at last taken credit to themselves for the fastest locomotive run on record. Returning to the speed attained by Mr Pearson's Broad Gauge tank engine, we find that 81 miles an hour was the highest rate of travelling officially credited for one of these splendid locomotives. This was forty-one years ago, and it has taken our go-a-head cousins across the 'herring pond,' nearly this number of years before they claim to have beaten this speed record of the old time Bristol and Exeter Tank. These engines had ten wheels, and the principal dimensions were—a leading and trailing bogie, each with four wheels of 4 feet diameter, and a pair of 9 feet driving wheels without flanges ; the boiler was 4 feet $\frac{1}{2}$ inch diameter, 10 feet 9 inches long, and contained 180 tubes of $1\frac{15}{16}$ inch diameter ; the cylinders were $16\frac{1}{2}$ inches diameter by 24 inch stroke ; weight of engine, 42 tons. When the Bristol and Exeter and Great Western Railways were amalgamated in 1876, these 9 feet tanks were rebuilt, the diameter of the driving wheels was reduced to 8 feet, the trailing bogie was removed, and a pair of wheels substituted, and lastly a tender was added—a complete metamorphosis of a locomotive from a tank to a tender engine—a practice not usually followed, but which the Great Western Railway again did a few years back, when the 'Cornishman' was inaugurated, which train, not stopping between Exeter and Plymouth, and the line beyond Newton being very severe for passenger tender engines, three of the tank engines used on this section had tenders added to

A LOCOMOTIVE METAMORPHOSIS. (*From a Photograph by F. Moore, London.*)

A Bristol and Exeter, 9-ft. tank, rebuilt, driving wheels reduced to 8-ft. diameter, and tender added.

enable sufficient water to be carried, so that the whole 53 miles could be run without a stop.

These engines were built at Swindon in 1885, and had a pair of leading wheels 3 feet 6 inches in diameter, 4 coupled wheels 5 feet diameter, cylinders 18 inches by 26 inches, their wheel base being, leading to driving, 9 feet 3 inches, driving to trailing, 7 feet 9 inches. Ten of them were built, and Nos. 3502, 3505 and 3508 were, in 1890, converted into tender engines, for the purpose above mentioned. The tenders were of the type used with the 2080 class of goods engines.

Another innovation in railway locomotion introduced by the Bristol and Exeter Railway was that of combined engine and carriage for branch line traffic. This combination was constructed by Mr Adams, of Fairfield Works, Bow, E., and was called the 'Fairfield,' and was first used on the Tiverton branch on 25th December 1848; its length was 39 feet, and the boiler was placed in a vertical position. The driving wheels were 4 feet 6 inches diameter, and made of solid wrought iron; and trailing wheels 3 feet 6 inches, of wood, and running independently on their axles as well as their journals, the middle wheel having a lateral transverse of 6 inches. The boiler was tubular and vertical, 3 feet in diameter and 6 feet high; the firebox 2 feet high and 2 feet 6 inches in diameter. The cylinder was 8 inches diameter, with 12 inch stroke; the connecting rods worked a separate crank shaft, which communicated with the driving wheels by side rods, the axle of the driving wheels being straight, with crank pins on the outside. The boiler was placed behind the driving axle; the tank, capable of holding 220 gallons of water, being in front of it, and the coke box was attached to the front part of the carriage behind the driver.

'The bottom of the framing is within 9 inches of the rails, so that, by keeping the centre of gravity low, greater safety may be insured at high speed, and freedom from oscillation obtained. The first-class carriage is in the form of a saloon, and accommodates sixteen passengers, while the second-class compartment is seated for thirty-two.   The entire weight of the machine was about 10 tons, when occupied with forty-eight passengers it will amount to about 12½ tons.   On the experimental trip, on the 8th December 1848, the 'Fairfield' left Paddington Station at 10.30. A.M. for Swindon, 77 miles down the line, with a party of gentlemen connected with various railways.   Mr Gooch officiated as driver on both the up and down journeys.   Though the rails were greasy from the prevailing rain, in addition to a head wind, and, what was worse, a leak in the boiler, the machine soon attained considerable speed, and for a portion of the way reached the rate of 49 miles an hour.   On arriving at Swindon the fire was extinguished, the leak partially repaired, and after a reasonable sojourn the party returned to town.   The run back was exceedingly satisfactory, the speed of 49 miles being maintained for a considerable part of the way.   The passage from Slough to Paddington being performed in 30 minutes.'

Mr Gooch also designed and built at Swindon a very powerful class of saddle tank engines—probably the first saddle tank locomotives constructed.   The engines of this class, and of which the 'Corsair' was the prototype, and which were further developed in the 'Pluto' class, were used for hauling the trains over the severe gradients on the South Devon Railway until the conversion of the line to the Narrow Gauge.   The principal features were a leading bogie; wheels, 3 feet 6 inches diameter, and four coupled wheels, 6 feet diameter; inside cylinders, 17 inch by 24 inch stroke; boiler, 10 feet 6 inches long, with saddle tank on top; fire-box, 4 feet 11 inches in length; total length, 25 feet 10¾ inches, or over buffers, 27 feet 7 inches; extreme height, top of chimney to rail, 14 feet 10 inches; weight, 35¾ tons. The brake fitted to the early engines of this class was a curious contrivance, consisting of sledges of iron suspended over the rails between the driving and trailing wheels; it was applied by means of a screw which forced the iron blocks upon the surface of the rails, and this transferred the weight of the engine from the wheels to the sledge brake—the brakes used on the cable cars on Highgate Hill were on much the same principle. Another great innovation in locomo-

'THE HUNCHBACKS.' A South Devon Saddle Tank, designed by Mr D. Gooch.

tives introduced by Mr Gooch on the Broad Gauge was the coupling of two pairs of wheels, each 7 feet in diameter. This was in 1855, and such large coupled wheels were then unheard of, so that there is no doubt that at that time the Broad Gauge was still far ahead of its competitors in the matter of locomotive development. Ten of the engines were constructed by Robert Stephenson for the Great Western Railway, the general characteristics of which (excepting the coupled wheels) were similar to the renowned 'Great Western.'

While on the subject of Broad Gauge engines mention must be made of the celebrated tank locomotives used to work the heavy mineral traffic over the steep gradients on the Vale of Neath Railway, one bank of 1 in 50 being 4½ miles long—a loaded Broad Gauge truck weighed 15 tons—and to convey trains of these a class of six coupled tank engines was constructed with wheels 4 feet 9 inches diameter; cylinders, 17 inches diameter; stroke, 24 inches; gross weight, 40 tons. Upon one occasion one of these engines hauled a train of twenty-five loaded trucks, weighing 375 tons, or including the engine, a total weight of 415 tons upon a bank of 1 in 90 for a distance of 4½ miles. This remarkable and unsurpassed performance is equal to conveying a gross weight of 1245 tons on a level line; and at the present time, under the most favourable conditions attainable in summer, the London and North Western Railway consider a train of less than 700 tons travelling over the good gradients of its main line at an average speed of 15 miles an hour a noteworthy performance. Yet, in effect, the Broad Gauge engines exceeded this accomplishment more than forty years ago. But we have already written in praise of Broad Gauge engines *satis superque.*

The last Broad Gauge engines constructed were eight of the 'Ironclad' class, built at the end of 1891 and beginning of 1892. These were really Narrow Gauge engines, with the wheels placed outside the frames, to adapt them temporarily to the Broad Gauge.

CHAPTER XV.

THE Broad Gauge having extended its trunk line as far as Exeter, no time was lost by the promoters and adherents of the wide gauge in still further extending its lines to the westward, so, early in 1844, the South Devon Railway, from Exeter to Plymouth, was projected. The public being already familiar with the many advantages and increased speed of the Broad Gauge railways; two further novelties were introduced into the South Devon Railway, viz., the daring construction of a railway along the seashore from Starcross to Teignmouth, and the use of the atmospheric system in place of locomotives as a propelling power. The Bill was read a first time on 29th February 1844, but the Admiralty stopped the second reading of it on the 4th March, as it was alleged that the line along the front at Dawlish was dangerous to the local fishermen. Mr Walker, the engineer, was sent to Devonshire by the Admiralty to report on this line and an opposition line which took a more inland direction.

We extract from his report the following paragraphs :—' Notwithstanding that the coast line between Exeter and where it leaves the Teign is 3 miles longer than that portion of the inland line which would compare with it, I consider that its being nearly level for the whole length, and the much greater population upon it, whose convenience is to be considered, gives it a preference over the inland line, which, on leaving Exeter, has first a long rapid ascent of 1 in 75 for 3¾ miles, then a tunnel ¾ of a mile long, then a series of descents.'

'*First.* Keeping the general line of railway closer to the cliffs, cutting off the projections to enable this to be done, so that the necessary width may be obtained chiefly out of the cliff. *Second.* Forming at proper distances sloping ways of approach of sufficient length, from the beach to the level of the railway, wherever the coast is encroached upon. These would act as groynes or jetties, to stop and collect on either side of them the gravel or sand as it is driven along the shore by the heavy seas, so that the beach would probably be kept as high as the retaining wall. *Third.* As a parapet wall must be raised above the level of the railway to protect it and the trains from the winds, and occasionally the waves, I think that this parapet wall should, for the whole length upon the river and coast —say from Powderham to Teignmouth—be nowhere less than 6 or 8 feet inside the retaining or embankment wall, leaving the space between the embankment and the parapet as a public way for the convenience of fishermen and mariners, and as a public walk or communication. This might probably be considered by the inhabitants of the town an equivalent for the facilities which the railway may in other respects deprive them of, so as to leave the balance in their favour.'

The total length of the proposed line was 51 miles 72 chains, exclusive of a branch to Mill Bay, Plymouth (67 chains long), which had a fall of 1 in 24, and was not proposed to be worked by locomotives. In it was a stiff rise of 1 in 42 for 2¼ miles up the Dainton Bank beyond Newton Abbot. There would be four tunnels through the hard, red conglomerate, and the town of Teignmouth would be cut in two, there being no less than fourteen road bridges there. Twelve miles of the course was along the border of Dartmoor. It crossed the Yealm Valley on two wooden viaducts, each 240 yards long, one of which was on a curve of 25 chains radius, and on an incline of 1 in 236. The estimated cost of constructing the line was £1,000,000. Such were the facts as given in evidence. This Bill sought powers to buy up the Plymouth and Dartmoor Railway, and to alter the gauge of same, it being a Narrow Gauge line used to bring granite from the quarries on Dartmoor to Sutton Harbour at Plymouth.

The railway was duly incorporated, the Act receiving the royal assent 4th July 1844, with a capital of £1,000,000, of which the Great Western Railway subscribed £150,000, the Bristol and Exeter £200,000, and the Midland (or more properly the Birmingham and Gloucester) £50,000. There were ten directors, of which the Great Western sent four, Bristol and Exeter Railway five, and the Midland two.

The work of constructing the line was commenced immediately after the Act was obtained, the line commencing with a viaduct through Exeter. Beyond this the line has a very level stretch until it approaches the river bank at Powderham Castle. The construction of the line at this point was brought to a complete standstill for four months by a curious natural phenomenon. The stone to form this river wall was sent in ships, which were to be unloaded at the spots where the material was required. Usually at high tide there would be sufficient water to enable the boats to approach close to the river bank for the purpose of unloading, but, unfortunately, for four months, a strong contrary wind continued to blow, which prevented the tides rising to their normal height, and, therefore, the ships were unable to unload the stone, and were compelled to wait in mid-stream during the whole period; but at last the wind died away, and the boats could then approach the shore to unload the stone, and the work of building the embankment was commenced and everything possible done to make up for the extraordinary delay. The next portion of the line between Starcross and Langstone Cliff was also difficult to construct. The traveller over this part of the line will notice, at high tide, on either hand, the sea water, and at low tide, in place of water, a large expanse of mud.

The original idea was to construct an embankment across the Cockwood Swamp, and although the soil was excavated to a depth of 40 feet, no firm foundation could be found ; then the idea of George Stephenson, of laying down faggots, which he successfully carried out at Chat Moss, was tried, with no better success, until at last a wooden viaduct was constructed over the swamp, being finished in December 1845. From Langstone Cliff to Dawlish the line is constructed upon a raised terrace built on the seashore, with the red cliffs for a background. At Dawlish the railway is continued on an embankment, which entirely separates the town from the seashore, so that the houses on the front facing the sea have immediately in front of them a railway (instead of the usual marine promenade) and beyond this the sea. The work of construction beyond Dawlish was more difficult, consisting of several short tunnels cut through the cliff, these tunnels being connected by terraces cut out of the face of the cliff, the seashore being on the other hand. The principal one of these tunnels is the last, known as the Parson's Rock Tunnel, 366 yards long. From this point to Teignmouth a massive sea wall was constructed of stone, the railway being on the side immediately under the cliffs, a parapet wall separating the line from the other half of the sea wall, which was laid out for a public promenade. The construction of this part of the line was attended with many difficulties, as although extensive stone breakwaters were built, several times large portions of the massive embankment were washed away during the gales in the winter of 1845. To break the force of the waves as much as possible, the wall facing the sea was built with a concave front. Turning inland, we arrive at the Teignmouth Station. The original headquarters of the South Devon Railway Company, the primitive apology for a station, or 'Noah's Ark' as it is locally called, disgraced the Great Western Railway until very recently; but better things are in store, for eighteen months ago the foundation for a new station was commenced, and the modern structure will very shortly be completed. Beyond Teignmouth Station the line curves to the right and runs up the bank of the Teign to Newton Abbot.

Up to this point the line is practically level, the ruling gradient being 1 in 660, but beyond, the conformation of the country is very unsuitable for the purposes of constructing a railway with good gradients. This drawback did not at the time trouble Mr Brunel, the engineer to the South Devon Railway Company, since he proposed to work the line on the atmospheric principle, and one of the advantages claimed for the system being that steep banks were as easy to work as a level. Therefore the rise of 1 in 43 for a distance of nearly 4 miles, with the Dainton Tunnel at the summit, was constructed; the line then falls for 5 miles at 1 in 40, and then, after passing Totnes, for a further 5 miles, there is a rise of 1 in 48, terminating with the Marley Tunnel. The inhabitants of this part of the country, being unacquainted with railway works, took a great interest in the construction of this short tunnel, not half a mile in length, and on the last length of masonry being completed, on 23d December 1846, a procession was arranged, the contractor and engineer driving through the tunnel, and over twenty of the neighbouring gentry accompanying them on horseback. The tunnel was lighted by torchlight, and 'upon the cavalcade emerging from the west end of the tunnel, it was heartily cheered by the crowds assembled, while Lady Carew, a local landowner, was much pleased with the proceeding, and gave the workmen engaged a dinner in commemoration of the event.'

Even at this early period a railway was proposed to Kingsbridge, and a station erected at Wrangerton (now called Kingsbridge Road), selected for the convenient approach of the projected branch from Kingsbridge.   Never has so long a time elapsed in railway history before the realization of the project has been fulfilled, for the opening of the line is one of the latest events in the history of the Great Western Railway, only taking place in the autumn of 1893.   Up to that time very many of the natives had never seen a railway or locomotive engine, although it was in 1845 when the line was first projected.

We now come to the most remarkable portion of the South Devon Railway, Brunel's wonderful wooden trestle viaducts, of which there are four in the next few miles of line.   The construction of these considerably delayed the opening of this line; at first, when it was intended to work the line by the atmospheric system, fir was the wood used, but after Brunel's remarkable change of opinion, when he decided on using locomotives, these viaducts had to be rebuilt of American oak, and indeed afterwards iron girders were inserted within the woodwork, so that the frailty of these curious structures was more fanciful than real.   Their construction is thus described in Mr Brunel's interesting life of his father :—

' The piers are formed of plain walls built up to 35 feet below the level of the rails, those of the more lofty viaducts being strengthened by buttresses.   St Pinnock is the loftiest viaduct on the Cornwall Railway, the rails being at a height of 153 feet above the ground.   A description of the superstructure will serve to explain the design of the principal viaducts on the line.

The roadway planking rests on three beams, which run longitudinally throughout the whole length of the viaduct.   Each of these beams consists of two pieces of timber, one above the other, fastened together by bolts and joggles. The piers are 66 feet apart, centre to centre, and the longitudinal beams are supported at four nearly equi-distant points in this space by straight single timbers radiating from the tops of the piers. The feet of the timbers, which rest on the masonry in cast-iron shoes, are connected together by wrought-iron tie bars, and the framework is made rigid by iron diagonals. The diagonal braces which are attached to each set of the main timbers give transverse stability to the superstructure.'

Although most of these viaducts are found on the Cornwall Railway we may as well here describe them. When the South Devon and Cornwall Railways were completed there were some sixty of these wooden viaducts in Devon and Cornwall, forty-two of them being found in the 66 miles between Plymouth and Falmouth, nine of which occur in the 8 miles between Devonport and St Germans, and seven in the 12 miles from Truro to Falmouth. Two of these trestle bridges are each more than a 1000 feet long, and at Truro is a pair close together, the combined length of which is nearly half a mile. The following are the principal viaducts :—The 'Rattery,' between Totnes and Brent, consists of six spans of 50 feet each, at an elevation of 50 feet, while beyond Brent is another, 72 feet high ; The 'Erme' Viaduct, near Ivy Bridge, 110 feet in height ; the 'Moorewater,' near Liskeard, 147 feet high. This is the largest and highest, but it is now rebuilt in granite. While among the seven on the Falmouth branch are the 'Carnon,' 766 feet long, and nearly 100 feet high ; the 'Ponsanooth,' 140 feet high, and the 'Treberer' Viaducts. A temporary station was opened at Laira (Plymouth), and this was the terminus of the line for some time. The original station was to have been erected near the site of the present Devonport (Great Western) Station ; but upon the Cornwall Railway being incorporated, this portion of the line was sold to that company, and a new site for a joint terminus chosen at Mill Bay. The progress of this extension was for a time stopped by a dispute which arose between the South Devon Railway Company and the mortgagee in possession of the Dartmoor Railway, a line 24 miles long, constructed in 1820. This railway was crossed on the level at right angles by the South Devon line. The mortgagee, not getting the terms he asked from the South Devon Railway, brought immense blocks of granite from his Dartmoor quarries, and deposited them on his line, where the South Devon wished to cross. This effectually prevented the railway from proceeding with the line, and they soon arranged a compromise, which had the desired effect, the granite blocks being then removed by the mortgagee of the Dartmoor Railway. The South Devon Railway scheme proved, in a measure, disastrous to the reputations of two of the principal figures of the Broad Gauge party, for even the undoubted genius of Mr Brunel, which was clearly exemplified in so many stupenduous engineering feats, was not sufficient to cause the public to forget and forgive his unexampled change of front in connection with the atmospheric system.

We now proceed to deal with the subject that makes the South Devon Railway one of the most interesting lines, not only in the history of the Broad Gauge railways but in the history of the railway system of the world, viz., the atmospheric principle of propulsion.

The Act of Incorporation received the royal assent on 4th July 1844, and within six weeks after, the Directors reported to the shareholders :—'Since the passing of the Act a proposal has been received by your Directors from Messrs Samuda Brothers, the patentees of the atmospheric railway, to apply their system of traction to the South Devon line. After much deliberation the Board were induced to refer the question to their engineer, Mr Brunel, for his opinion thereon as well, in reference to the application of the principle as to the economy stated to be the consequence of its adoption. It was likewise deemed to be desirable that a deputation of the Directors should visit the atmospheric railway now in operation, from Kingstown to Dalkey, with a view to inform themselves and their colleagues of its peculiar mode of working, and of the actual expenses attendant thereupon. In pursuing these inquiries every facility was politely afforded by the Directors and engineer of that line. From the careful consideration given to the subject by Mr Brunel, as well as from the deliberate and very decided opinion in favour of the system which he has expressed to the Board, added to the favourable report of the deputation, and also keeping in view the fact that at many points of the line both gradients and curves will render the application of this principle peculiarly advantageous, your Directors, in the belief that it will be greatly to the interest of the company, have resolved that the atmospheric system, including the construction of an electric telegraph, should be adopted upon the whole line of the South Devon Railway. On reviewing the circumstances to which the Directors have already adverted, viz., the reduced cost of construction, and (if the atmospheric principle be adopted) the diminished expense of working, added to the probability of an increased traffic, they trust they shall not be deemed too sanguine in stating, as their firm conviction, that there are few railways yet in operation, or, in contemplation, that offer fairer prospects of success than the South Devon line.' There can be no doubt that both the Directors and Mr Brunel had from the first decided upon working the line by atmospheric propulsion. At the annual meeting of the South Devon Railway, held on 30th August 1845, the following report from Mr Samuda was read :—

    ' 1. That we obtained a vacuum of 27½ inches in 5 miles of pipe, working only one engine over the two sections to obtain it, not only once, but every time, with ease.

' 2. When the engine is stopped, and the vacuum allowed to be destroyed by leakage, it takes two hours to reduce the barometer to zero (though at Dalkey 15 minutes would be all the time it could be maintained above the zero point), the leakage being here less than half horse power per mile.

' 3. The facility of obtaining the vacuum is greater, having regard to the length, than anything we have hitherto done.

' 4. We have travelled over the 5 miles in 6 minutes 45 seconds when working one engine only, and in 6 minutes 14 seconds when working engines at both stations, as intended in practice, viz., at the middle and the end to propel the train.

' 5. To do the distance in the above time, which includes the time of obtaining our speed and coming to rest, the maximum speed was 70 miles an hour.

' 6. The practical result of our working was to beat the Brighton quick train ; having given it one minute's law, and then started from rest while the Brighton train passed the spot where we were standing at full speed, drawn by two locomotives, and continued with unabated speed, and was, in fact, going as fast as it could when we overhauled it 4 miles beyond where we started.

' 7. With a train of eight carriages and about 200 persons we stopped with the brakes on an incline rising 1 in 50, and started again nearly as free as on the level. On the whole the results are beyond what we led anyone to expect, and I trust it will not be long before I have an opportunity of showing them to the South Devon Directors.'

This report immediately caused the South Devon

shares to rise £5 in value, so great was the faith of the public in this system of propulsion.

After very many delays (the real reason for which, although not openly acknowledged, was Mr Brunel's desire to see how the atmospheric system answered on the Croydon Railway) the first section of the South Devon Railway from Exeter to Teignmouth was opened on 3d May 1846. The line was, however, worked by locomotive engines supplied by the Great Western Railway. Nor would this portion of the line have been opened at this date had not the inhabitants of the districts been so loud in their complaints as to the inconvenience caused by the delay in opening. On the opening day the first train left Exeter at 12.10 P.M., and returned from Teignmouth at 1.15 P.M. There were then but two intermediate stations, Starcross and Dawlish. The following was the original service of trains :—

ON WEEK DAYS.

UP TRAINS.

Leaving Teignmouth at	7.10 A.M.	arrive Exeter	7.55	A.M.
,,	,,	9.10 ,,	,,	9.55 ,,
,,	,,	11.10 ,,	,,	11.55 ,,
,,	,,	1.15 P.M.	,,	2.0 P.M.
,,	,,	4.25 ,,	,,	5.10 ,,
,,	,,	6.45 ,,	,,	7.30 ,,
,,	,,	8.45 ,,	,,	9.30 ,,

DOWN TRAINS.

Leaving Exeter at	8.10 A.M.	arrive Teignmouth	8.55	A.M.
,,	,,	12.10 P.M.	,,	12.55 P.M.
,,	,,	2.20 ,,	,,	3.5 ,,
,,	,,	3.25 ,,	,,	4.10 ,,
,,	,,	5.40 ,,	,,	6.25 ,,
,,	,,	7.40 ,,	,,	8.25 ,,
,,	,,	10.10 ,,	,,	10.55 ,

SUNDAY TRAINS.

UP TRAINS.

Leaving Teignmouth at	7.15 A.M.	arrive Exeter	8.0	A.M.
,,	,,	9.30 ,,	,,	10.18 ,,
,,	,,	8.30 P.M.	,,	9.25 P.M.

Down Trains.

Leaving Exeter at 8.20 A.M. arrive Teignmouth 9.15 A.M.
„ „ 5.40 P.M. „ 6.25 P.M.
„ „ 10.5 „ „ 10.50 „

Fares, from Exeter to Teignmouth,
First-class, 2s. 6d. ; second-class, 2s. ; third-class, 1s. 2d.
By order of the Directors.

W. Carr, *Secretary.*

Exeter, 18*th May* 1846.

'Note.—Horses, carriages and dogs will be conveyed by rail-way, and also fish ; but for the present no other description of goods.'

The fares were the cheapest of any then charged, being only 2d. for first-class, 1½d. for second-class, and 1d. for third-class per mile, and the traffic much exceeded the expectation of the Directors, amounting to from the first 12,000 passengers per week, and the receipts to £600 per week.

The Great Western Railway charged 1s. 4d. per mile for locomotive power, but with the atmospheric system the Directors told the shareholders the expense would not exceed 6d. per mile for haulage. The first experiment of the atmospheric system on the South Devon line was made on 26th February 1847, when a train of two carriages went from Exeter to Turf and back, upon which occasion Mr Brunel said everything gave him full satisfaction. During the half year to 31st December 1846 the receipts amounted to £15,620, and the expenditure to £10,124, of which £3269 had been paid the Great Western Railway for locomotive hire.

At a meeting in Plymouth in May 1847, the Chairman said that they had attained a speed of 70 miles an hour with a light train, and 33 miles an hour with a train weighing 100 tons (this was the weight of the train itself, as, of course, no locomotives were used). He also stated that it was 'the great desire of the Directors to extend to the public the benefit of the opening to Plymouth at as early a period as

possible, that they would use the locomotive temporarily from Totnes to this town.'

On 18th August a goods train of eleven trucks,
weighing 120 tons, travelled the 8¼ miles, Exeter to
Starcross, in 15 minutes. On 8th September 1847,
besides the usual service of trains hauled by locomotives, four extra ones commenced running, these being
propelled by the atmospheric system. This was the
first public use of the system on the South Devon
Railway. Shortly after, three of the regular trains
were also propelled by means of the atmospheric
apparatus. Although the line was opened as far
as Newton Abbot, between that station and Teignmouth locomotives were employed, but the piston
carriage on the down train went on to Newton,
where it was taken off with the superfluous carriages
and placed on a convenient line to be attached to the
up train when required, so that, on arriving at Teignmouth, where the locomotive was removed, the piston
carriage started the train when the signal was given ;
and on the down atmospheric train arriving at Teignmouth, the engine that had to run in front was instantly
attached to the piston carriage, and was ready for the
start at all times before the guard was ready or the
passengers seated.

A traveller thus relates his experience of the
system :—' The trains ran up to the respective stations,
and were stopped and started again with the utmost
ease and with as much regularity as we ever witnessed
in those propelled by steam power. In travelling
the passengers experience scarcely any oscillation.
We tested the steadiness of the piston carriage when
the train was at its greatest speed, by placing a half-
penny on a narrow ledge of the sliding sash, and for
a distance of 3 miles it never shook or moved from its
position.' On 9th November trains worked on the
atmospheric system commenced running to Newton
Abbot.

On 10th January 1848 all the trains except the

first and last each way commenced running by atmospheric power, and the trial fully answered all the expectations. Notwithstanding the disadvantages attending the commencement of every new undertaking, not a single instance of stoppage or delay occurred on the new piece of road from Teignmouth to Newton. On the first day the express train was unusually heavy, and it started from Newton 6 minutes after its proper time, but reached Exeter at the regular period, gaining 6 minutes on the 20 miles. On the 12th the down express train was 30 minutes late at Exeter, but on arriving at Newton 10 minutes had been recovered—so much therefore in praise of the system. On 29th February the general meeting of the company was held, and the Chairman then stated 'the atmospheric had proved so successful that the locomotive had been entirely withdrawn from the line between Newton and Exeter. Out of 884 trains which had then been run 790 had either gained time or performed the journey in the exact time. Of the remainder 70 lost from 1 to 5 minutes, 14 from 6 to 10 minutes, 3 from 11 to 15 minutes, 7 from 16 minutes and upwards.'

After all these eulogistic speeches and reports, the shareholders and the public were very greatly surprised to find in the report for the half year to 30th June 1848, that a loss of £2489 had occurred in working the line during the six months, and that the Directors recommended the suspension of the atmospheric system.

Mr Brunel presented an exhaustive report on the failure of the system (*see* Appendix). This remarkable change of front on behalf of Mr Brunel had a disastrous effect on his reputation, a dead set being made against him at the meeting, one shareholder stating,—'On the system which is now to be abandoned the company have already expended from £300,000 to £400,000. Mr Brunel had received warning upon warning from engineers as eminent as himself, but had recklessly entered upon this extravagant expenditure, not at his own expense, but that of others—at the expense of persons of small means, widows and others who had invested their all in such enterprises, and who could ill afford to pay the cost of his playing in this manner with their property. So the South Devon Line was left with bad gradients —a long bank of 1 in 40, which was laid down by Mr Brunel in the certainty that locomotive power would not be used ; and the tremendous inclines were left to be worked as best they could be by locomotive power, and the Great Western Railway route to the far west was for ever debarred from being worked at anything like the express speed that had made this line from London to Exeter world famous ; and so that after exactly a year's trial the experiment was abandoned, and locomotives only were employed to haul the trains, Mr Brunel, in his report to the Directors, advising the withdrawal of the atmospheric system, basing his decision principally on the fact that the leather of the longitudinal valve was perished, and required renewing, which would have cost some £1600 a mile, or £32,000 for the section then open. He attributed the deterioration of the leather to the chemical action set up by the wet iron on the tannin of the leather ; to the absorption of the natural grease of the leather by the immense suction of the air pump, and to the injurious properties of the sealing composition on the leather ; these facts together making the leather so brittle that it was easily torn by the coulter connecting the piston and the carriage, and the leather had from the same causes become so sponge-like that it failed as an air-tight covering to the valve, and so prevented the formation of an effective vacuum in the traction pipe.

The Directors decided to act upon Mr Brunel's recommendation, in consequence of which Mr Gill, the Chairman, resigned his position on the Board. The majority of the South Devon Directors were the nominees of the Great Western Railway, which company held a large proportion of the South Devon shares, and it was to the advantage of the Great Western Railway that the South Devon Railway should use locomotive power, as the Great Western Railway supplied the engines on hire to it, and so made a considerable profit out of the substitution of locomotives for the atmospheric system. Mr Gill wrote a lengthy pamphlet urging the retention of atmospheric traction. The Directors for some months did not answer this attack on their policy, but the agitation led by Mr Gill compelled them at last to do so, and to call a special meeting of shareholders to finally decide as to what systen should be used—locomotive or atmospheric. This meeting was held at Exeter, on 6th January 1849. At it Mr Gill stated that the cost of locomotive traction on their line was 1s. 7½d. per mile; while he had an. offer from Clark and Varley to spend £10,000 of their own money on experimenting with their patent valve on two miles of the line, and, if successful, they would enter into a contract for five or seven years to complete the system at a cost of only £5000 a mile, and that they would take a considerable portion of this price in South Devon stock. They also undertook that the cost of working on their system should not exceed more than 1s. a mile. Mr Gill also stated that he had offers from twenty-five different inventors who were willing to have their atmospheric systems tried on somewhat similar terms. Samuda's valve, which was the one the South Devon Railway had used, Mr Gill considered the worst of all those submitted to him. After the meeting had lasted eight hours a poll was taken, with the following result:—For abandoning the atmospheric — present 576 shares, proxies 5324 shares, total 5900; against the abandonment—present 645 shares, proxies 1230 shares, total 1875. It will be seen, therefore, that there were a majority of 69 shares present at the meeting in favour of the retention of the atmospheric, but the immense number of shares held by the Great Western and Bristol and Exeter Railways, who were interested in supplying locomotive power to the South Devon Railway, completely swamped the ordinary shareholders, so that the final abandonment of the atmospheric system was carried by a majority of 4025 shares. The plant, which had cost the company over £300,000, was sold for about £50,000.

Clark and Varley's system, which Mr Gill proposed should be used on the South Devon Railway, consisted of the tube being made of wrought sheet iron, and constructed so as to form a powerful spring; the edges were provided with tips of india-rubber, about $1\frac{1}{2}$ inches high, and the circular form of the sheet iron pressed them close together, while the weight of the train on the lines, to which the edges of the tube were attached, opened the valve sufficiently for the coulter to enter, and as the train proceeded, and its weight was withdrawn from the metals, the valve closed automatically behind it.

The South Devon line was opened to Laira (a temporary station at Plymouth) on 1st May 1848, the service consisting of six trains each way. As already stated, the Great Western Railway provided the locomotive power to work the South Devon Railway, Mr Brunel building engines of the 'Corsair' type; but after some years the South Devon shareholders thought they could do better, and contracted with Messrs Geach, Evans and Company to work this line and the Cornwall jointly. Mr Daniel Gooch had a considerable interest in this firm of engine builders, and most probably designed the locomotives supplied by Evans and Company. But the South Devon Railway fared, perhaps, even worse under Evans and Company. This firm was paid 1s. 8d. per train mile run for locomotive power, and they must have made enormous profits out of the contract, for, with their drivers, the coal used was reduced to a minimum.

Liberal premiums were paid the engine drivers for the coal saved, and to see one of the goods trains ascending a bank at less than 6 miles an hour, and running down the other side of the incline with steam off, was certainly a vivid example of economy. After twenty-one years this contract was determined, and the railway took over the locomotives at a valuation, and worked the line itself, when the cost of locomotive power was found to work out at only 10d. per mile, so that Evans and Company had been making about half of their 'little bill' clear profit every year. Although the line has such severe gradients, these lend themselves to economical working of the goods traffic, as the trains crawl up one side of the bank (the Great Western now do this at 10 miles an hour against Evans and Company's 6 miles an hour), and run down the other side by the force of gravity.

It was at the end of 1866 that Evans and Company's contract was determined, and the South Devon and Cornwall Railways decided to provide joint locomotives to work their systems. In 1867 the Avonside Engine Company constructed saddle tank engines with a leading bogie, from the design of Mr Slaughter. These locomotives, known as the 'Pluto' class, were for some time the standard type engines west of Newton.

The Torquay branch was opened on 18th December 1848. In 1857 the Dartmouth and Torbay Railway was formed, and the line from Torquay to Paignton opened on 2d August 1859, while the second portion to Brixham Road (now called Churston) was opened for passenger traffic on 14th March, and for goods on 1st April 1861. From Churston, branches the Torbay and Brixham Railway. While writing about the South Devon Railway, we take the opportunity to shortly describe the romantic career of the Torbay and Brixham Railway, a line but 2¼ miles long, but interesting from the fact that it was constructed by a private gentleman, who, to help the fishing town of

Brixham, spent the whole of his fortune on making this railway, and completely ruined himself in the laudable attempt to benefit his fellowmen. A local company then took over the line, and worked it independently of the South Devon Railway, which latter company, year by year, delivered accounts by which the Brixham line appeared to be more and more in debt to it, and so greatly pressed for money was this little railway, that it mortgaged its only locomotive, 'The Queen,' to the South Devon Railway for £350. But money matters went from bad to worse, till the Brixham Directors appealed to the Railway Commissioners, who went into the case fully, and found that the debt was entirely on the other side, the South Devon Railway having to pay the Torbay and Brixham Railway over £2000, less the £350 already advanced on its engine. At one time the Brixham Company was so exasperated that, in 1875, it obtained Parliamentary sanction to alter the gauge of its line, the idea being that if the gauges of the lines were different, no interchange of traffic could take place, and the South Devon Railway would be effectually prevented from making any charges for such accommodation; but this change of gauge was not carried out until the final conversion of the Great Western Railway in 1892.

This small railway had another hardship to contend against, as although it had never made enough money to pay even the debenture interest, yet year by year the Government charged it £50 for passenger duty, based on the fact that the third-class passengers were charged 3d. each for the journey of 2¼ miles, which, however, was the fare authorized by its Act of Parliament.

CHAPTER XVI.

THE CORNWALL RAILWAY.

EARLY in 1844, a meeting was called at Truro, at which it was decided to form a company to construct a railway through Cornwall, and a provisional committee was appointed at a meeting held on 6th August. The report of this committee was adopted. The principal recommendations were, the construction of a coast line from Plymouth to Falmouth; the adoption of the atmospheric system of propulsion; the crossing of the Tamar by means of a steam bridge, the train being itself thus ferried across, so that passengers would have the advantage of through carriages from London, etc.

The traffic was estimated to produce £105,655 per annum, the expenses of an atmospheric line were put down at £38,000, and the profit at £67,000, or sufficient to pay 7 per cent. on the capital of £900,000. If worked by locomotives the annual expenses were estimated at £46,000.

The capital was divided into 18,000 shares of £50, of which the Great Western Railway and its associated companies took 5000, the local capitalists took 3000, and the remaining 10,000 were subscribed for four times over in two months. As might be expected, the London and South Western Railway immediately started an opposition line, 'The Cornwall and Devon Central,' commencing at Exeter and passing through Crediton, Bow, Hatherleigh, Okehampton, Launceston, Bodmin, and Truro to Falmouth, a line 98 miles in length, or 20 miles shorter than the South

Devon and Cornwall route. This line was to be double throughout. The capital of this line was £1,500,000, and the London and South Western Railway undertook to provide £450,000. On the 4th of March 1845 the railway department of the Board of Trade reported on these rival schemes ; the defects of the central line are thus dealt with :—'Throughout its whole length it has hardly a mile running at or near the natural surface of the ground. It has nine tunnels, whose united length amounts to 4820 yards, 8 miles of cutting at depths exceeding 50 feet, 9 miles of embankment of a height exceeding 70 feet, and 1076 yards of viaduct at heights of 83 and 45 feet. The difficulty and expense of such immense works are greatly enhanced by the geological character of the district through which they would have to be constructed. It appears from statements submitted to us that one tunnel of 700 yards, at a depth of 146 feet below the surface, is through granite, a cutting of $1\frac{3}{4}$ miles, as deep in parts as 70 feet, is through granite and hard greenstone.'

While the report was extremely favourable to the Cornwall line, 'we are of opinion that the extension of the coast line from Plymouth to Falmouth may fairly be sanctioned as a commercial speculation, and that, in this point of view, it affords the only practicable means at present of extending railway communication to the county of Cornwall.' After a long hearing the Lord's Committee reported,— ' That they were of opinion that the construction of a railway from Plymouth to Falmouth, with a branch to Bodmin, would be of great public advantage. But they were also of opinion, that without a further and more accurate survey, with the view to procure gradients of a more favourable character, and to avoid, if possible, the crossing of the Hamoaze, the Bill should not now be further proceeded with.'

In the Bill introduced in 1846, the gradients were greatly improved, none being steeper than 1 in 60, while the proposal to ferry the trains across the Tamar was withdrawn, and a high level bridge at Saltash substituted.   Before the Lord's Committee, a Cornishman, who was giving evidence in favour of the Bill, was one too many for Mr Sergeant Kinslake, who appeared for the opposition scheme.   The witness was cross-examined as to the passenger traffic between St Austell and Truro, conveyed by vans, and he stated they were chiefly used by people of a low class.   'Now be careful, have you never travelled by one of those vans?' asked the learned sergeant.   'No,' was the reply.   'Just think again and be sure.'   'I never have,' responded the witness, 'although I have heard of barristers who have.'   This reply raised a general laugh at the counsel's expense.   The Bill received the royal assent in August 1846.   The opposition line (The Cornwall and Devon Central Railway), promoted by the London and South Western Railway, failed to obtain their Bill, and was left in a curious predicament in consequence.   Both the Cornwall lines had made offers for the Bodmin and Wadebridge Railway, and that of the Central Company being the better, it was accepted, the purchase price being £35,000.   What to do with this line was the question that exercised the minds of the officials of the Central Company, and after various negotiations, rather than it should fall into the hands of the Cornwall Railway, the London and South Western Railway took it over.   The history of this little line is interesting.   It was opened in 1834, and constructed to convey sand to and from the mouth of the Camal, to enrich the meadow land round about Wenford and Bodmin.   It began by being remarkable in being built for less than the estimated cost, as with a capital of £35,000 it had £106, 8s. 5d. in hand when completed.   The Great Western, in 1845, although more than 100 miles from the Bodmin and Wadebridge Railway, and although it was not paying a dividend, offered to buy it at a considerable profit on the cost of its construction, provided they got their Bill passed; while the London and South Western offered to buy it, if their Bill passed or not, but at a less price than the Great Western. Their offer was accepted, and it has been South Western property ever since, although it is not even yet connected with their system. The passenger rolling stock consisted of a first and second composite and two open thirds. The train went from Wadebridge to Bodmin on Monday, Wednesday and Friday, and returned on Tuesday, Thursday and Saturday. The line was $14\frac{3}{4}$ miles long. Recently the Great Western constructed a branch about 4 miles long from Bodmin Road, on their Cornwall line, to Bodmin, and so connected this early line with the great rival of its owning company, and so, since the abolition of the Broad Gauge, with the rest of the lines in this country. But although the Cornwall Railway had been legally incorporated, nothing was done towards constructing the line for some years. The disastrous financial failures and general commercial depression in 1847-48 prevented the construction of the line being actively proceeded with, $7\frac{1}{2}$ miles of the course had been purchased and the works were commenced in the end of 1847, but in the middle of the next year they were wholly abandoned. To preserve the benefits of the Act, upon obtaining which an immense sum of money had been expended, a supplementary Act was obtained in 1847 extending the time for the completion of the line to 23d June 1860. The project was then left in complete abeyance until 1853, when another start was made with the construction of the line between Plymouth and Truro, $53\frac{3}{4}$ miles, an Act having been obtained allowing until August 1864 for the completion of the line from Truro to Falmouth.

The line was formally opened by Prince Consort on 4th May 1859. It was a single one throughout, but is now being doubled. The principal work is the Saltash Suspension Bridge, Brunel's great masterpiece. The appended description of the construction and

opening of this colossal engineering feat is from the
Life of I. K. Brunel.

ROYAL ALBERT BRIDGE.

The great cylinder, having been constructed on
the river bank, was moved down to low water on
launching-ways, and floated off by the rising tide.

BRUNEL'S MASTERPIECE—The ' ROYAL ALBERT BRIDGE,' Saltash,
connecting Cornwall and ' England.'

Guided between four pontoons, it was finally sunk in
correct position in June 1854.

Some delay in penetrating the mud was caused by
a bed of oyster shells which had to be cut through by
one edge of the cylinder. In consequence of some
irregularities of the surface of the rock, the cylinder
at first deviated considerably from an upright position,
and it was necessary to use the pneumatic apparatus to

gain access to the rock and excavate it. The height of the annulus below the dome was such that it was not quite filled by the mud when the cylinder rested on the bottom. The work of getting the mud out of the annular space was much faciliated by the division of it into compartments.

By February 1855, the cylinder had been sunk to its full depth in an upright position, and it then rested everywhere on the rock, its lowest point being 87 feet 6 inches below high water. Much trouble was given by a spring of water issuing out of a fissure in the rock, in one of the compartments, but the flow was stopped by driving close sheet piles into the fissure. The rock in the annulus was dressed, and the space filled by a ring of granite ashlar masonry, which was built to a height of about 7 feet all round. The rock consisted of greenstone trap, so hard that tools could with difficulty be got to work it. When the ring of masonry was completed, it was expected that the bottom might be sufficiently watertight to act as a coffer-dam, and allow of the mud being taken out from the central part of the cylinder below the dome. But the pumping power was not at first sufficient for this purpose, and it was thought that it would be necessary to employ the pneumatic process in this space also. However, by rapid and incessant pumping, the water was lowered so as to allow of the mud and rock being excavated, and the masonry in the central space built without having again recourse to the use of air pressure. The leakage water was conveyed to two wells formed of cast-iron pipes built into the masonry, from which the water was pumped. The inner plates of the annulus were cut out, and the work in the centre, which consisted of granite ashlar set in cement, was throughly bonded into the ring of masonry already built. When the work was carried up to the level of the dome, both the dome and the internal 10 feet cylinder were cut out and removed. When the building had been carried up some height, the pump wells were filled with cement concrete, and the influx of water stopped. Finally, about the end of 1856, when the masonry was completed to the cap of the pier, the upper part of the great cylinder was unbolted and taken ashore, it having been made in two halves with that object. Thus the most difficult part of the undertaking was successfully completed.

The centre pier of the Saltash Bridge is, like many great engineering works, out of sight, and little regarded by any but professional men. The rest of the bridge forms a striking feature in a beautiful landscape, and its appearance is well known. The whole length of the bridge is about 2200 feet, and is divided into two great spans over the river of 455 feet each, and seventeen side spans, varying from 70 to 90 feet, which are on sharp curves. The piers of the side spans, as well as the two large piers carrying the land ends of the main trusses, are of masonry. The masonry of the centre pier is 35 feet in diameter, and is carried up about 12 feet above high water level. On it stand four cast-iron octagonal columns, rising up to the level of the railway. The piers which support the ends of the great trusses are constructed with arched openings through which the trains pass.

The upper part of the centre pier is a cast-iron standard, and that of the land piers is of masonry cases with cast-iron. The highest part of the truss is 260 feet above the lowest point of the foundations.

The railway is carried over each of the smaller openings between two longitudinal girders, and over the main spans it is carried between similar longitudinal girders, which are suspended at intervals from the main truss. Each truss consists of a wrought-iron oval tube, which forms an arch, and of two suspension chains, one on either side of the tube, connecting its two ends.

The rise of the arched tube above its abutments on the top of the piers is the same as the fall of the suspension chains below the same level. At eleven points in the length of the truss the chains are connected to the tube by upright standards, which are braced together by diagonal bars in order to resist the strains due to unequal loading. The roadway girders are suspended from the truss at the upright standards already mentioned, and at an intermediate point between each of them.

The truss has the great depth of 56 feet in the centre; this conduces materially to the economy of the construction as it diminishes the strain upon the principal parts, the tube and the chains, and so enables them to be made of smaller dimensions. The truss may be described as a combination of an arch and a suspension bridge, half the weight being placed on the one and half on the other, the outward thrust of the arch on the abutments being counterbalanced by the inward drag on the chains. The mechanical arrangement of the Saltash truss is similiar to that of the one at Chepstow, the tube resting on standards, the railway passing beneath, the suspension chains hung from either side of the tube, the upright standards and the diagonal bracing are common to the two structures. The total weight of wrought-iron work in the superstructure of each span is 1060 tons. When the truss for the Cornwall or western span was completed, temporary piers were erected to support the ends, and the scaffolding having been removed, the roadway was loaded with 1190 tons uniformly distributed. This test having proved satisfactory, preparations were made for floating the truss. Docks were made underneath it near the two ends, and in each of these docks two iron pontoons were placed, valves were then opened to admit water, and the pontoons were allowed to sink on timbers prepared to receive them.

Upon each pair of pontoons was erected an elaborate framework of timber to carry the weight of half the truss, or between 500 and 600 tons. The framework consisted of stout timber props, some of them 40 feet long, extending from the pontoon to the arched tube, and was attached to the tube by iron suspension rods, so that when the operation of floating was completed the pontoons would be free to pass from underneath the truss. In order to haul the truss out warps were laid from the pontoons to a gun brig hulk near the centre pier and to a barge higher up the river. On this barge were also placed, ready for use, the ends of four warps leading to capstans and crabs on board vessels moored at various points. To keep the truss from being drifted up or down the river while being moved out, radius lines were laid from the pontoons to moorings, with arrangements for hauling in on them if required.

In order to ensure his directions being clearly understood and promptly attended to, Mr Brunel assembled a number of his assistants, one of whom was placed as 'captain' in each of the vessels containing the hauling capstans to superintend the men and to execute orders. These orders were given by signals. It was most important that the attention of the captain should not be diverted by looking out for the signals, and that there should be no chance of a signal not being seen by him because he was attending to some other of his duties.

There was therefore in each vessel an assistant whose sole duty it was to watch for the signals, to give the appropriate interpretation to the captain, and to acknowledge the signal by a flag corresponding to that by which it was given.

Mr Brunel directed the operations from a platform in the centre of the truss. The signals were given from a smaller platform immediately above, and were made by red and white flags held in front of black boards, which were turned toward the vessel signalled to. Printed papers containing instructions were dis-

tributed to all engaged, the signalling was carefully
rehearsed, as also was every other part of the operations which could be tried beforehand.

1st September was the day fixed for the floating.

During the morning the men, about 500 in number,
assembled at their stations on the vessel and pontoons.
At about one o'clock in the afternoon signals from the
tops of the temporary piers on which the truss rested
showed that the ends had been lifted 3 inches clear.
Mr Brunel then gave the signal for the men in the pontoons to haul on the warps, and the great structure glided
slowly out to the centre of the river. A pause was
then made, while the warps which were to swing the
truss round into its place were being attached to the
pontoon which was farthest from the centre pier.
When this was done the different ropes were hauled
upon in obedience to signals, so as to keep the other
pontoon close to the centre pier, upon which, as a
pivot, the truss swung round in a quarter circle till it
occupied the whole of the western half of the river,
and was brought close to its appointed resting place.
It was finally adjusted to its exact position by strong
tackles attached to the piers. Water was then admitted into the pontoons; and as the tide fell they
were allowed to drift away, leaving the truss resting on
the piers, the roadway girders being but a few feet
above the water.

The whole operation was conducted with the most
perfect order and regularity,

Under each end of the truss were three hydraulic
presses; the two outside presses combined, or the
middle one by itself, were sufficient to lift the weight.
Mr Brunel had also at first intended to have strong
screw-jacks, which were to be kept screwed up underneath the truss, and so to support the weight, if by any
accident the presses failed. A modification of this plan
was adopted; the rams of the presses had a screw
thread cut on them, and a large nut on each was kept
screwed up hard against the top of the press as the ram

emerged from it.   As an additional precaution, timber packing, in thin layers, was placed in the space between the completed portion of the pier and the end of the truss as it was lifted.   Great care was thus taken to guard against any mishap.   The tube was lifted 3 feet at a time at each end.   The operation went on slowly in order to allow the masonry of the land pier to set after it had been built up underneath the truss.

Mr Brunel was only able to be present during one of the lifting operations as he was then engaged in the 'launch' of the 'Great Eastern,' so that it was superintended by Mr Brereton.

By July 1858 the first truss had been lifted to its full height, and the second truss was ready for floating. Mr Brunel was obliged to remain abroad from ill health, and Mr Brereton conducted the operations. Although the weather was not favourable, and the wind high, the truss was safely landed on the piers, and was afterwards raised in the same manner as the first one.   On the Devonshire side, the side spans pass over fields, and on the Cornwall side over the town of Saltash.

The general effect of the bridge is in no way heightened by an expenditure of money on architectural ornament ; for with the exception of a few unimportant mouldings, the bridge is absolutely unadorned. The total cost was £225,000, a very moderate expenditure, especially when the difficult work at the centre pier is taken into consideration.   This result is due not only to the careful manner in which all the details of the design were prepared, but also to the great attention given throughout to its construction.

His Royal Highness the Prince Consort, as Lord Warden of the Stannaries, permitted the bridge to be called the Royal Albert Bridge, and consented to open it in person.   The ceremony was performed on 3d May 1859.   Mr Brunel was on the Continent at the time, but on his return to England paid a hurried visit to the Cornwall Railway, and saw for the first and last time in its completed state the great work on which he had expended so much thought and care.'

The other remarkable works are the numerous timber viaducts, the construction of which we have already specified in the chapter describing the South Devon Railway. The entire line to Falmouth was opened in 1863. On the 12 miles between Truro and Falmouth, there are seven trestle viaducts, two tunnels, many deep cuttings, high embankments, and sharp curves.

Just before Perranwell, we cross at right angles the little railway constructed for the purpose of bringing minerals from the Chacewater and St Day districts to the shipping port of Devoran on the Truro River. This small mineral line has been used for this sole purpose for many years. The Falmouth Station is nearly a mile beyond the town, quite a unique experience, but just as inconvenient as the usual one of building a station a mile before the town is reached. Its position, however, adjoins the docks, which were expected to become of great importance; hence the reason for this site being chosen for the station. The Great Western leased the line in 1861 for a term of a thousand years, to date from 3d May 1859, so that the Cornwall Railway practically formed a part of their system; but the 'Sleepy Giant' on different occasions purchased the connecting railways; but in 1889 the lease was cancelled and the Great Western Railway purchased the Cornwall Railway, so that now the Great Western Railway owns the whole line from London to Penzance.

The West Cornwall Railway reversed the order of the gauges, and is, with the exception of the length of line, less than 7 miles between Gloucester and Cheltenham, already mentioned, the only example of a Narrow Gauge line that was made a Mixed Gauge for the purpose of accommodating the Broad Gauge, the introduction of the Mixed Gauge upon other lines being the precursor for the abolition of the 7 feet gauge,

The West Cornwall Railway purchased, for £80,000, the Hayle Railway, a company formed as early as 1834, with a capital of £20,000, its system being 9½ miles long, and its rolling stock comprising five locomotives, six passenger carriages, and one hundred and nineteen trucks, waggons, etc., besides two stationary engines to work the inclined planes of 1 in 9½. The Hayle Company made no profit, but formed branch lines to the various mines for the accommodation of the mine owners, who were also the shareholders of the railway company. It was at first only a mineral line, but the great success of the Manchester and Liverpool Railway in the carrying of passengers caused the Directors of this West County Railway to have a coach for passengers linked at the rear of the mineral trucks.

The train took 1 hour to cover the 9½ miles from Redruth to Hayle.

The West Cornwall Railway was formed in 1844, and applied for their Act in 1845. The Board of Trade reported in favour of it. The usual result followed, the Bill being thrown out. The lines proposed to be constructed were two, one at each end of the Hayle Railway, and both single track, in all 22 miles 6 furlongs in length, and was to be worked partly by locomotives and partly by atmospheric power. The 11½ miles from Truro to Redruth were to be worked by the latter system. The whole line was estimated to cost only £180,000. In the next year's Bill the capital was increased to £500,000, and the Act was obtained on 3d August 1846 to construct a Broad Gauge line from Truro Quay to Penzance, with a branch to the Truro Station of the Cornwall Railway Company; but the Cornwall Company delayed the construction of their line for so long, that in 1850 an Act was obtained to allow the West Cornwall to construct their line on the Narrow Gauge, and the construction of the West Cornwall Railway was then commenced. This Act had a clause requiring either the West Cornwall Railway to alter their gauge when the Cornwall line joined it at Truro, or to lay down a third rail for the accommodation of the Broad Gauge. This third rail completed a continuous Broad Gauge railway from London to Penzance. The Narrow Gauge line was still used for local mineral and timber traffic between Penzance and Truro. The trucks used for this traffic were of small size and of peculiar design, the axles of the rear and leading wheels being so close together that only a few inches separated their tyres. When the whole line was converted to the Narrow Gauge, these trucks were lettered, 'not to run east of Truro,' so that these are still only used for local traffic, and unless the curious reader makes a journey west of Truro, he is not likely to see these old time vehicles.

The Broad Gauge branch from St Erth to St Ives was not opened for many years after, although the construction of it was proposed as early as 1844. From the 1st August 1878, the West Cornwall Railway became part of the Great Western Railway system, as also did various mineral branches which abound in the district, those in connection with the West Cornwall Railway being Broad Gauge and those connected with the Cornwall Minerals Railway being of the Narrow Gauge.

Par is the junction for the Cornwall mineral lines, the loop from that station to St Blazey, the junction on the Cornwall Minerals Railway being a double line, although the distance is less than half a mile, but it is nevertheless remarkable as, until a few months back, being the only length of double line in Cornwall except the crossings. The Cornwall Minerals Railway was formed in 1873, and consists of 47 miles of line running from Fowey, on the South Coast, to Newquay on the north, with numerous branches to the various mines and china clay works, some of which are very extensive. The streams of water in this part of Cornwall are mostly quite white through the china clay, which seems very plentiful, and we begin to fancy we have at length come 'to a land flowing with milk;' but the china clay industry is accountable for this whiteness. The water is used for washing the clay, most of which falls to the bottom, and is collected, while enough to discolour the water and make it milk white is carried off by the streams. The Cornwall Minerals Railway consisted of a number of private and semi-private lines connecting the various tin mines, china clay works, etc., with Newquay on the north and Fowey on the south, and so provided means of shipping the produce to its destination. The line from East Wheal Rose Mine to Newquay was the property of Mr Treefry, and its opening, on 28th January 1849, is thus described :—'The Newquay Viaduct was opened by Mr J. T. Treefry riding over it, and afterwards sending his loaded waggons across with supplies for the line beyond it. At a later period of the day barley was sent over it for shipment at Newquay. The viaduct, an exceedingly light yet very strong structure, is 98 feet high from the base of the piers, and 630 feet long.'

We therefore see that when first constructed the Cornwall Minerals Railway was purely a mineral line, but since it did not answer as such, from 1st July 1877 the Great Western Railway took over the system on lease for 999 years at a rental of £18,800 a year, payable half yearly. Most of the trucks used for conveyance of china clay are the original ones belonging to the Minerals Railway. They are constructed of iron, and are less than 11 feet 6 inches in length over the buffers, and carry 10 tons each. Many of the gradients on the line are very severe, from St Blazey to Bridges it is 1 in 34, and between Victoria and St Denis Junction 1 in 39, other sections vary between 46 and 73. Near Newquay is a branch, at present not worked, to Newlyn, the gradients of which are so severe that the engines are not allowed to take more than eight loaded vehicles including brakes. Slate is so plentiful in this district that on parts of the line immense slabs of it are used to fence the railway. At Newquay the line crosses the public street twice by an S curve, to enable it to approach the harbour, which is reached by a very steep descent through a short tunnel. The trucks are let down and pulled up on this part of the line by means of a wire rope and a stationary steam winding engine with two locomotive boilers, each with a smaller one on top for a steam reservoir, and resembling somewhat in appearance the engine lately introduced on the Paris, Lyons and Mediterranean Railway; only one loaded and one empty truck are allowed to be pulled up or let down at the same time. China clay is shipped at Newquay, and the ships unload coal for the mines. Having described the Great Western trunk line, we will reserve for another chapter the particulars of the most important branch of the Broad Gauge—the South Wales Railway.

CHAPTER XVII.

THE SOUTH WALES RAILWAY.

In 1844, the Great Western Railway revived the proposition of constructing a railway from Stonehouse, across the Severn, along its western bank, through Chepstow, Newport, Cardiff, Swansea and Carmarthen, with a branch right and left, one to Milford Haven and the other to Fishguard, from whence a service of steamers were to run to Waterford. The following were the lines proposed to be constructed :—

	Miles.	Chains.
The main line, from Standish to Fishguard,	162	0
Pembroke Branch, ...	19	32
Newport to Monmouth, . . .	22	35
Forest of Dean, ...	7	0
In connection with these lines were the Monmouth and Hereford Railway, from Hereford to Gloucester, . .	32	15
Monmouth Branch, . . .	8	20
Forest of Dean, ...	4	26
Total, .	255	48

It was proposed to cross the Severn by a bridge 2000 feet long at a horseshoe bend, and to cut a ship canal across the bend for the passage of large ships ; the railway would cross this canal by a swing bridge, so that no inconvenience would result to the navigation of the river. There would be a tunnel near Swansea 1320 yards long, and another near Kidwelly 1463 yards in length. The total cost of construction was estimated at £2,800,000, and the 250 miles between

London and Fishguard was expected to be covered in 5 hours.

The time taken to-day (fifty years later) to perform this journey from London to New Milford, 272½ miles, over exactly the same course—with the substitution of the Narrow Gauge—is 7 hours 10 minutes, while other trains take as long as 10 hours 40 minutes to cover the distance.

The Committee of the House of Commons declared the preamble of the Bill proved, but the Admiralty having decided against the bridge across the Severn, the Chairman said they had come to the following decision :—' That, although the preamble of the Bill is proved, the success of the whole scheme of the South Wales Railway so entirely depends upon that part of the work to which the Admiralty object, that they cannot consent to proceed in the investigation of a measure which the promoters have not the power of accomplishing.'

The whole House then discussed the Bill, and referred it back to the Committee. The Opposition urged that as it was not now proposed to make a railway according to the preamble, the Bill did not comply with the standing orders, and, therefore, could not be proceeded with. The preamble was allowed to be altered, to allow of a line being constructed from Chepstow to Pembroke, and this received the royal assent 4th August 1845. In their Bill the next year the South Wales Railway proposed alternative modes of crossing the Severn, but neither of these methods was sanctioned, the Admiralty being in favour of a bridge and the House of Commons of a tunnel, so that the South Wales Railway had to avail itself of a clause in another of their Bills and construct a railway along the Welsh side of the Severn to Gloucester. This made the distance to London considerably longer, and, therefore, another line was projected from Gloucester to Cheltenham, and thence through Chipping Norton to Oxford.

In 1846, the Great Western Railway agreed to lease the South Wales Railway in perpetuity, as the various sections were completed.   The construction of the line was immediately proceeded with, and the boring of the Hillfield Tunnel caused the good folks of Newport considerable inconvenience.   This tunnel is 200 feet below the surface, and lower than all the wells supplying the town, so that all the wells ran dry, and the inhabitants had to obtain a supply of water from elsewhere at a large expense, so they did not think the South Wales Railway an unmixed blessing.   Mr Brunel was at this time constructing many timber viaducts on the lines of which he was engineer, and he did not neglect the South Wales Railway in this particular, the principal one being that at Landore, over a mile long and 160 feet high.   The original bridge across the Usk was a wooden one 1200 feet long, the centre span being 99 feet and the other 70 feet wide.

When this bridge was almost completed, it was, unfortunately, burnt down, and gave a vivid illustration of the saw that 'great events from little actions spring.'   On 31st May 1848, at 6 P.M. the workmen engaged in completing the central arch, which was on an immense pile, consisting of several tons weight of timber and iron bolts, were busy at work driving in the bolts, when one man used a bolt which had been heated to an extraordinary degree.   This immediately ignited the adjoining timber, which, being highly kyanized or " pickled," was as ignitible as gunpowder. The man had a bucket of water at hand, as was always usual, but it was useless, for the flames leaped along on each side from the centre to each end of the bridge, and the whole extent was instantly in a terrible blaze. The men with difficulty escaped with their lives.   A team of trams was passing at the time, and the horses, put to their utmost gallop, were obliged to dash through the flames to escape.   The whole town rushed to the great stone bridge adjacent, and hundreds of navvies, carpenters, masons, labourers, tradesmen and gentlemen were quickly on the spot, but it was of no avail. The town fire-engines were brought, but acted with no effect on the awful flames bursting from the surface of the piles, the rails, the arches, and in fact wherever the fire could lay hold of wood to burn. The timber work was so enormous that it took a considerable time to burn any portion wholly away, while the patent composition used to preserve the wood lent assistance to the flames, which rose up with blue and black smoke, filling all the heavens. At about 9 P.M. the ponderous work of the central arch gave way with a terrible crash, and soon after this; portion after portion fell, until, with the exception of here and there a solitary black and charred fragment, with some portion on the banks, the whole of this magnificent work was totally destroyed. The river was black with burning wood, and the banks became strewed with enormous pieces of half-burnt wood like the coast after a wreck. The fire-engine from the barracks did great execution, worked by two companies of soldiers under the command of officers, and the town engines did all they could, but it was a physical impossibility to save even a fragment; we might as well suppose a portion of a barrel of gunpowder could be found after the ignition of the barrel. The bridge was almost completed when this unfortunate calamity occurred. It had been built of kyanized timber by the eminent contractors Messrs Rennie, Logan and Company, and cost upwards of £20,000 in the erection. Fortunately for the contractors, the terms of their contract with the railway company necessitated them insuring the timber bridges during construction, so that the Fire Insurance Company bore the loss.

Near Llansamlet, between Neath and Swansea, Mr Brunel introduced a novel method to prevent the earth, which forms the side of the deep cutting, from slipping. The usual procedure is to build retaining walls, but, as these must be very massive and solidly built, to save expense, Mr Brunel designed four flying arches over the cutting.   The thrust of both sides of this cutting would be concentrated on the arch of these bridges, so that they were likely to be forced up at the crown and so destroyed.   To prevent such a *contre-temps*, Mr Brunel weighted the centres of the arches with masses of heavy copper slag, and by this means the thrust of the arches on the sides of the cutting balanced the thrust of the cutting on the crown of the arch, and the purpose in view, viz., the non-erection of expensive retaining walls, was successfully accomplished.

The *chef d'œuvre* of the South Wales Railway is the Chepstow Bridge over the Wye, which Mr Williams, in his interesting work, *Our Iron Roads*, thus describes :—

WYE BRIDGE.

A tubular bridge has been constructed over the Wye at Chepstow, on the South Wales Railway, to which allusion must be made.   It consists of four spans, three of about 100 feet each, and one of 290 feet, extending altogether from bank to bank for 610 feet.

The chief span is a modification of the suspension principle, the great length of the girders requiring more support than that afforded by the piers alone at each extremity.   Mr Brunel accordingly contrived that this should be given by means of a tube 309 feet in length and 9 in diameter, which, having been raised to the summit of piers erected on the east bank and in the centre of the river, is strengthened by massive chains secured to the girders.   These girders are 50 feet above high water mark at spring tides, which here rise from 50 to 60 feet, being more than any other river in the kingdom.

In sinking the cylinders to form the piers of the

bridge, the workmen had first to pass through 29 feet of blue clay and sand, below which they met with a thin bed of peat containing timber, some solid oak, hazel-nuts, and other similar substances. They next came to several feet of fine blue gravel, and then they reached a bed of boulders, upon which the cylinders were originally intended to rest. After this was a bed of red marl, beneath which was solid rock like millstone grit, and into this the cylinders were sunk. The mode in which this part of the work was performed was curious. The cylinders were placed on planks to prevent their cutting into the soft mud. One by one cylinders were added until they had reached the top of the stage (about 100 feet in height) which had been erected for the purpose of sinking them. The weight of the column now cut through the planks, and the cylinder sank about 6 feet into the mud. Two or three men then descended into it, and, as they removed the contents, the cylinder continued to sink, and as it descended fresh cylinders were added at the top. This process continued without interruption till a depth of about 17 feet was attained, and then a spring was tapped, and without a moment's notice the water broke in from below in such force as to require the constant action of two 13-inch pumps worked by an engine. A remarkable fact attending this occurence was, that the spring water invariably rose in the cylinder exactly at that height to which the tube was standing in the river at the moment. That it was not an interruption from the Wye was considered to be beyond dispute, inasmuch as the river at this point, from the action of the tide, was always heavily tainted with mud, while the water which rushed into the cylinder from below was of exceeding purity, and did not contain a particle of salt.'

The first locomotive engine on the South Wales Railway, named the ' Dove,' and a tender were hauled from Gloucester on a carriage built purposely, and drawn by eighteen fine grey horses. Four superior black horses hauled the tender. The novelty of the load and the beauty of the teams drew the attention of a number of people.   In August 1849, a committee of shareholders was appointed, who recommended the abandonment of the line from Whitland to Fishguard, and, consequently, this portion of the line was not constructed, so that the Irish connection is *viâ* Milford. The Great Western Railway leased the South Wales Railway as soon as the various sections were opened. At first a rent of £46,000 per annum for the whole line was paid, together with two-thirds of net profit—the Great Western Railway providing rolling stock.   This arrangement did not, however, work well, and in 1861 a rather serious quarrel arose between the two companies, because the Great Western Railway contended that the Barlow saddle rail was not suitable for the traffic, and they renewed it with their ordinary pattern rail, charging the expenses to renewal of permanent way, and so reducing the net profit considerably.   The two railways thereupon went to arbitration, and a new arrangement was entered into, which finally resulted in the Great Western Railway absorbing the South Wales Railway into its own system.

The route to South Wales *viâ* Gloucester was from the very first constructed as one necessary from the force of circumstances, or in other words it was felt that the direct route should branch from the Great Western system in the neighbourhood of Bristol, but the river Severn debarred the physical continuation of such a direct line.   The Bristol and South Wales Union Railway was therefore formed in 1846, to construct a line, 14½ miles long, from Bristol to New Passage, thence a steam ferry across the Severn to Portskewett, which joined the South Wales Railway by a short branch.   This shortened route was not opened until 1863, and although the distance between London and Newport and stations below on the South Wales Railway was thereby shortened by some miles, the route, save for the local traffic between Bristol and

South Wales, was never popular in consequence of the ferry. Brunel is incorrectly reported to have proposed ferrying the first-class railway carriages across to save the passengers the trouble of changing to and from the steamers. The mistake arose through an error of a newspaper reporter, who, in giving an account of a meeting of shareholders of the Bristol and South Wales Union Railway, held at Bristol on 9th March 1847, attributed such a statement to Mr Brunel, when, as a fact, he was not present at the meeting at all.

The observation as to the railway carriages crossing the river was made by one of the Directors, who said ' He believed that Mr Brunel expected to be able,' etc. The reporter failed to note that it was a Director speaking, which, together with the omission of the three words, 'he believed that,' caused the mistake and led to rather an awkward *contretemps* a few months later, when Mr Brunel was under cross-examination before a Parliamentary Committee.

The Great Western Railway took over this short connecting line and ferry in 1868, after which the proposals for a Severn Tunnel assumed a practical shape. Much has been written on this gigantic engineering undertaking—a gigantic one even for the Great Western Railway, with its wealth of colossal engineering achievements. The history of the venture is truly romantic, and has been delightfully told by the late Mr Walker, the contractor, in his book.

This is the most modern engineering triumph in the history of the Great Western Railway, and at present no other great works in connection with the Great Western Railway are contemplated, nor indeed are any such (so far as can be judged) likely again to occur on its system. If long lines of figures can convey even an approximate idea of the colossal nature of the engineering feat accomplished by the triumphant construction of this subaqueous tunnel, we will, before giving an outline of the trials and difficulties which were so successfully overcome in the construction of the Severn Tunnel, present to our readers' notice the following :—3100 men employed in its construction, 76,400,000 bricks used to line it, 36,794 tons of Portland cement used in setting the bricks, 250 tons of explosives used to blast the rock, 30,000,000 gallons of water pumped per day, and 23,000,000 gallons of water the average quantity pumped daily during construction.

The tunnel beneath the Severn was not the first proposal of the Great Western Railway as a means of obtaining a shorter route to South Wales, the original idea being a bridge at Chepstow, an Act for which was duly obtained. The plans for the tunnel were adopted in 1871, and next year an Act of Parliament authorising its construction was obtained, and the necessary works were commenced in 1873. At this time there was not a single house at Sudbrook—the headquarters of the Tunnel Works—but when operations were commenced a small office and six cottages were erected, and a temporary line laid down to Portskewett Station. Little progress was made in the construction of the tunnel, and in 1877 the Great Western Railway advertised for tenders. Only three firms tendered, and as the Directors considered them all too high, they determined to proceed with the tunnel themselves ; but the progress was still very slow, for by 18th October 1879 only 130 yards of a tunnel 7 feet in diameter had been constructed on the Welsh side, when an underground spring of water was unexpectedly tapped, and the whole works were completely flooded. This accident caused another change in the Directors' plans, and they now determined to accept, with slight modifications, the tender of Mr T. A. Walker, one of the three previously mentioned. Mr Walker commenced operations on 18th December 1879. The specification stated that the tunnel was to be 7942 yards in length, and the railway through the tunnel and the connecting lines 7 miles 5 furlongs long. It was to be lined throughout with brickwork, 2 feet 3 inches thick, with a brick invert for half the way through the tunnel. The permanent way was to be sleepered, and the rails to weigh 86 lbs. per yard. Afterwards it was decided to increase the brick lining to 3 feet in thickness, and to have an invert the whole length of the tunnel, to lay it with the famed longitudinal sleepers and Great Western bridge rails, 68 lbs. to the yard. The lowest level of the tunnel in the centre of the river was also increased by 15 feet, and the line fell from the Welsh side by a continuing gradient of 1 in 100, and on the English side 1 in 90. A considerable part of the roof of the tunnel had already been bricked in before the decision to alter the level was arrived at, and Mr Walker adopted a novel and successful plan to utilise the brickwork already executed. This he supported, and then built under it continuing side walls down to the new level, and the invert under this.

The colossal new pump provided to drain the tunnel burst on 2d July 1880, and the works were again completely flooded. The Great Western Railway provided another new pump of immense power, which was got to work on 12th October 1880. But, despite the millions of gallons of water pumped from the tunnel daily, the workings could not be emptied of water, so a diver was sent to shut a sluice door in the middle of the tunnel, his instructions being to turn the screw governing the sluice a certain number of times one way. After several exciting attempts he reached the sluice and carried out his instructions, but to the surprise of everyone this made no difference in the amount of water to be dealt with. Some time after, when the water had been lowered sufficiently to allow of the sluice being visited, the door was found wide open, but the mystery was explained. It was found that the screw controlling the door was a left-handed one instead of a right-handed one, as it was believed to be, so that when Lambert, the diver, turned the screw the number of times as directed, he really opened the sluice wider instead of shutting it, as he would have done had it been a right-handed screw. Upon another occasion this intrepid diver, when in the water, was drawn by the power of the pump against the wind box of the suction pipe, and it required the united efforts of three men to haul him out of this dangerous position.

The work was further delayed by a strike of the men in May 1881, but this was of short duration, and for some time the work progressed in a satisfactory manner until the junction of the two headings was successfully accomplished at 10 o'clock on the night of 26th September 1883. Everything now seemed to point to a speedy conclusion of the great undertaking, when, on 10th October 1883, the spring again broke out and flooded the whole tunnel. Efforts were immediately taken to obtain the mastery of the water, and with success, but the liquid element was hard to conquer, for when the subterranean spring had thus been finally vanquished, on the 17th October 1883, an immense tidal wave swept the Severn, broke down the river wall built to protect the land from the effect of these waves, which are the highest in Europe, for as far up the Severn as its junction with the Wye the normal rise of the tide is 50 feet.

Such an inundation was totally unexpected, the water rushed down the shaft and imprisoned the men, who retreated before it to the highest point in the tunnel, and their lives were saved by the natural law, which prevented the water rising further in consequence of the resistance of the air which had been driven by the inrush of the water to this spot, and as it had no outlet it resisted the advance of the water, and the men were consequently saved from a watery grave.

This was the last of the series of untoward events that retarded the completion of this mammoth work, and by the 5th of September 1885 the tunnel was far

enough advanced to allow of a special train, conveying the late Sir D. Gooch, to pass through from England to Wales, 50 feet under the bed of the river, and
145 feet below the level of high water spring tides.
The line was opened for goods traffic on 1st September 1886, and for passenger trains on 1st December
of the same year, while the regular service of passenger trains between London and South Wales
viâ the Severn Tunnel was inaugurated 1st July
1889. Such is the history of this remarkable triumph
of subaqueous tunnelling.

CHAPTER XVIII.

THE EARLY CONVERSIONS FROM BROAD TO NARROW GAUGE.

THE great scarcity of money in the early fifties, and the reaction that had set in against railway investments, together caused the stocks of the Great Western Railway and its Broad Gauge allies to be at considerable discounts, so that it was at that time useless to propose further extension of the Broad Gauge lines towards Liverpool, Manchester, and York, as were originally intended, while the principle of the Mixed Gauge, having been settled in the West Midland and Midland district, and all the through traffic from the North and North West being of necessity conveyed by Narrow Gauge until it reached the Mixed Gauge, over which lines, as a matter of convenience, it was conveyed as far as possible in Narrow Gauge vehicles. It will therefore be readily understood that under these circumstances the Broad Gauge traffic over the Mixed Gauge system was principally of a local character, the remainder for Broad Gauge destinations being of but small volume, so that, although both gauges were provided, the Broad Gauge was little used, and the increasing demand for Narrow Gauge accommodation on the Mixed Gauge had a tendency to cause the remaining Broad Gauge traffic to be still less catered for, so that the traffic was in a measure forced into the Narrow Gauge; for which traffic the management were providing ample accommodation.

The alteration of the gauge on the Oxford and Birmingham line presents a curious problem to the student who endeavours to fathom and account for the peculiar phase of human incongruity exhibited by the Great Western Railway Directors in connection with this section of their system.

The most important fight between the 7 feet and 4 feet 8½ inch rivals, indeed *the* Battle of the Gauges was fought over this line, and after each side had done its very utmost, the result was a complete triumph for the sesquipedalians, who thereby gained admittance to Birmingham and Wolverhampton—the very centre of the London and North Western preserves, while the victory also gave the Great Western means of competing with its rival the Midland, which had, by obtaining the railway from Birmingham to Bristol, entered into direct conflict with the Great Western Railway. The Broad Gauge lines, therefore, had at this time all the advantages they could desire to enable them to compete for the traffic between the North Western districts and London, and the West and South of England, yet it was on this very section, after so fierce a fight, and a victory so hardly gained, that the retrograde movement was first inaugurated. Nations and individuals speak proudly of any hard-earned advantage they have gained, and talk of dying to defend such privileges rather than surrender them; but with the Broad Gauge lines *tout cela changé,* for the whole advantage of the Battle of the Gauges was quietly surrendered; for after exactly nine years' experience of the Broad Gauge to Birmingham, the 7 feet gauge trains were withdrawn and the Narrow Gauge ones only were to be found North of Oxford. In August 1859, the Oxford and Worcester and Wolverhampton Railway obtained Parliamentary sanction to abandon the Broad Gauge on its system, and to use the capital raised for Broad Gauge purposes to extend Narrow Gauge branches; this alteration of gauge was speedily carried out. In 1860 the various lines, 217 miles in length, constructed in connection with the Oxford, Worcester and Wolverhampton Railway, were amalgamated and called the West Midland Railway, and on 1st July 1861 the Great Western Railway leased the West Midland Railway for a term of 999 years.   This lease provided for 'the Narrow Gauge to be laid down between Reading and Paddington, and from the junction near Bull's Bridge to Brentford, with all reasonable despatch, so as, if possible, to be ready for the reception of Narrow Gauge traffic on the opening of the Worcester and Hereford and Severn Valley.   On and after the opening of the Narrow Gauge to London, through and express trains are to be worked over the two systems, so as to thoroughly develop the traffic, as if they were one system.'

In 1861 the Wycombe Railway obtained an Act to construct a branch from Princes Risborough to Aylesbury, a distance of 7 miles, which was constructed and opened for traffic in about two years.   The Wycombe Railway was amalgamated with the Great Western Railway on 1st February 1867 ; the Aylesbury branch thus became part of the Great Western system.   It was on this short section that the conversion of gauge was first undertaken, it taking place in 1868 (this branch was for two years entirely cut off from the other parts of the Great Western system, as the main line of the Wycombe Railway was not converted till 1870).

The next year, 1869, the first important conversion was made.   This was not an alteration of the line from the Broad to Narrow Gauge, but only consisted in removing the third rail from the Mixed Gauge lines North of Oxford.   This was immediately followed by the actual conversion of the line from Grange Court to Hereford, a line constructed by an independent company (the Hereford, Ross and Gloucester Railway), and opened 1st June 1855, and with an annual revenue of about £16,000.   At Hereford there was already a Narrow Gauge line to Worcester, opened in 1861, which was one of the companies forming the West

Midland Railway, and was therefore part of the lines leased by the Great Western Railway, so that the narrow gauging of this portion of the line opened a shorter route to the Western Narrow Gauge portions of the Great Western system.

The first complete conversion consisted of (A.) The mixing of the gauge in the extensive Gloucester Station Yard—a most difficult undertaking, in consequence of all trains arriving at and departing from a single platform at Gloucester.

(B.) Mixing the gauges from Gloucester to Grange Court, 22½ miles, at which point the single Broad Gauge line to Hereford branches off. This work was successfully carried out, and now the line had to be closed for the purpose of altering the lines from the Broad to the Narrow Gauge. To minimise the inconvenience as much as possible, the Great Western Railway arranged with Mr Hughes, of Bayswater, to supply ten omnibuses to convey the passengers between Hereford and Ross. This service commenced on Monday, 16th August 1869.

Four hundred and fifty permanent way men were conveyed in three special trains to Barr's Court Station on the Saturday, and a train of forty Broad Gauge covered goods waggons was provided for the men to sleep in, the vehicles were white-washed within, and clean straw and new sacks provided for the men's bedding. A first-class carriage was provided for the accommodation of the staff. Operations commenced at 4 A.M. on the Sunday morning, when an engineer placed flags along the line to mark out each gang's work for the day. Each gang consisted of twenty-two men and a ganger. For their use the company provided a cask of water, a 'devil' iron pot, and the requisite fuel for cooking. The men were paid their usual wages for 9½ hours work instead of 12, the other 2½ hours being paid as overtime. An additional 15d. per day was also paid them for ration money. By Monday evening the conversion was completed as far as Fawley, and to Ross on Tuesday night, on Wednesday at 10.30 P.M. the Narrow Gauge had reached Mitcheldean Road, and the whole work to Grange Court was completed by Thursday night, and the next morning a service of Narrow Gauge trains commenced to run. It had taken but five days to convert the whole 22½ miles. The work consisted of withdrawing 3800 bolts in each mile, or 85,500 in all, drilling the same number of holes in the sleepers and refixing the bolts, and screwing the nuts up taut, and lifting the rails sideways 27½ inches. The metals consisted of four kinds, and different tools were required to deal with each class, so that caused additional labour and preparation.

All the conversion was not carried out on one side of the line, as of necessity, when stations were on opposite sides of the line, the rail further from the platform was the one which had to be shifted. This caused the changing of sides three times during the operation. A mile and a half of the work was done in tunnels, and this naturally added to the difficulty of the undertaking. The officials were extremely pleased with the behaviour of the men, who never took their clothes off the whole time, and during the five days only had 3½ hours rest each night, 20½ hours of every 24 being either spent in working, getting to work, or by short stops for meals. On the Wednesday night the men were so tired that they preferred to camp out at the spot where they were working rather than return to the sleeping train at Grange Court.

Thus was the first complete change of gauge carried out on the Great Western Railway, and, alas, this was but the beginning of a retrogressive policy, and as is usual after the accomplishment of a first bad action, to stifle reproach, the evil ways are persevered in and still further injustice is done to the whole system.

So was it with the conversion of the gauge on

the Great Western Railway. A new generation of officials had arisen who were not knit closely together by that *esprit de corps* begotten of a determination to succeed and overcome all opposition, which spirit had been so noticeable in the original band of Great Western Railway pioneers who had fought so many long and resolute battles for the grand 7 feet gauge. Therefore, having once commenced the alteration of the gauge, other conversions soon followed. The table below gives particulars in chronological order of the alterations in gauge.

Date.	Section.	Miles.
1868	Princes Risborough to Aylesbury, . .	7
1869	Grange Court (Gloucester) to Hereford, .	22½
1869	Oxford to Wolverhampton, with Stratford and Great Bridge branches, . .	89¾
1869	Reading to Basingstoke, ...	16
1870	Maidenhead to Oxford, ...	37
1871	West Drayton to Uxbridge, . . .	2½
1871	Whitland to Carmarthen, . . .	13¾
1872	Swindon to Milford, with all branches, .	239½
1872	Vale of Neath, Merthyr Tydvil branch, and Grange Court to Cheltenham, . .	60½
1872	Radley to Abingdon, ...	2
1872	Didcot to Oxford, ...	10¼
1873	Bristol and South Wales Union, . .	12
1874	Thingley Junction to Dorchester, Westbury to Salisbury, Barthampton to Bradford Junction, North Somerset Junction (Bristol) to Frome, Reading to Holt, with Marlborough and other branches, ...	197¼
1874	Dorchester to Weymouth, . . .	6½
1874	Southcote Junction to Reading, . .	1¾
1875	Southall to Brentford, ...	4
1876	Twyford to Henley-on-Thames . .	4½
1878	Uffington to Farringdon, . . .	3½
1880	Yatton to Clevedon, ...	3½
1880	Durston to Penn Mill (Yeovil), . . .	20¼
1881	Norton Fitzwarren to Barnstaple, . .	42¾
1882	Norton Fitzwarren to Minehead, . .	22¾
1884	Tiverton Junction to Tiverton, . .	4¾
1891	Creech Junction to Chard, . . .	12

Date.	Section.	Miles.
1892	Penzance to Truro (Mixed Gauge line), .	27¾
1892	Truro to Exeter, ...	106¼
1892	St Erth to St Ives, Truro to Falmouth, Burngallow to Drinnick Mill, Plymouth to Tavistock (Mixed Gauge), Tavistock to Launceston, Laira to Sutton Harbour, Totnes and Totnes Quay to Ashburton, Churston to Brixham, Newton Abbot to Kingswear, Newton Abbot to Moretonhampstead, . . .	92½

The Devon and Somerset Railway (Norton Fitzwarren to Barnstaple), 42¾ miles long, had a very short existence as a Broad Gauge line; it was only opened in November 1873, and converted in May 1881. There must have been something radically wrong in its management to allow of such a gigantic blunder being perpetrated. If it were necessary to build the railway Broad Gauge in 1873, why had it become necessary to alter its gauge seven and a half years later, while the line from which it branched remained the Broad Gauge until the final conversion in May 1892?

With such management it will not be surprising to learn, that of the entire capital raised on behalf of the Devon and Somerset Railway, amounting to some £1,390,000, considerably over one-third, or £512,000, represents arrears of debenture interest capitalised.

Even when the gauge of this line was altered, the Great Western Railway gave it no better service, and at the present time, with a difference of 3 miles in favour of the Great Western Railway route between London and Barnstaple, the best train on the London and South Western Railway, over a very much harder line, performs the journey in 25 minutes less time than the Great Western Railway's quickest train, thus,—

London and South Western Railway, 210½ miles; quickest train, 5 hours 30 minutes. Great Western Railway, 207½ miles; quickest train, 5 hours 55 minutes.

The Devon and Somerset Railway is now worked

and maintained by the Great Western Railway for 50 per cent. of the receipts. The agreement, which is perpetual, was entered into with the Bristol and Exeter Railway, and was made binding on the Great Western Railway by the Great Western and Bristol and Exeter Amalgamation Act, 1876.

CHAPTER XIX.

THE LATER DEVELOPMENT OF THE RAILWAY.

IN 1854, the Temple Meads joint station was laid down with Narrow Guage lines for the accommodation of the Midland Railway, who had in 1844 obained an entrance to Bristol by absorbing the Bristol and Gloucester Railway, then Broad Gauge, but soon after narrowed by the Midland. But two years earlier the Broad Gauge route to Birmingham had been opened by the completion of the line from Fenny Compton. The Great Western trains reached Birmingham in the same time as the London and North Western, although the route was 16 miles longer than the rival London and North Western.

In July of the following year the Great Western and its Broad Gauge allies sustained a great loss by the retirement from the chairmanship of Mr C. Russell, M.P. for Reading, and who had so ably forwarded the fortune of the 7 feet gauge by his energetic Parliamentary action, and the great personal interest he took in the details of the railway he had presided over for sixteen years. At this time the half-yearly meetings of shareholders used to be held alternately at London and Bristol, but for many years now past they have been all held in London.

The Great Western Railway shareholders were considerably agitated in 1856 as to the connection of Mr Gooch and other of their officials with the Ruabon Coal Company, and although full explanations were given at the time, the matter smouldered for many years, and when nothing of sufficient importance could be discovered with which to find fault, the grumblers promptly trotted out this 'old man of the sea.' We therefore extract from Sir D. Gooch's diaries the following lucid explanation of the whole matter :—'It had been found impossible to get a regular coal trade on our line, and I proposed to my company to have some collieries of their own, and went to Wrexham to look at those belonging to Mr Henry Robertson, and also some property of Sir Watkin W. Wynn's, where a colliery might be sunk. Having obtained the best information I could, I advised the Directors to buy up Robertson's works, as they were in operation and could be made available for our purpose at once. This was finally agreed upon by the Directors, and the price settled, but at this time a decision in regard to a similar plan in operation on the Eastern Counties Railway showed it not to be within the powers of the company, and stopped our plan. Mr Walpole, our Chairman, then asked me if I could find private parties to form a company, and enter into an agreement with the Great Western Company to send a large fixed quantity of coal over their line. This I agreed to do, and took a large stake in the coal company myself, and was to be the chairman. Feeling that this might conflict with my position as an officer of the railway company, I placed my resignation in the hands of Mr Walpole, but he and the Directors did not think it right to accept it. I, however, left it in their hands to accept at any time, should circumstances make it desirable.

'I felt there were interests in the coal trade amongst the shareholders of the railway who would no doubt object to what had been done, and such proved to be the case. Some parties went to the Court of Chancery to put an end to the agreement. In this they failed, and the Court expressed themselves strongly that what had been done was perfectly legal and right. I thus got a great deal of abuse by trying to do a good turn to the shareholders of the railway, and risking a good deal of money in doing so.'

The question of railway rates has been one which has exercised the traders on one hand, and railway officials and shareholders on the other, for very many years. As long ago as 1858 the Great Western ran amuck of its customers with regard to the legality of their charges for goods carriage, and in that year the railway introduced a Bill to Parliament to obtain a better definition of their powers, but the Bill was withdrawn, and again in 1881-82, when the celebrated Commission on railway rates was sitting, it was Mr Grierson, the late general manager of the Great Western Railway, who was the principal witness tendered by the associated railways, thus showing they considered the Great Western Railway to be the principal line. Some very interesting figures were given in evidence as to the amount of traffic dealt with by the Great Western Railway in twelve months at some of their stations. London was accredited with 657,000 tons (Paddington, 513,000 tons, and Smithfield 144,000 tons); Bristol, 495,000 tons; Birmingham, 250,000 tons; Bilston, 120,000 tons; Bath, 51,000 tons; and Evesham, 22,000 tons.

Mr Grierson died in October 1887, after being connected with the Broad Gauge railways for very many years. In May 1861, the Great Western Railway, upon the advice of Mr D. Gooch, put down plant at Swindon Works, for the purpose of making their own rails, at a cost of £25,000, but in 1878 the making of rails at Swindon was discontinued.

In 1853 a railway was incorporated as the North Metropolitan, the next year a new Act was obtained, and the title changed to the Metropolitan. This authorized the construction of a railway from the Great Western Railway at Paddington to the General Post Office; powers were afterwards obtained to allow the City terminus to be in Farringdon Street instead of the Post Office. The Great Western Railway sub-

scribed £175,000 of the capital, and for the convenience of that company's through traffic the
Metropolitan was laid out on the Mixed Gauge, and
when it was first opened it was worked on the Broad
Gauge only, by the Great Western Railway—a most
sensible arrangement, and one which ought never to
have been relinquished, seeing how well adapted the
wider vehicles are for conveying the immense crowds
that travel by every train on this line. With Broad
Gauge vehicles each train could seat 152 more passengers, or nearly 40,000 additional passengers could
be properly conveyed every day on this line without
any increase of expense. But the wonderful wisdom
of the advocates of the 'Coal Waggon Gauge' lost
London the great boon of having the most important
of its local lines Broad Gauge.

The Act of Incorporation specially provided that the
line was to be worked without annoyance from steam
or fire. At first it was proposed to heat the water
by means of red-hot bricks placed round the boiler,
and an eminent engineer designed such a locomotive,
which was built by a Newcastle firm ; but after £4000
had been expended in experimenting with this 'hot-
brick engine' it was given up as a failure, as the experiments that were made conclusively proved that
the bricks would have required replacing by fresh
ones at nearly every station, so soon would they have
cooled. But Mr D. Gooch was, as usual, in the van
of locomotive improvements, and in 1862 he designed
and built suitable tank engines for working this line.
By means of a specially-contrived fire-box and baffle
plate, the engines consumed their own smoke. With
regard to the blast, he fitted these engines with tanks
under the boiler, into which he discharged the waste
steam by reversing a valve at the bottom of the blast
pipe, so that when the engine was in an open cutting
she worked like any other engine ; but when in the
tunnel the blast was stopped, and a good ash-pan
damper destroyed the blast. For some reason or other

the Great Western Railway did not appear to try to work in harmony with the Metropolitan Company, and raised several difficulties, which did not tend to the smooth working of the traffic. The Great Western said it was not possible to work this underground system with less than 20 minutes' intervals between the trains; while the Metropolitan rightly contended that the trains could safely follow each other with but 5 minutes' intervals. The Great Western Company then agreed to run trains every quarter of an hour, and commenced to do so on 10th January 1863. At first the Great Western worked the Metropolitan, as many lines are now worked, for a percentage of the receipts, the working Company providing rolling stock and locomotives and station staff—in fact, everything but the line and stations. The then Directors of the Great Western Railway early foresaw that this underground line was sure to prove a most profitable one, and they therefore, having subscribed a part of the capital, and working the line as well, considered that they had the upper hand of the Metropolitan, and thought by putting pressure on them they would be enabled to get complete control of the line and absorb it into their own system; so acting on the advice of Sir Robert Baxter, their Parliamentary counsel, the Great Western gave the Metropolitan three months' notice that they would cease to work the line after 30th October 1863.

The Metropolitan Railway Directors, with commendable promptitude, got Narrow Gauge rolling stock and locomotives contracted for, to be delivered by that date. What the Great Western Railway did next, we are sorry to say, does not in any way tend to reflect credit on those who then controlled the policy of that company; for, to the astonishment of the Metropolitan Directors, they received notice from the Great Western Railway stating that their trains would cease to run over the Metropolitan lines after 9th August 1863. The second notice was only given on the 1st of August, and doubtless the majority of the then Great Western Directors thought by this *coup* the Metropolitan would be entirely at their mercy, and that the smaller line would be obliged to accept their terms of compromise, as not only were the trains to be withdrawn, but the Great Western threatened to withdraw the staff at all the stations as well, who were, of course, their servants.   In justice to the then Great Western Board, we mention that this latter threat they did not carry out; had they done so, there is little doubt that the Metropolitan would have been paralyzed for a time at least.   Our readers will perhaps think that there must have been some error in the agreement, which allowed the Great Western to act in this arbitrary manner, and so there was, for neither of the railway companies had affixed their seals to the working agreement, which was therefore of no more value than waste paper, and was binding on neither company.

This startling difficulty was, however, most successfully met by the energy and resource of Mr (now Sir) Myles Fenton, the then manager of the Metropolitan Company, who, at a few hours' notice, arranged for an emergency service of Narrow Gauge trains to commence running between Bishop's Road and Farringdon Street on the morning of 10th August. This he did by borrowing the passenger carriages from the London and North Western, and the locomotives from the Great Northern Railway.   These latter were old main line tender engines, and were not adapted for working the traffic ; but in cases like these, the maxim, ' If one cannot get what one wants one must take what one can get,' is a most useful one.

Sir Myles Fenton gave the writer a vivid account of these preparations.   For the whole nine nights between the date of the Great Western notice and the commencement of the Narrow Gauge trains he never had his clothes off, nor slept in a bed, but snatched an hour or so of repose in his office chair, as opportunity offered. The difficulty was to provide some kind of condensing apparatus on the Great Northern tender engines, it being necessary to use flexible connecting pipes between the engine and tender, strong enough to withstand the steam pressure; but Mr Sturrock, the then locomotive superintendent of the Great Northern Railway (to which line he came from the Great Western Railway), just two days before the Narrow Gauge service was to commence, was successful enough to contrive the necessary flexible pipes by which the exhaust steam was conveyed from the engine to the water tank of the tender, but these pipes very frequently burst, and all concerned were far from sorry when the proper engines were delivered.

Every evening, as soon as the Great Western service of trains for the day was over, the anxious officials were experimenting with the Great Northern tender engines, which experiments were carried on until the next morning's service commenced. This introduction of the Narrow Gauge on the Metropolitan was certainly made under rather inauspicious circumstances, for the Great Northern engine of almost the first train ran off the line soon after leaving Bishop's Road; while once during the day both an up and down train were off the lines at the same time at the Gower Street Station. In all, six trains ran off the line on this fateful 10th August. The reason for these derailments was not hard to find. On a line like the Metropolitan, the permanent way can only be attended to at night after the traffic is over, and while the line was worked Broad Gauge only, no attention was given to the packing of the middle rail, so that it was not properly ballasted, and therefore spread out when the trains went over it. Naturally these *contretemps* disorganised the service during the whole of the day. In fact, so alarming were the rumours of accidents to the Narrow Gauge trains, that at some of the stations the booking-clerks refused to issue tickets for a time. Luckily, the trains were soon got on the line again, and in a few days the service was working as regularly as if no sudden alterations had been made. Had the connecting line between the Great Northern and Metropolitan Railway at King's Cross, by which the Narrow Gauge rolling stock and locomotives gained access to the Metropolitan system, been in a less forward condition when the Great Western Railway so suddenly refused to work the underground trains, London would have been deprived of this newly-inaugurated means of conveyance which had already obtained an immense amount of public favour, and all because the Great Western officials were not allowed to do just as they liked with the Metropolitan Railway.

The remarkable acuteness of Sir Myles Fenton at this critical time secured the complete independence of the Metropolitan Railway, and the Great Western were repaid their £175,000 as soon as possible. The great tax of these nine busy days and nights told on Sir Myles Fenton, for after all was arranged the reaction came, and he was seriously ill for a month after.

The Metropolitan Directors at their next meeting passed a hearty vote of thanks to their energetic General Manager for the clever way in which he had overcome what threatened to be a serious episode in the history of their railway, and handsomely recognised his services at this critical period of the undertaking.

The Great Western Narrow Gauge engines built in later years for the Metropolitan traffic, and which are still working, are yet unequalled for quickly obtaining a good rate of speed and for sharp stopping, containing, as they do, all the requisites of good tank engines, and are eminently suited for the class of work, in addition to which their handsome exterior, with the profusion of bright brass work, at once marks them out for general admiration, especially when compared with the dingy monsters of other companies using the underground. A cab for the men's protection would be a great improvement to these Great Western engines. Having said so much in favour of the Great Western Narrow Gauge Metropolitan tanks, we are sorry we cannot say the same for the rolling stock that until recently formed the middle circle trains. It seemed as if the Great Western wished to give the London public a daily object lesson of the superiority of the Broad Gauge so far as passenger vehicles were concerned, and for this purpose provided some of the worst Narrow Gauge coaches possible, they were but 7 feet wide, and although the third-class ones were not labelled 'to seat five a side,' yet this being the usual number, five people usually squeezed on each side, with the result of general discomfort and mutual recrimination as to taking more than one's share of the allotted space; to meet the Government requirements these vehicles should have been 7 feet 6 inches wide. There was a space of but 18 inches between the seats, so that the passengers generally, and long-limbed ones in particular, had great difficulty in properly disposing of their legs. Unhappily placed was the individual (and his fellow-travellers also) who wished to alight from a seat near the off side in a full vehicle of this description.

The extension of the Metropolitan system to Hammersmith for some years after it was opened, was a source of considerable delay to the Great Western trains, as the two railways crossed one another on the level between Bishop's Road and Westbourne Park Stations, and as the Metropolitan trains amounted to sixteen an hour, the inconvenience was very great. To prevent these delays the Hammersmith line was diverted, and made to pass under the Great Western lines, so that the working of the services do not now interfere with each other. The Great Western Railway has recently provided very superior vehicles for their services on the Metropolitan system, and these trains are quite equal to any other third-class ones now in use. A noticeable part of their construction is the long wheel base of the third-class brake carriages, these vehicles having five wide passenger compartments and a guards' compartment; quite equal to the six compartments, and yet only have four wheels. There must therefore be a great strain on the axles, and it would appear to be unadvisable to run such vehicles at high speed. The Great Western Railway has also further augmented their Metropolitan services, by running trains from Aldgate to Hammersmith and Richmond in addition to the middle circle trains, and during the rebuilding of Moorgate Street Station the Great Western main line trains from the Metropolitan Railway also arrive and depart from Aldgate.

Upon the resignation of Mr Saunders in 1863, the dual office of secretary and general superintendent, which he had filled, were made two distinct positions.

To show how completely the Great Western kept aloof from its Narrow Gauge neighbours, at this time (1863) it was only connected with the London and South Western at Yeovil by a line then recently opened, and with the London and North Western at Oxford, Banbury and Leamington.

In September 1864 Mr D. Gooch retired from the Great Western Railway after twenty-seven years service, and Mr Armstrong was appointed locomotive superintendent, which position the latter held until his death in June 1877.

When it became known that Mr Gooch had determined to retire, the officers and servants of the railway made preparations to present him with an address, and Mrs Gooch with a present. The presentations took place at Swindon, on 3d June 1865, and Mr Gooch thus feelingly alludes to the occasion :—' I hope those who succeed me will value that address more than anything I can leave behind me, and also preserve the brooch and earrings as heirlooms in the family for ever. Man can receive no higher reward on earth than that of the goodwill and esteem of those with whom he has been associated through life, and my life has been passed in daily communication, both as master and brother officer, with those who gave expression to their feelings on this occasion. I count this 3d of June as the brightest day in my life.'

1865 saw the completion of the Broad Gauge to Milford Haven, and a few years later the Great Western services of steamboats to the Irish ports were inaugurated.

The Channel Islands service from Weymouth is now worked by the Great Western Railway and under the present improved management is gaining greatly in public favour.

The advantage of the Weymouth route to the Channel Islands is the short sea passage, the distance to Jersey being only 112 miles, against 160 from Southampton ; but against this advantage is the long time spent on the railway journey of 168 miles from London to Weymouth, while under the old conditions there was also the inconvenience and expense of a conveyance from the railway station to the steamer.

The Great Western could certainly save an hour in the railway journey to Weymouth. Already there is one train doing the distance in 4 hours 5 minutes (which is only $41\frac{1}{4}$ miles an hour), while the boat express takes 4 hours 55 minutes. If the trains ran *viâ* the Berks and Hants line, the distance would only be 160 miles, and the 10-minute refreshment stop at Swindon would be saved also ; then, the journey ought to be easily done in $3\frac{1}{2}$ hours.

The service used to be performed six days a week in each direction during the summer, three times weekly in the autumn and spring, and but twice a week during the winter months. The boats used to be paddle-wheel steamers belonging to the Weymouth and Channel Islands Steamship Company. These boats were originally built of wood, but, when repairs were necessary, iron was used to replace the wood, so that, after many years of this system of repair, the original fabric disappeared, and the boats became iron steamships.   As long as the steamers belonged to an independent company, the Great Western Railway took no pains to develop the traffic.

The last train for Weymouth used to leave Paddington at 5.45 P.M., and in the summer the boat left Weymouth at 11.15 P.M., soon after the train arrived.   But the difficulty and danger of entering Guernsey Harbour except in daylight caused the departure of the steamer from Weymouth to be delayed till 2.15 A.M. during the winter, and so prolonged the time spent *en route ;* while the same difficulty at Guernsey made it necessary for the return voyage to be made in the morning. For some summers, the Weymouth company's boats left Jersey at 5 P.M., and were still able to clear from Guernsey before darkness set in, but this meant an uncomfortable stay in Weymouth for several hours in the early morning, while, by the usual day service, passengers always had to spend a night there.   During the latter years of its existence, the steamboat company only managed to struggle on by the help afforded by the Great Western Railway, and matters were hastened to a conclusion by the loss of the ' Brighton,' which struck on the rocks near Guernsey in the uncertain light of a winter's morning.   This accident reduced the fleet to two ships, and for the 1887 summer traffic the Great Western Railway assisted with a third boat, the ' Great Western,' one of their New Milford boats engaged in the Irish service.

We visited Jersey that year, leaving there at 10 A.M.   We arrived at Weymouth about 9 P.M., and, of course, had to spend the night there.   The next day at Swindon we saw a fellow-passenger, who was travelling third class, give the officials at that junction a lesson as to the rights of the third-class passengers. This passenger left Weymouth about 3.30 P.M., arrived at Swindon about 6.15—this was in the days before third-class passengers were conveyed by all trains of the Great Western—and the next up train from Swindon was the West of England express at 6.42 P.M., due at Paddington at 8.10.   By the Great Western official time-table, third-class passengers from Weymouth were due at Paddington at 9.40 P.M., while the next third-class train from Swindon left at 8.20, and arrived in London at 10.20.   The officials told him he must wait for this train, but he saw a third-class coach being added to the rear of the express, and he took his seat in it.   The ticket-collector wanted him to come out, saying, 'the coach was slipped at Didcot, and it was only for the convenience of passengers travelling to Birmingham and the Midlands generally,' but the gentleman refused to leave, and the station-master was fetched.   This official fumed, threatened, and was about to summon help to carry out the ejectment, when the knowing traveller produced the Great Western Railway official time-book, showing he was due at Paddington at 9.40.   This took the station-master by surprise, and after considering, he said, ' All right ; change from this slip coach at Didcot,' and he gave instructions that Weymouth line passengers were in future to be allowed to travel by the slip to Didcot, and so arrived there before the 5.40 from Swindon, which used to shunt on the way to allow the express to pass.   So the knowing passenger triumphed, and arrived in London by the 9.40 P.M.

After the ' Brighton' struck on the rocks off Guernsey and foundered, the ' Aquila' and 'Cygnus,' the two boats of the Weymouth Company, were fitted with gear and dials indicating the number of revolutions performed by the paddles, so that the officers might know something of the ship's position when ordinary observations were impossible, and so prevent a similar mishap.   When the Great Western took over the steamers, these two boats were sold, and one now sails between Plymouth and the Channel Islands, while the other is used for pleasure excursions at Llandudno. At first the Great Western provided three large screw steamers, the 'Gazelle,' 'Lynx,' and 'Antelope,' built a passenger station on the landing-stage at Weymouth, and started a special boat-express from Paddington at 9.15 P.M., running direct to the steamer, which left at 2.20 A.M. The sea passage was accelerated, Guernsey being reached in about 5 hours, and including the wait to unload cargo there, Jersey in about $7\frac{1}{2}$ hours. By this means passengers were landed in Jersey in about $12\frac{1}{2}$ hours, or in less time than by the London and South Western route. But swifter boats were again provided by that company, performing the sea trip to Jersey in about $9\frac{1}{2}$ hours, or the whole journey under 12 hours. The London and South Western 'Lydia' was, in 1890, the fastest ship in existence. Upon trial her quickest run was at the rate of $24\frac{1}{2}$ statute miles per hour, and the average of four trips $22\frac{1}{2}$ miles an hour. But the Great Western could not allow of being second in the race, and a new twin-screw ship, the 'Ibex,' was built, which has, on several occasions, covered the $82\frac{1}{4}$ miles between Guernsey and Weymouth in $3\frac{1}{2}$ hours, or an average speed of $23\frac{1}{2}$ miles an hour for the whole voyage. By this accelerated service Guernsey was reached in $9\frac{1}{2}$ hours, and Jersey in $11\frac{3}{4}$ hours from London by the Great Western Railway.

This summer (1894) excursion tickets were issued by both routes, available by the boat trains on Saturday night, to return in 8, 10, 15, or 17 days, at a return fare of 24s. 6d., third class.

With regard to the improvement of the service, the Great Western (which made the first move) had the better arrangements—namely, separate steamers to and from both Guernsey and Jersey, with an independent vessel for the local traffic between the two islands, by means of which visitors staying at Jersey can make a trip to Guernsey and back the same day, instead of having to spend a night as formerly. But the London and South Western work their improved service more economically, by having the same passenger steamer to and from both islands, and a separate one for conveying cargo. It was the time taken *en route* at Guernsey in loading and unloading cargo that formerly made the voyage to Jersey so long. Thus the Great Western advertised the sea passage to Guernsey as 4½ hours, and Guernsey and Jersey 1½ hours, but the total time *en voyage*—Weymouth to Jersey—was not 6 hours, but, including the detention at Guernsey, 7 to 8 hours.

The Great Western has also given its Jersey passengers another concession. At low water the steamers cannot enter the harbour at St Heliers, and upon such occasions passengers both embarking and disembarking were put to the expense and inconvenience of engaging a row-boat to take them to or from the steamers ; the Great Western now provides this service gratis.

The tables below show the improvements in the services this summer :—

		June.	1894.	July.	
Paddington,	depart,	9.15 P.M.		9.15 P.M.	
Weymouth,	arrive,	2.10 A.M.		2.0 A.M.	
Weymouth,	depart,	2.20 ,,		2.10 ,,	2.30 A.M.
Guernsey, .	arrive,	6.45 ,,		7.0 ,,	
Jersey, .	,,	9.0 ,,			8.0 ,,
Jersey, .	depart,	8.30 A.M.		9.30 A.M.	
Guernsey, .	,,	10.30 ,,			10.45 ,,
Weymouth,	arrive,	3.0 P.M.		3.30	3.15 P.M.
Paddington,	,,	7.45 ,,		7.45 P.M.	

The up passengers were conveyed from Weymouth Landing Stage to Swindon by a special train running as soon after the arrival of the steamers as possible, from Swindon they travelled to London by the express due at Paddington at 7.45 P.M.

During the winter months the service, as shown above for June, has been reverted to.

THE BOURTON DISASTER, 1876.

(The Broad Gauge carriages did not leave the metals.)

While mentioning excursion facilities, it will not be out of place to notice the arrangements made in the summer of 1894, whereby passengers could travel every Saturday to North Wales and spend a week or fortnight there at very cheap fares. These excursions are on the same plan as those to the West of England, which have been popular for so many years.

In February 1874 a most serious collision occurred in the fog at West Drayton, between the up 'Flying Dutchman' (drawn by 'Prometheus') and a goods train which was stationary. Had it happened on the Standard Gauge, the results would have been most appalling, but thanks to the wide base of the vehicles, the express never left the line, and only the guard lost his life in consequence of the tender of his train being hurled on to the 'cab' of its locomotive and being caught by a passing engine and thrown back on a contingent van.

Our personal reminiscence of this disastrous collision was, at the time, not of a pleasant nature. In those days the useful postal order had not been invented, and small remittances sent by post were usually made by means of postage stamps. We had an uncle who used to keep the feast of St Valentine in a very practical way, by remitting his nephews at school, postage stamps on the anniversary of that saint's day. Our school was situated a few miles from West Drayton, and instead of the mail bag containing our letter being safely deposited in the apparatus near the station, it was shot into the canal, so that when we received the letter, the stamps were all stuck together, and it was a matter of some difficulty negotiating to obtain in exchange for them a sum anywhere near their full value.

While we are on the subject of collisions on the Broad Gauge, we take the opportunity of remarking, upon the well-established fact, that although the trains were heavier and travelling at much higher speeds than Narrow Gauge trains under similar circumstances, yet the consequences on the Broad Gauge were always much less disastrous in consequence of the wider gauge giving greater stability to the trains, which generally did not even leave the metals, as instance the accident near Langley in 1845, referred to in a previous chapter, that at Bullo in 1868, and Bourton in 1876, where only the driver and fireman were killed.   On 26th November 1852, a down express, drawn by the ' Lord of the Isles,' ran at full speed into a train shunting across its path at Heyford.   Again only the driver was killed, and the engine did not leave the metals.   Yet·again in November 1890, a special passenger train, conveying the Cape mail from Plymouth to London, worked by a Bristol and Exeter tank engine, No. 2051, but which had been rebuilt and a tender added, collided with the engine of a Narrow Gauge goods train at Norton Fitzwarren, near Taunton.   The goods train was stationary, while the express was travelling at 60 miles an hour, yet neither the engine nor any of the coaches left the rails.   Through the unfortunate forgetfulness of the signalman, ten passengers lost their lives on this occasion, but had a van been next the engine, as should have been the case, no loss of life would probably have resulted.

Many years ago, a van at the tail of a goods train got off the metals near Reading, ran along the longitudinal sleepers for 5 miles, and then righted itself at a level crossing.   The engine driver was unaware of the mishap, until, in consequence of the report of some platelayers who saw the occurrence, the line was examined and the indentations on the timber caused by the wheels were observed.

In 1847 an extraordinary accident happened to the Exeter express—the ' crack' train of those days—when passing Southall, one of the driving wheel tyres of the ' Queen' engine broke.   A piece flew in the air and descended upon a down train, killing two cattle drovers in it, whilst another piece threw the down train off the rails.   Although he had to cross a high embank-

THE NORTON FITZWARREN COLLISION.

Narrow Gauge Goods Locomotive No. 1100 charged *vis-à-vis* by Broad Gauge Express Engine No. 2051.

ment and the Brent Viaduct, the driver of the 'Queen' went on to the next station (Hanwell), where he examined his engine, and proceeded to Paddington minus the tyre. The last accident to a Broad Gauge train happened to the 2.15 up express on 14th May 1892. As the train was passing over the points of Lipson Junction, near Plymouth, the axle of the engine broke, and although the train was travelling down an incline at high speed, fortunately none of the carriages were derailed, although, of course, the engine left the line.

While any old Broad Gauge driver was always able to give his own experience of accidents that happened to himself, which were far more miraculous than the cases previously narrated by his *confrères*, but as most of these accidents never obtained official publicity, we only accept them *cum grano salis.*

Most travellers can give an account of some one or another remarkable journey they have performed, but few, we think, can equal the experience of a poor man who arrived in a most exhausted and dirty condition at Swindon, having ridden from Paddington underneath one of the coaches of a fast train bound for the West of England. He was discovered at Swindon lying across the brake rods, on which he hoped to have made his journey home as far as Bristol. Being out of work and penniless, his appearance caused great excitement and pity amongst the passengers, who made a collection for the unfortunate man to enable him to complete his journey in a more comfortable way.

Another remarkable case of railway travelling on the Great Western Railway was the involuntary journey, or rather series of journeys, performed in January 1877, half a dozen children, each about ten years of age, were charged before the Bristol magistrates with having travelled without taking their tickets or paying their fares on the Great Western Railway in the truck of a goods train for three days and three nights. It was found that they had been playing in the goods station yard at Plymouth when a guard shouted to them, and they became so frightened that they hid themselves in one of the trucks. Keeping very quiet, so as not to be detected, they fell asleep. During the night the truck was attached to a goods train which was being formed for Penzance. The train then started without anyone knowing that the stowaways were there. The truck was shunted when the train reached Truro in the night, and there the urchins woke up, and being much frightened, they stole out of the station and tried to walk back towards Plymouth. They had only gone a short way when the rain came down in torrents, and so drenched them that they determined to go back to the railway station, where, unobserved, they got into another covered truck which they thought would take them back to Plymouth. This truck was booked through to Bristol with a load of general goods ; it was consequently not shunted at Plymouth, but with numerous delays and shuntings in the course of the goods traffic *en route* it arrived at Bristol. The urchins slept a good deal of the time, but were so exhausted when discovered that three or four of them could not stand. They soon recovered under the attention they received, but appeared in the most bewildered state of mind. They were taken to the police station and cared for during the night. Their names and addresses were telegraphed to Plymouth, and the Plymouth police discovered that inquiries had been made at the police station for two or three of the little travellers, and their parents were in great distress at their loss. The magistrates expressed their astonishment that the boys' hunger had not caused them to declare themselves. They were eventually dismissed, the bench expressing the opinion that it was hardly a case of fraud.

At Christmas 1880, the Paddington Station was lighted by the electric light on the Brush system, this was a forward step indeed, seeing how little this method of illumination was then in vogue.

Most of us have personal experiences of a very unpleasant kind in connection with the tremendous snow storms of January 1881, but although all the railways suffered severely, the Great Western far the worst. At the meeting of shareholders in February, Mr Gooch gave them the following account of the difficulties experienced on the line :—'We had every reason up to the middle of January to anticipate that we might have been able to offer the shareholders a dividend in excess of what they had previously received, but you all know in the middle of January a snowstorm occurred, the first we have had in the history of this railway to interfere with our traffic, and wiped off something like £56,000 of the amount available for dividend. Had we had that £56,000 in our pockets, we should have been able to give you from a half to three-quarters per cent. more dividend than we are now doing. We did not make the storm, we did our best under the circumstances, so I hope you will all be satisfied that the 5 per cent. we now offer you is as much as we could reasonably be expected to give. There is no doubt that the storm was much more severe on our line than on any other. Its great weight fell in the counties of Berks, Wilts, and down towards Weymouth and that district. We had to excavate 111 miles of snow, varying according to the drift from 3 feet down to 10 feet in depth. We had, unfortunately, fifty-one passenger trains and thirteen goods trains buried in the snow, making a total of sixty-four, and we had blocks on one hundred and forty-one different parts of the system. Great credit is due to the skill and zeal of our officers, and not only to the officers but to every man engaged in the service for accomplishing what they did. They had a very difficult service to perform, and we had no accident to any person during the whole period.'

In October 1882 the Teign Valley Railway, a Narrow Gauge line, was opened ; it was the first Narrow Gauge branch on the South Devon Railway, and was a shadow of the complete narrow gauging of the Great Western which took place nearly ten years later.

In 1886 the superintendent of the line (Mr Tyrrell) retired; he had been with the Great Western for forty-six years, and it is really remarkable how long-lived the old Great Western officials were, and how intensely they believed in the undoubted advantage of the Broad Gauge. Mr Higgins, the secretary, died just before the final conversion, and Mr Mills, the present secretary, was appointed 16th May 1892, so that he may claim the proud honour of being the last of the Broad Gauge officials, for had the appointment taken place a few days later, the Great Western Railway would have then been an ordinary Narrow Gauge line. In 1894, Mr Burlinson, the then superintendent of the line, retired after fifty years' service.

On 1st October 1890, the Great Western fell into line with the other great railways, and commenced to carry third-class passengers by all trains, although it was not until 1st July 1894 that third class, as distinguished from Parliamentary fares, were abolished on the system, and third-class passengers were carried by all trains at 1d. per mile. In the early days of railways, besides the opposition of landowners and the general public, these companies had also to fight against two other opponents, and these were the most determined and aggressive of all those who battled against the introduction and extension of railways; the resistance of these two was the more bitter and relentless, since it was patent that if the railways were successful, then the utility of the stage coach and canal would be most materially decreased. The stage coaches more easily succumbed to the railway attack, since, in most cases, they were but single proprietors fighting against a powerful combination of capital, and the travelling public soon perceived the great superiority of railway travelling as compared with the stage coach.   But with regard to the · canal companies, the case was different; these were themselves huge and wealthy corporations in possession of immense capital and enjoying a valuable and lucrative monopoly, which was guarded by a number of Parliamentary protections which almost freed them from competition in the carrying of merchandise, while the income derived from the various canals was so large that no railway ever has, nor ever can hope, to pay a rate of interest at all commensurate with those paid by canal companies before the introduction of railways.   The magnitude of these annual dividends can, in a measure be gauged when we mention that, in 1846, and in the face of railway competition, the dividends paid by the following canals were :—Duke of Bridgewater, 30 per cent. ; Trent and Mersey, 30 per cent. ; Oxford, 26 per cent. ; Coventry, 25 per cent. ; and Old Birmingham, 16 per cent. ; while the average railway dividend for the same year, 1846, was only £13, 12s. 4¼d., per cent.   Therefore it is not at all surprising to find that the fights between the old water carriers and the new steam ones were of so severe and unyielding a nature, since the former had everything to lose and the latter all to gain, if only the railways were allowed to be constructed.   The railway companies were, however, no match for the already established canal proprietors, so that they were compelled to enter into some kind of arrangements with the companies owning the canals, and these latter were shrewd enough to foresee that the defeat of the railway schemes was but of a temporary nature, and that in a few years at most, railways would be constructed over the country in all directions ; therefore they took advantage of the railway companies' desire to commence construction without delay by arranging with them to purchase the canals, and in this way they were enabled to sell their concerns at a good price, and secure themselves, knowing that if they did not do so, when the railways were willing to buy off their opposition, in a few years the railways would refuse to purchase their undertakings, and possibly they would be left with costly works to maintain which would produce but a small income. By this means the Great Western Railway Company became possessed of a considerable canal mileage to the evident satisfaction of the original canal proprietors, while, doubtless, our legislators considered that they had well guarded against a monopoly in the carriage of goods by requiring the railway companies to maintain these canals in a suitable condition for the conveyance of traffic at the scheduled charges. So far from this arrangement being of any utility, it has become a source of great loss to the railway and of not the slightest advantage to the public; therefore, as soon as such an anomalous system is put an end to so much the better will it be for all concerned.

The Great Western Railway Company is owner of the following canals:—Bridgewater and Taunton, Great Western, Kennett and Avon, Monmouthshire, Stourbridge Extension, Stratford-on-Avon, and Swansea. The *bête noir* of the Great Western Railway Company's canals is the Kennett and Avon, along the side of which the Berks and Hants line is constructed. This canal was authorised by Acts 34, 36, 38, 41, and 45 of George III., and its general direction is from west to east for a distance of 55½ miles in Somerset, Wilts, and Berkshire. When the Great Western Railway was opened to Bath and Bristol, this canal was a competitive route for goods traffic between those places and London, so that the purchase of it was considered to be advantageous to the interests of the Great Western Railway. We are not aware of the indirect benefits derived by the railway shareholders by the acquisition of this canal, but the direct loss they incur yearly in the working of the undertaking is very considerable.

The deserted appearance of this canal is notorious ; in fact, the sight of a barge upon its waters is an almost rare event. To make matters still worse, the Great Western Railway Company not only maintain the canal, but also a railway—the Berks and Hants line—which, as we have already stated, for a considerable distance runs side by side with the canal. The railway itself can scarcely be a prosperous one, as, although some 60 miles in length, it has but four down and five up through trains daily, besides four local ones each way, none of the towns on it being of much importance. The company, however, hope, when the new lines from Woodborough to Westbury, and from Castle Cary to Athelney are completed, to make use of the Berks and Hants line for the express traffic to the West of England, as this route will then be 19 miles shorter than the present way *viâ* Swindon and Bristol ; while the distance between London and Westbury, Frome, and the other stations on the Weymouth branch, will be lessened to the same extent, so that the competition with the London and South Western Railway will be very considerably increased. The single portions of the line will, however, require doubling before any practical use can be made of the route for through express traffic. Yet what a great saving of capital would have resulted had the Berks and Hants line been constructed along the course of the useless Kennett and Avon Canal, instead of as an independent adjacent route. There is the faint hope that in the far future, when the traffic on this section of the Great Western system has increased so much that the present line is incapable of carrying it all, that the canal will then be utilised, like so many others have been, by being converted into a railway. We fear, however, this is looking very far ahead.

CHAPTER XX.

THE FINAL CONVERSION.

'TO-DAY'S ARRANGEMENTS.—The Great Western Railway substitute the Narrow for the Broad Gauge.'—(*Daily Telegraph, 21st May* 1892.)

THE partisans of the Narrow Gauge always professed that sooner or later the Broad Gauge must give way to the Narrow Gauge; but, somehow, although they always expected this event to happen in the near future, it was a very long time before their opinions were verified. After the battle of 1845-46 they expected an immediate conversion; but, not only was the Narrow Gauge party signally disappointed, but year by year the Broad Gauge lines increased in mileage and also in power until, in 1867, the Broad Gauge lines had reached the important total of 1456 miles, with no less than 700 locomotives of the 7 feet gauge. In London, with Paddington as headquarters, the Broad Gauge trains were found at Kensington, Moorgate, and even Victoria (one half of which station is jointly leased by the London, Chatham and Dover and Great Western Railways); but years ago the Broad Gauge rail had been removed from the Metropolitan Railway, the West London line, and the Great Western route to Victoria *viâ* Clapham and the London and South Western. But at this time, when at its zenith, and with the voices of the Narrow Gauge adherents almost silenced from hope deferred, as narrated in a previous chapter, the change commenced, and no doubt the Great Western Railway shareholders were ready to change any and everything in the hope of improving their dividend, well-knowing that, come what might, they could not be worse off, and by the change their position might be improved; for while the Great Western Railway was paying a dividend of but 1⅞ per cent., its neighbours, the London and South Western on one side, the London and North Western on the other, were returning their shareholders 4⅝ per cent. and 6 per cent. respectively. So the various changes, as already chronicled, were duly carried out; and when almost everybody had nearly forgotten the probability of the Great Western Railway ever changing the gauge of its main line, early in 1891 it began to be whispered round the railway world that the Directors of the 'Sleepy Giant' were seriously considering the advisability of a complete withdrawal of the Broad Gauge. From being whispered in railway circles it soon became a matter of public speculation. The then recent death of Sir Daniel Gooch, the last of the Broad Gauge pioneers, gave a *raison d'être* for the change, for while he was the nominal head of the Great Western system, it was not likely that the complete rejection of the Broad Gauge would be seriously entertained at all. But, in the spring of 1891, it was officially announced that this great engineering feat would be accomplished on 21st and 22d May 1892, and for a year the railway and engineering papers were constantly giving particulars, more or less correct, of how the conversion was to be carried out. At the half-yearly meeting of the Great Western shareholders, held on 11th February 1892, Mr F. G. Saunders, the Chairman, preached the funeral sermon, as he called it, of the Broad Gauge. We extract the following from this 'sermon':—'With regard to the gauge he need not tell them a long story. It was unfortunately left to the Board of 1892 to carry out the abolition of the Broad Gauge on their system. It was a matter of regret that the time had nearly arrived when that should be done; but they had for many years past made preparations for that which they knew was imminent. The alteration at Exeter from the Broad to the Narrow Gauge was a very large and serious operation, and involved a great deal of preparation. . . . More than three-fourths of their passenger stock was already constructed so as to be ready to be convertible from the Broad to the Narrow Gauge. He was of opinion that the Broad Gauge would have been more suited to the comfort of the travelling public, who now required dining and sleeping saloons and other luxuries such as could be obtained at West End Clubs.'

The following is the opening stanza of a poetical history of the Broad Gauge written by one of the numerous Broad Gauge enthusiasts :—

> ' The fiat's gone forth that the giants of yore,
> The sires that gave breath to the Dutchman's loud roar,
> Shall be buried in life, and they've tolled the death knell
> Of the noble creations of Gooch and Brunel.
> We mourn for thy death, dear old Broad Gauge and sigh
> For the exquisite forms which were balm to the eye;
> Creations superb of a far-seeing brain,
> No more shall we look on your equals again.'

That the inhabitants of the Broad Gauge districts firmly believed in the undoubted superiority of the 7 feet gauge is unquestionable, and the public opinion of the locality is well expressed in a series of articles which appeared in the leading West of England paper at the time of the final conversion. We extract the following from these interesting articles :—

' Sentiment is often more potent than argument, and it is not without some pangs of regret that Devon and Cornwall have bid adieu to their old friend and ally the Broad Gauge. By the hour when these lines meet the eyes of our readers every Broad Gauge engine, carriage and truck will have been removed beyond the limits of the western counties, most of them being destined for Swindon, either to be there converted into Narrow Gauge vehicles or to be broken up. So much of comfort and celerity has for many years been associated in the minds of travellers with these ponderous and substantial carriages that it will be long before the older portion of the travelling public will fully reconcile themselves to the Narrow Gauge. The Broad Gauge was doomed, not through any deficiency, but rather in spite of its superiority, and in order to facilitate the transit of commercial produce by a uniformity of gauge. There being a greater mileage of Narrow than Broad Gauge the latter was necessarily the one to give way, though even in the present day Brunel's contention would be widely echoed :—" I believe we travel much quicker at the same cost and with more ease, and certainly the wear and tear of the carriages is very much less with us than with the other lines."

'Although engineering talent has been concentrated on improving Narrow Gauge engines, and the Broad Gauge locomotives have been allowed to rest on their laurels of past days, the average speeds per hour for various Narrow Gauge engines on the great lines between London and their first stopping places are respectively :—Great Northern, 51.88 miles ; Midland, 51.78 ; and the London and North-Western, 49.15. Compare these speeds with that of the Great Western Railway. The Broad Gauge express (on the improvement of which the engineer has lavished no pains in recent years), which leaves Paddington for Penzance at 10.15 A.M., maintains an average speed of 53.28 miles as far as Swindon. This will bear comparison even with the 54.1 miles per hour of the Great Northern, Manchester and Sheffield express. In face of such facts it were foolish to argue that the ' Battle of the Gauges ' has been decided on merit :—

'It is a curious fact that there is no scientific theory to support the adoption of the 4 feet 8½ inches, or Narrow Gauge, in preference to any other measurement. On the other hand, much has been, and can still be, said in favour of the Broad Gauge of Isambard Brunel, since the gauge determines the width across each pair of wheels of the engines and carriages, and, to a certain extent, the width of the engines and carriages themselves. It is patent that increased width of gauge must give more room for the play of the machinery of the engine, and for the comfortable accommodation of the passengers. Upon a Broad Gauge line—7 feet—carriages measuring 10 feet 6 inches across are run, whilst Narrow Gauge carriages are but 8 feet 6 inches. West Country people have found the Broad Gauge exceedingly comfortable, and they naturally regret its extinction. Travelling was done with smoothness and speed. The speed was in advance of other lines for years; but since the Broad Gauge was doomed, the development of engines of this class has not been continued, else we should ere this be travelling 80 miles per hour instead of 60 miles, so engineers tell us. It is also worth noting that Brunel's rails, bolted down to wood, running longitudinally, has proved the safest road, perhaps, all the world over. The West of England has consequently gained no notoriety by reason of frequent accidents: especially is this the case with reference to express trains. No accidents with grave fatal results have ever happened to the " Flying Dutchman," the " Cornishman," or " Zulu "'

We purpose to sub-divide this chapter under four heads—(*a*) The traffic arrangements; (*b*) The conversion of the line; (*c*) The conversion of the rolling stock; (*d*) The result of the conversion.

(*a*) THE TRAFFIC ARRANGEMENTS.

These were of a most extensive character, a special pamphlet clearly defining the running of the trains west of Exeter before, during, and immediately after the conversion was issued for the use of the public, while, for the guidance of the staff, a handbook of fifty-five 8vo pages was issued on 30th April 1892 containing

'GENERAL INSTRUCTIONS
FOR THE USE OF THE COMPANY'S SERVANTS
IN CONNECTION WITH THE
CONVERSION OF THE MAIN LINE
FROM
BROAD TO NARROW GAUGE
BETWEEN
EXETER AND TRURO,
AND OF
THE FOLLOWING BRANCHES—

Newton Abbot	to Moretonhampstead.
Newton Abbot	to Kingswear.
Churston	to Brixham.
Totnes and Totnes Quay	to Ashburton.
Laira Junction	to Sutton Harbour.
Lidford	to Launceston.
Burngallow	to Drinnick Mill.
Truro	to Falmouth.
St Erth	to St Ives.

The Conversion will take place on

SATURDAY AND SUNDAY, 21st and 22d MAY 1892.

During which days these lines will be entirely closed for traffic purposes.'

The goods traffic for stations west of Exeter began to be refused as early as 7th May, and continued to be so until the 25th, but goods traffic from Broad Gauge Stations was received up to 17th. The London and South Western Railway took compassion on its life-long rival during the conversion, and arranged to convey Great Western traffic to and from Plymouth over its system between that place and Exeter, where it was transferred to the Great Western Narrow Gauge line. Although no down Broad Gauge goods trains were run west of Exeter after the departure of the 7.30 A.M. on 18th May, the Broad Gauge engines and brakes were worked down according to time table for the purpose of bringing back the enormous amount of Broad Gauge vehicles to be brought off the lines about to be converted. Some of the fish merchants at Penzance nearly lost their

market on the Friday, the catch had been exceptionally heavy, and as the merchants knew the
supply of fish trucks was very low (only sufficient
having been kept back to form the ordinary 12.35
P.M. up fish), there was a general rush and hurry
to the station to secure accommodation, 'first come,
first served,' being the order.   After a deal of difficulty the whole consignment was duly loaded, but
not a single Broad Gauge vehicle remained over.
About 2000 empty Broad Gauge trucks were worked
from off the West Cornwall line during the first
half of the conversion week, and as not more than
16 trucks are allowed for any one train over one
portion, the traffic over the Cornwall and South
Devon lines was pretty brisk.   While the west
county lines were thus engaged in sending out its
Broad Gauge stock, London was not behindhand, for,
on Thursday night, 19th May, the sidings at Swindon must have been pretty full, as a special of twenty-
eight trucks (Broad Gauge), and two engines, which
left London at 9.20, were sent to Didcot instead of
Swindon as previously arranged.

Coming to the passenger trains, the last through
Broad Gauge one to leave Paddington was the 'Cornishman,' on Friday, 20th May.   The terminus was
all bustle and excitement as soon as daylight dawned
on this eventful morning, the most unobservant person could not fail to notice a curious and unusual
expression on the countenances of the railway
officials from the highest to the lowest, who seemed
to be gathering on the platforms in increasing numbers, and as the morning wore on these were joined
by a large number of the general public, many
of whom certainly had not prepared for a railway
journey.   Then 'gentlemen of the press' were unmistakably *en evidence*, artists were not wanting in the
increasing crowd, while photographers—amateurs and
professionals—were well represented, and so matters
went on until the 'Cornishman' was drawn up at the

departure platform, when the suppressed excitement began to be openly expressed, reporters were trying to get hold of all and every official who appeared likely to be willing to impart any information as to the proceedings, while the guards, driver and fireman were each surrounded by small crowds of curious, sympathising and inquiring individuals, who came to pay their last respects to the expiring 7 feet gauge. No little excitement was caused among the mourners by the premature departure of the train, but after journeying a few yards it was brought to a standstill, and inquiry showed that it was solely for the benefit of photographers that this forward movement was made.

As the hands of the clock showed that the time of departure was near at hand, it appeared as if every employé at Paddington Station were congregated on the various platforms to see the 'Cornishman' depart. Among the officials could be distinguished Viscount Emlyn, the Deputy Chairman of the Company, and Mr Hubbard, another Director. While Colonel Edgcumbe, another Director, and Mr Lambert, the General Manager, travelled through to Penzance. Punctually to time the famous 'Great Britain,' rebuilt in 1888, started on this fateful career—the train consisted of seven bogie coaches, and the last through Broad Gauge train glided out of the station amid the cheers of passengers and spectators. As the last van passed the platform, the veteran guard, who had travelled thousands and thousands of miles in Broad Gauge trains, leaned his head out of the window and cried,— 'One cheer all together for the last.' This brought forth what is called a 'rouser.'

The following is the timing of this train to Swindon :—

	h.	m.	s.			h.	m.	s.
Paddington, dep., .	10	15	0	Castle Hill,	.	10	26	4
Westbourne, pass.,.	10	18	15	Hanwell,	.	10	27	3
2 mile post, .	10	19	45	Southall.	.	10	29	20
Acton, .	10	22	53	Hayes, .	.	10	31	50
Ealing, .	10	24	55	West Drayton,	.	10	34	43

T

	h.	m.	s.		h.	m.	s.
Langley,	10	38	15	48 mile post,	11	16	55
Slough,	10	40	55	52 ,, ,,	11	21	20
19 mile post,	10	41	35	Didcot,	11	22	30
Taplow,	10	45	50	54 mile post,	11	23	40
Maidenhead, .	10	48	10	56 ,, ,,	11	26	5
24½ mile post,	10	48	45	Steventon,	11	26	50
26 ,, ,,	10	50	20	58 mile post, .	11	28	30
26½ ,, ,,	10	51	10	60 ,, ,,	11	30	45
27¾ ,, ,,	10	52	55	61 mile post,	11	31	55
28¼ ,, ,,	10	53	30	62 ,, ,,	11	33	4
29¼ ,, ,,	10	54	46	63 ,, ,,	11	34	7
30 ,, ,,	10	55	46	65 ,, ,,	11	36	40
Twyford,	10	57	5	66 ,, ,,	11	37	55
32 mile post,	10	58	30	68 ,, ,,	11	40	55
Reading,	11	3	20	70 ,, ,,	11	42	25
Tilehurst,	11	6	10	71 ,, ,,	11	43	40
Pangbourne, .	11	9	40	72 ,, ,,	11	44	45
42 mile post,	11	10	30	75 ,, ,,	11	48	10
44 ,, ,,	11	12	20	76 ,, ,,	11	49	20
Goring,	11	13	10	Swindon,	11	51	20

At Swindon two fog-signals were detonated by the engine as she entered the station. Here again was another crowd of regretful admirers and photographers, more cheering as the train started for the west, and quite a volley of fog-signals were discharged as the train left the station. Much the same scene was enacted at every station on the journey, and it was stated that this train was photographed at over a hundred different places. This train was timed to call at several additional stations, and was not due at Penzance till 8.20 P.M., over an hour later than usual, but as a fact it was 9 P.M. before the last Broad Gauge 'Cornishman' reached its western destination. A large crowd took tickets from Penzance by the last local train to Truro, and, alighting at Marazion, caught the "Cornishman,"' thus riding back to Penzance by the last Broad Gauge passenger train. On the arrival of this train, arrangements were at once made for the return to Swindon of a train which should clear the whole of the Broad Gauge traffic from the line. This train was made up of two engines, six coaches, and a breakdown van containing a gang of men supplied from Newton Abbot, and the necessary tools which were provided in view of any accident, the object being to clear the line of all possible obstruction.

The last through up passenger train from Penzance was the mail, on Friday afternoon. This train was also late, and at Plymouth was nearly an hour behind, not leaving the Mill Bay Station till 9.17 P.M. There was great competition among the through guards as to who should have the honour of working this last Broad Gauge train to London. The fortunate one received a present at Mutley collected from a few passengers during the journey from Mill Bay.

As the train proceeded on its course to Totnes, the first stopping place, there were at each station clusters of people assembled, and the platelayers turned out of their tents to give it a hearty cheer and a respectful farewell, which was clearly heard above its vibrating roar. At Exeter, notwithstanding that it was near midnight, and the train was 1 hour 15 minutes late, it was the subject of a farewell demonstration, a large crowd having patiently waited to see the last of the Broads.

It was the last of its kind to leave the city, and those present wished it a hearty good-bye. It had met the down train at Dawlish, where there was much shaking of hands through the windows, the passengers singing 'Auld Lang Syne.' One of the coaches which came up bore the inscription—

> Good-bye to this old body of mine,
> I've knocked about for many a time;
> B.G. I am, B.G. I'll stay,
> Until I'm turned the narrow way.

Another less poetical, but more tragic sentiment on a goods truck was, ' Good riddance, old boy, you nearly killed me two years ago.'

As it left Exeter, shortly before the stroke of twelve o'clock, following the lead of the 'Amazon,' it received the last cheer raised by the public.   Thence to Swindon its course was as usual.   Here it was taken up by the 'Bulkeley,' which had brought down the last Broad Gauge from London the previous afternoon, and as it passed out of the station a salute of exploding fog-signals announced the departure of the last train on the Broad Gauge.   On arrival at Paddington the passengers on turning out, feeling that they had taken an indirect part in the final performance of the Broad Gauge service, lingered to see the emptied carriages back out of the station, in preparation for their last Broad run to the sidings at Swindon.

The very last Broad Gauge passenger train to leave Paddington was the 5 P.M. for Plymouth, many people placed coins on the line for the train to run over, and now treasure them up as mementoes of the journey of this historic train.

At Exeter a gentleman took his stand by the side of the 'Iron Duke,' which had brought the train from Bristol, and delivered an oration on the great advantages of the Broad Gauge.   This train did not arrive at Plymouth till 1.15 on Saturday morning, over an hour late, but a crowd kept vigil to see the last of it.

The Portreeve of Ashburton enveloped the locomotive of the last Broad Gauge train from that station in black crape, and so decked in mourning it accomplished its last journey to Totnes, and thence to Swindon.

From Torquay crowds of people travelled by the last train to Torre, many taking two tickets and keeping one in memory of the eventful journey. After the public traffic was over, many special trains of empty Broad Gauge stock and dead engines of ancient design were run to Swindon, there to await their turn of conversion or extinction.

From Plymouth such trains left at 7.10, 9.20, 11.20,
               11.35, P.M., and 12.55 A.M.

    ,,   Moretonhampstead   ,,   .,   10.0 P.M.

    ,,   Ashburton   ,,   ,,   10.0 ,,

    ,,   Liskeard   ,,   .,   9.50 ,,

    ,,   Kingswear   ,,   ,,   8.15 ,,
        and 12.45 A.M. on Saturday, which train
        also included the Brixham branch train
        and engine.

    ,,   Penzance   ,,   ., at 7.5 P.M.

    ,,   Launceston ,,   ,,   9.35 ,,

    ,,   Falmouth   ,,   ,,   8.15 ,,

    ,,   St Ives   ,,   ,,   8.50 ,,

As already stated, the last Broad Gauge train, consisting of the stock of the down 'Cornishman,' and a
breakdown van drawn by two locomotives was timed
to leave Penzance at 9.10 P.M., and to reach Swindon
at 9.45 A.M. on Saturday morning. The departure of
this train did not take place till 10 P.M., it stopped at
every station and an inspector travelled with it, and
when he had ascertained from each stationmaster
that all Broad Gauge stock had been worked away,
and he had also satisfied himself that the whole
of the trains timed to leave their respective junctions in advance of him had departed, and having
done this, he issued a notice in the following printed
form to every stationmaster between Penzance and
Exeter :—

    'This is the last Broad Gauge train to travel
over the line between Penzance and Exeter.'

    On receipt of this notice the stationmasters, at
the stations between Penzance and Exeter, gave a
printed notice to the representative of the Engineering
Department in the following form, that he could take
possession of the line :—

    'This is to certify that the last Broad Gauge train
from Penzance has left this station, and the Engineering Department can now take possession of the line

from the station in the rear up to this station, for the purpose of converting the gauge.'

Similar forms were given and received from the last Broad Gauge trains on the branch lines.

The mail service to and from Cornwall, during the time of the conversion, was performed partly by rail, partly by steamer, and partly by coach. The 9 P.M. mail train was Narrow Gauge for the first time on the Friday, and was consequently the first train (usually Broad Gauge) to run Narrow Gauge. Leaving Exeter at 2.45 A.M., this train was handed over to the London and South Western, and was conveyed over their line to Plymouth (North Road), arriving there at 4.20 A.M. Here the passengers, mails and parcels were transferred to waggonettes and conveyed to the Mill Bay Docks, whence the Great Western Railway steamer 'Gazelle' (one of the new boats employed in the Weymouth and Channel Islands service) left at 5.30 A.M., and was due at Fowey at 7.30, and Falmouth 9.30. The steamer, however, made quicker voyages than was expected, and arrived at Fowey at 7.17, and Falmouth at 8.45. There was quite a busy scene on her arrival at the latter port. There were coaches and four, waggonettes and other vehicles in readiness to receive the mails. As the heavily-laden coaches passed through the streets of the town, the remark was frequently heard,—'It reminds one of olden times,' or words to that effect. West of Truro, to which city the mails were conveyed from Falmouth by coach, the usual order of things was reversed as the up mail left before the down one arrived, thus a reply to a letter by Friday's night mail, from London to Penzance, could not be despatched from Penzance until Sunday morning instead of Saturday morning. The London night mail was despatched by train leaving Penzance at 11.15 A.M. in charge of a mail guard. This officer received and put out mails at all stations as far as Truro, and there met and took charge of the down night mail, performing the same duties on the homeward journey, reaching Penzance at 2.20 P.M. On Sunday the same officer took charge of the mails, conveyed by coach and four leaving Penzance post office at 8 A.M., by way of Marazion, Hayle, Camborne, Carn Brea, etc., to Redruth, picking up mails at each office. The down night mail was timed to arrive at Redruth shortly after the up mail left there, as soon as the coaches had exchanged their respective mails, the down service was performed in the same manner as the up mail service, reaching Penzance office at 3.5 P.M.

The steamer, on her return voyages on Saturday and Sunday, was again before time. Leaving Falmouth at 3.30 P.M., she arrived at Plymouth at 6.42 instead of 7.30, from thence to Exeter the mail was forwarded by the London and South Western Railway.

So satisfied were the Great Western officials that the colossal work of converting the gauge on the Cornwall Railway between Plymouth and Penzance would be successfully carried out within 48 hours, that the mail train leaving London at 9 P.M. on Sunday (arriving at Plymouth *viâ* London and South Western from Exeter) was booked to leave North Road at 4.40 A.M., and travel over the line just narrowed, and arrive at Penzance at 8.17 on Monday morning, calling at all intermediate stations. This journey was duly run to time.

The London and South Western also conveyed empty Great Western Narrow Gauge stock from Exeter to Plymouth on the Friday morning. These vehicles stood at Laira until Monday morning, and formed the first Narrow Gauge trains. The Narrow Gauge coaches to work the Brixham, Kingswear, Moretonhampstead and Ashburton branches were sent over the South Devon line from Exeter by specials at 3.15 and 4.40 A.M. on the Monday morning. The ordinary Narrow Gauge rolling stock of the Cornwall Minerals line provided the coaches for trains on Monday from Truro, Falmouth and Penzance.

The amount of Narrow Gauge rolling stock was so restricted on the Monday that no through vehicles were run from the Falmouth branch to London.

The Helston Narrow Gauge branch was 'commandeered' to the extent of one *tri-compo* and two third-class coaches, to form the St Ives branch train, while, to provide for the early up trains from Penzance, Narrow Gauge coaches were worked down from Plymouth (North Road) to Carn Brea yard on crocodile trucks, which, as soon as unloaded, were returned for two more coaches, and this was repeated until sixteen coaches had been thus conveyed.

On Saturday, 21st May, the inhabitants of the district between Truro and Penzance, after an interval of nearly thirty years, again saw Narrow Gauge passenger trains running over the West Cornwall Railway, for a special service of Narrow Gauge trains was provided on this line, which had still preserved the Narrow Gauge line on which it was built, and was the only Mixed Gauge line in Cornwall. This section was closed on the Sunday for alterations. The conversion did not affect the following Narrow Gauge branches :—

> Helston Branch ;
> Cornwall Minerals Line ;
> Bodmin and Wadebridge Branches ;
> Princetown Branch ;
> Teign Valley Branch ;

while a service of Narrow Gauge trains was run between Plymouth (North Road) and Tavistock, the gauge on this line having been mixed to accommodate the London and South Western some years previously.

The full usual service of Narrow Gauge trains was advertised to run on Monday, 23d May. Mr Foxwell, of 'Express train' celebrity, travelled from Penzance by the up 'Cornishman,' and wrote to the *Pall Mall Gazette* the following epigrammic account of that journey :—

' It has been said that sudden conversions are

never to be relied on. No one would assent to this proposition after travelling in the 'up Cornishman' to-day. This train is timed to leave Penzance at 11.10, and to reach Paddington at 7.50. Considering the extraordinary character of the line from Penzance to Exeter (132 miles), this represents a sufficiently hard task. To-day, therefore, being the first on which the Cornish express was to run Narrow Gauge, over a track which had just been changed from Broad Gauge in the twinkling of an eye, no one (except the drivers) thought it possible for the train to keep time, at any rate along the section from Truro to Plymouth, which is composed (or discomposed) on incessant curves and thirty-three trestle viaducts. However, it was on this section that we did best, for at each stopping station we had to wait till our time was up, and then we ran into North Road too soon. Not once were we checked by any weak spot in the road so recently relaid. Finally, after being snubbed all the way up for being too forward, we shut off steam 2½ miles outside Paddington, and stopped at the platform at 7.46—that is, 4 minutes before our time. In spite of all temptations to belong to other nations, I am content to be an Englishman just now.—Yours truly,

'E. FOXWELL.'

(*b*) THE CONVERSION OF THE LINE.

The arrangements made by Mr Trench, the Great Western engineer for the stupendous work of converting some 230 miles of line from the safe, comfortable and convenient 7 feet gauge to the cramped coal-wain wheel track, now almost universal in this country, were of such a complete and exhaustive nature that they rightly deserve a foremost place in the annals of engineering triumphs, as an example of a gigantic task successfully carried out in an exceedingly short time, without hitch or accident. The success of the work is

undoubtedly due to the very careful way in which
every detail of the work to be performed had been
mapped out most minutely and scheduled many
months beforehand, and it only required obedience to
orders on the part of the men employed to enable the
undertaking to be carried through without mishap; and
so well was the army of workers disciplined in this
desideratum of immediate and exact attention to orders,
that failure was an unknown quantity. The result
would have been quite otherwise had there been any
indecision or want of cohesion among the men or their
superiors. The many permanent way hands usually
employed on the 230 miles of line to be converted,
were assisted in the work by importations of fellow-
workmen from all parts of the Great Western system.
These left their various districts on Thursday, 19th
May, as follows :—

From	No. of Men.	Destination.
Chester, . .	441	Main line—Exeter to Newton and Ashburton branch.
New Milford, .	315	Totnes and Rattery.
Bristol, . .	462	Moretonhampstead, Kingswear and Brixham branches.
Crewe, . .	378	Main line—Totnes to Plymouth.
Paddington, .	447	Main line—Plymouth to St Austell.
Weymouth, .	414	Lidford to Launceston; Bodmin Road to St Austell.
Tondu, . .	483	Par to Falmouth.
Total,	2940	

Exaggerated accounts appeared in many papers as
to the number of men imported to do the work, some
putting it as high as 5000. The total number engaged, including those in the district, did not exceed
4200. The men were billeted in gangs of about
sixty, accommodation being found them in the goods

sheds, waiting-rooms, and other offices, or in tents
erected for the purpose along the line. Each man
had a straw mattress for a bed and two rugs, provided
by the company; and on arrival at the allotted posts
hot gruel (oatmeal and water), was served out, the
Directors having supplied 10 tons of oatmeal, and this
was the only refreshment they attempted to supply,
every man being required to provide himself with a
week's supply of food. Mr Wills, of Bristol, of the
firm of W. and H. O. Wills, who is also a Director of
this company, very generously gave five thousand two
ounce packets of the celebrated 'Westward Ho' brand
tobacco for distribution among the men, and each man
received a packet before commencing work. The
cost of this gift amounted to £150. Undoubtedly
this was a capital advertisement, and those who indulged in the fragrant weed extolled its virtues.
Every three gangs had an inspector over them, this
official being responsible for the conversion of about 3½
miles of way. Forty-six miles of the length to be converted was laid with cross sleepers instead of the
famous safety longitudinal ones. On these parts the
line had already been prepared for the Narrow Gauge,
not only by placing the chairs in position, but a third
rail was actually laid, so that the real length to be
altered during the period allowed for the final conversion was considerably less than popularly supposed.
Had the whole of the line to be converted been laid
with cross sleepers it would have been impossible to
have altered their position in anything like the short
time allowed for conversion. Indeed, it is quite possible that the whole line would have been 'mixed'
instead of converted, but as the great cost was the
principal factor in preventing the mixing of the gauge
through Devon and Cornwall, the travellers have the
longitudinal sleepers to thank for the minimum of inconvenience caused by the alteration of the gauge.
The actual work to be done consisted of four distinct
operations :—

1. Removing the ballast.
2. Cross-cutting the transoms and removing the tie-rods.
3. Slewing the sleeper and rail.
4. Bolting up the rails and rough ballasting.

On many sections of the line this work was actually accomplished in the incredibly short space of 31 hours. The advanced preparations were of a more complete character than can be appreciated by many of the travelling public. When the South Wales conversion was made none of the transoms between the longitudinal permanent way were cut entirely through. Of every three transoms two were cut three parts through, and the other was left intact until the traffic stopped. On this occasion every alternate transom was cut partly through, and the others entirely through. In many cases where the transoms were strengthened by iron rods alongside, these were shortened and a fresh worm made so as to be in readiness. Besides which the ballast had been removed from around the sleeper to be moved, and also from the new position the sleeper was to occupy. So that during the last days before the conversion the lines were on rather shaky bases. On the Thursday and Friday the workmen found plenty of occupation in connection with the station sidings, the transformation of which from Broad to Narrow Gauge was considerably advanced. At daybreak on the Saturday the army of workmen was astir, and a few minutes later each man was busily engaged in carrying out the particular duty allocated to him, and so the work of wiping out the noble conception of Brunel proceeded apace, some hammering, others slewing, then the more particular work of adjusting the newly positioned line. The work was of a many-sided character, fairly easy where there was a straight length of line to be dealt with, but fraught with difficulty where the railroad curves, and where at crossings, with their network of rails, the points had to be readjusted. In dealing with the longitudinal sleeper, the transoms which held the long lengths of timber together were cut off to the required gauge length, and the rail and sleeper shifted in bodily and readjusted. Preparations had already been made for the work. At the points much ingenuity and care was necessary. Great difficulties had to be surmounted in altering the gauge at junctions and goods yards where the lines intertwine in a perfect maze. Short sections of the new lines where points occur were carefully prepared and substituted for the old sections. Where the line curved in rounding corners it was very difficult. Every curve of a rail is a segment of a true circle, hence, when the outer of the two lines is moved in, some portion of the rail had to be cut off, as by narrowing the gauge and drawing in the outer line the outer line was found too long.

So rapidly had the change been effected that by one o'clock on the Saturday afternoon the South Devon line, which when first constructed was never expected to have a locomotive on it, had reached the level of all other railways in the country, and a Narrow Gauge locomotive was cautiously steaming over the erstwhile Atmospheric Railway, and so after 10 hours' work it became possible, with care and caution, to run Narrow Gauge trains over the various sections west of Exeter; not that the work was in any sense completed, but the whole of the rails had in that time been slewed into their new position.

The action of the Great Western Railway Company necessitated the Falmouth Docks Company narrow gauging their lines, the expense incurred in connection therewith being £4000. There were over 5 miles of line to be dealt with, including many crossings, etc. Two experienced foremen from the South Western Railway were engaged to render help in this conversion, which was carried out under the superintendence of the dock's engineer. The whole of the work at the docks was completed—without the aid of Sunday labour—by Tuesday morning.

More than a year after the 'abolition of the Broad Gauge' we noticed that the disused branch of the Cornwall Railway from Lostwithiel to Fowey was still unconverted, and may be still, for aught its proprietors seem to care, now the route to Fowey is *viâ* Par and St Blazey.

The sea was an object of wonder to many countrymen who had never seen the restless waves before, and some of the denser ones, whose ideas of autocratic and un-limited power did not go beyond their railway, were credited with the opinion that the daily variation of the tides was carried out from instructions received from the General Manager at Paddington, and this fairy tale was carried still further by the rejoinder that it was the Admiralty and not the Great Western Railway that was responsible for this natural phenomenon.

The abolition of the Broad Gauge was not carried out without some pathos, for at Torquay a ganger drowned himself rather than face the difficulty of the task allotted to him. This unfortunate man had been engaged in the narrow gauging of the line on the Torquay branch, and complained to his wife of the pressure of work, stating that it required a great deal of study. He also talked to men under him about the work, and wondered whether the $2\frac{1}{4}$ miles of line for which he was responsible would turn out all right. He also said he was afraid he would not have enough tools for the men who were to be sent down. He was very quiet on Monday night, but ate his supper and went to bed in his usual health. On the following morning he went to work in the Torquay Station Yard, where he remained until half-past nine. He then walked away down the line, and was not seen again alive. So the poor man sought for rest beneath the blue waves of Torbay, and saw not the 4 feet $8\frac{1}{2}$ inch gauge laid in his native place.

The arrangements for bringing back the extra men from the West of Exeter to their own districts were of a more minute character than those made for conveying them to the scene of operations. On Monday and Tuesday, 23d and 24th May, seven empty trains left Bristol and Weston for the various points to fetch men back, and soon after 6 A.M. on Tuesday morning the homeward trip was commenced, and a half an hour after noon on that day the whole of the imported men were again east of Exeter, and quickly journeying to their respective destinations. From some branches and stations as few as two men were required for the conversion, yet there were printed instructions as to which branch trains they were to travel by on their return journey, many not reaching home till nearly mid-day on the 25th.

The minute arrangements made for the five men from Brentford we fancy were hardly likely to have been appreciated or even carried out by those concerned; thus the special train was due at West Drayton at 9.46 P.M., and the five men for Uxbridge left by the 10.19 P.M. ordinary. The same special was due at Southall at 10.2 P.M., but as the last train to Brentford left Southall at 9.18 P.M., these five unfortunate beings were directed by the red tapeism of the officials to spend a night at Southall Station, and leave there at 7.25 A.M next morning for Brentford; but as that town is only distant 4 miles from Southall it is more than likely that after five nights of bivouacing in Cornwall the men would journey home by 'shanks's mare,' and before midnight be enjoying the comfort of sleeping in their own beds instead of roughing it for another night, and so fully carrying out the too minute arrangements made on their behalf.

As soon as the conversion was carried out the engineer of the Great Western Railway retired, and as he was not a Broad Gauge man, but a native of the North of England and an advocate of the

Narrow Gauge, he was doubtless pleased to give up, seeing he had achieved such a complete *conversion.* Thus was the abolition of the 7 *feet* o¼ *inch* railway gauge completed, and its epitaph, as written in chalk on a sleeper by a large-hearted West Country platelayer, was, 'Good-bye, poor old Broad Gauge. God bless you.'

(*c*) CONVERSION OF THE ROLLING STOCK.

At the first blush the conversion of a large number of locomotives, waggons and carriages appears almost impossible.   At the very best one would expect the alteration of even a single vehicle to be a long and complicated proceeding, yet so complete were the arrangements, and for so many years had this alteration been contemplated, that stock, particularly engines, had been built and worn out long before the fateful day of conversion came round.   For over two years Swindon had been preparing for the conversion, and nearly 20 miles of Broad Gauge siding were laid down at Swindon to hold the numerous vehicles sent there.   At the date of the conversion the Broad Gauge stock consisted of—

197 engines, of which . .	130 convertible	67 unconvertible.
555 carriages and coaching vehicles, . . .	426 ,,	129	,,
3269 waggons and goods trucks	792 ,,	2477	,,
4021 Total B.G. Stock.	1348 ,,	2673	,,

Of the locomotives several were new ones, designed by Mr Dean, and constructed to work the West of England expresses when the Broad Gauge was no more.   These were Narrow Gauge engines in every particular except in the length of the axle.   For the few months these engines were running Broad Gauge they looked most ungainly with the wheels outside the

U

'CONVERTED.' (*From a Photograph by F. Moore, London.*)

Mr. Dean's 'STORM KING,' built for the Narrow Gauge, but for the first few months she had her wheels
7 ft. apart to run on the Broad Gauge.

frames and far away from the boiler, it has been said that there was really no occasion for these to have been built Broad Gauge at all, as the old style Broad Gauge express locomotives were capable of working the traffic during the few months these engines were in use as Broad Gauge locomotives. It is probable that no locomotives have evoked so much hostile criticism as these engines designed by Mr Dean to work the express trains made world-famous by the Broad Gauge. The weight of these new Narrow Gauge engines on six wheels is 44 tons 4 cwt., of which 13 tons 4 cwt. is on the leading axle.

It is, therefore, no wonder that these 'ironclads' break their leading axles, as three or more have already done, and that Mr Dean has now fitted leading bogies to these engines. Had Mr Gooch's experience with the 'Great Western' been remembered, and these locomotives been at first provided with a leading bogie, the company would have saved the expense of the subsequent alterations and the damages caused by the breaking of the axles. In consequence of the high centre of gravity of these engines, their safety at express speed has been questioned; the top of the smoke box is only half an inch nearer the rails than was that of the Broad Gauge engines, which had a base 7 feet wide, as against 4 feet $8\frac{1}{2}$ inches of the present engines, a very considerable factor, coupled with a high centre of gravity, when it comes to a case of an engine turning over or running off the rails. The diameter of the cylinders have also been reduced from 20 inches to 19 inches; while the addition of the bogie makes them too long for the usual turn-tables, so that another difficulty has arisen. These alterations have made the engines more popular, while to still further gain public favour they have all been named; very many after famous Broad Gauge engines, and others after well known Broad Gauge men.

The 426 carriages converted were of three kinds — carriages with Broad Gauge bodies, which had to be taken to pieces and closed in so as to bring them to the Narrow dimensions, 8 feet 6 inches, or 2 feet less in width than the old carriages; secondly, there were carriages with Narrow Gauge bodies and Broad Gauge frames and wheels; and thirdly, some carriages had Narrow Gauge bodies and frames, and merely Broad Gauge bogies and wheels. The process of converting the last-named had been carefully planned by the officials, and the machinery was so perfect that a carriage was transformed in 10 minutes, while no less than 25 were completely converted in 6¼ hours. The change was effected this wise :—Batches of six carriages were run into a shed set apart for the purpose. The floor where the wheels rested was capable of rising and falling. When the carriages were properly arranged, the bodies of the carriages were raised by hydraulic power clear of their bogies. They were stayed up from the surrounding stationary floor so as to stand when the wheels were removed. This completed, the platform on which were the Broad Gauge bogies was lowered beneath the level of the adjacent floor, and the bogies run underground on to the rails near by, elevated to the line level, and then despatched from the shed. Then the Narrow Gauge bogies were brought in which were run on to the platform, lowered along under their carriages, raised to the carriage bodies, and fitted. As another instance of the speed with which the transformation was actually effected, under ordinary circumstances, it may be stated that in one day twenty carriages were sent into the works in the morning, and left as Narrow Gauge in the evening. Nearly one-third of the Broad Gauge coaching stock has been used again. Of 3269 waggons only 792 were converted. Most of the remainder were broken up, and the iron and wheels utilised where possible.

Although most of the stock was sent to Swindon to be converted, some of the waggons were converted at

'BROAD GAUGE STABILITY.'

A comparison between Mr Gooch's Broad Gauge 'ROVER' and Mr Dean's Narrow Gauge 'ROVER' No. 3019.

Lostwithiel, Newton Abbot and Bridgewater — at which places the locomotive works of the old Cornwall, South Devon, and Bristol and Exeter Railways were respectively located. Only ten firms owned private Broad Gauge waggons (a proof of how completely the Great Western had the whole of the goods traffic on its Broad Gauge lines entirely in its own hands). Some of these firms engaged the Great Western Railway to convert their stock, while others had theirs converted by private waggon builders. After all the convertible stock had been attended to, there remained the unconvertible Broad Gauge engines and vehicles to be disposed of, and it was nearly eighteen months later before the whole was completed. It is stated that the whole loss to the company in connection with the conversion of the rolling stock *alone* was £374,000.

Soon after the introduction of the Narrow Gauge on the Great Western Railway a driver of a Broad Gauge engine was killed in an accident. His epitaph was :—

'When Narrow with Broad first began to entwine,
A grey-headed driver was killed on the line ;
His last feeble whisper was caught by his mate,
Thank God, 'twas Broad Gauge where I met with my fate.'

(*d*) THE RESULT OF THE CONVERSION.

And now that the conversion had been carried out, the coal waggon gauge partisans are able to rub their hands together, and gloat over the fact that this country must now be content that its yearly increasing volume of traffic must be carried over the miserable 4 feet 8½ inch gauge.

What now are the benefits or otherwise derived from the abolition of the Broad Gauge? Have extra trains been put on to convey the through traffic of foreign lines east of Exeter to Devonshire and Cornwall? Have large sums of money, formerly spent in the wages of 'trans-shippers,' been saved by the company? Are myriads of foreign companies' and private owners' trucks seen on the South Devon and Cornwall lines? On the contrary, are not 98 per cent. of the vehicles seen west of Exeter still the property of the Great Western Railway? Was it worth all the expense involved to make the change for 2 per cent. of the traffic?

The first appreciable result of the 'narrowing' was the almost immediate slowing of the West of England trains—the 'Cornishman' took 16 minutes longer, the 'Dutchman' half an hour, the 9 P.M. mail 25 minutes; the first up from Penzance 15 minutes, the up 'Cornishman' 20 minutes, and the up mail half an hour. This was in part explained by the fact that the Great Western had introduced the electric tablet for working their single lines in place of the old method while in the case of the up and down mails, which, both before and after the conversion, stopped at several stations *en route*, but after the conversion ceased to run into Mill Bay, and so saved at least 15 minutes, yet this is slowed half an hour, or including the saving at Mill Bay, equal to three-quarters of an hour, of which but a few minutes can be attributed to the tablet changing. Since the doubling of several of the sections on the South Devon and Cornwall lines, the 'Cornishman' has been accelerated. A description of the electric tablet system now much in vogue for working single lines being of interest, we shortly describe it. 'Say "A" and "B" are the two boxes at the ends of a section, and "A" has a train he wishes to send on to "B." "A" will forward the "Be ready" signal to "B." If "B" is clear to receive this train he repeats the "Be ready," then "A" holds his plunger in for "B" to draw out his empty slide in which he is to place the tablet when it arrives. Then "B" turns his commentator, and presses in his plunger for "A" to obtain a tablet, which done, he puts it in a pouch and hands it to the driver for the train to procced to " B." Arriving at " B " the driver delivers the tablet up, and " B " puts it on his empty slide and gives "train out " to " A," which " A " has to acknowledge by repeating with the same number of beats, holding his plunger in till " B " pushes in his slide containing the tablet. When this is done " B " turns his commentator, presses his plunger, holding it well in for " A " to push his empty slide in. When this is done " A " has to give " B " one ring to let him know he is right.'

The introduction of corridor trains for all classes of passengers is a recent innovation, and the Great Western Railway run eight per day as follows :— those leaving Paddington at 10.15 A.M. for Plymouth and Penzance, at 11.25 for Torquay, at 1.30 for Birmingham and Birkenhead, and at 3.15 for Cardiff and Swansea ; also those arriving at Paddington at 2.35 P.M. from Swansea and Cardiff, at 4.30 P.M. from Torquay; at 7.45 P.M. from Cornwall and Plymouth, and at 8.40 P.M. from Birkenhead and Birmingham. But how much better would the Broad Gauge have lent itself for corridor trains? with a passage down the centre, instead of at the side as now.

The Great Western Railway corridor trains are the only 'three class' corridor trains running in the country. The lavatory accommodation has been arranged neatly and economically. The carriages are, with the single exception of the third class, which are only 52 feet $\frac{3}{4}$ inch, all 56 feet $\frac{3}{4}$ inch long over the mouldings, and all of them are 8 feet 6$\frac{3}{4}$ inches wide outside. The clear width inside is 8 feet and the corridors are 22$\frac{1}{2}$ inches wide. The classes are divided by means of doors in the corridors fitted with private locks. There is seating accommodation in the train proper for seventy-six third-class, twenty-two first-class, and twenty-four second-class passengers, and each of the two composite carriages provides accommodation for twenty-four third class, eleven first-class, and seven second-class passengers, so that the total accommodation provided by the whole train is 224 third-class, forty-four first-class, and thirty-eight second-class seats.   The carriages have the usual lantern roof of the Great Western stock, and run on the standard Great Western bogies and underframes, thus the two great desiderata of railway carriages, and for which the Great Western is famous, namely, ventilation and smooth travelling, are as complete as possible.   The coaches are finished in dark oak with Lincrusta panels.   The first-class are upholstered with crimson plush and the second and third-class compartments with rep of the standard Great Western Railway patterns.

The weight of the coaches varies from 22 tons 10 cwt. to nearly 24 tons, according to class.

Amongst some of the ills of the present state of things may be mentioned several breakdowns that have happened to the new engines, principally the snapping of the axles—trains running off the lines—scarcely possible with the original longitudinal sleepers —the 'abolition of which the Chairman of the Great Western was deploring as late as August 1894, more especially as the alteration is still costing the shareholders an unnecessary outlay of about £60,000 a year.*
The really enormous monetary outlay involved in the abolition of the Broad Gauge and other alterations and improvements rendered necessary in consequence will never be definitely known, the expense having been subdivided under so many heads, and spread over a long period, but the yearly interest on the money thus sunk would have been more than sufficient to pay all the extra expenses incurred annually by the Great Western Railway consequent upon having two gauges. Would it not have been cheaper, more convenient and better in every way to have mixed the gauge over the whole system?   While the punctuality of the trains has certainly not improved since the alteration, although some of the single sections on the South

---

* For the half-year to December 1894, £37,766 was expended on relaying parts of the converted lines, and the Deputy Chairman said the expense would be spread over several more years.

Devon and Cornwall lines have been doubled, and many of the weak viaducts have been substantially rebuilt, both of which improvements ought at least to tend to increased punctuality, and had these works been carried out when the Broad Gauge was in existence, the result then would have been increased speed.

The West Country people are conservative and sentimental, and cling tenaciously to anything to which they have been attached, especially if it has done them good service. As the Broad Gauge gave them railways, and good ones too, with liberal services and quick trains, when the Narrow Gauge was far away, and not likely to reach them for many years, so the Broad Gauge was always popular with them, and they looked upon it as something apart ; and when other parts of the Great Western system had been converted or mixed, and the Broad Gauge was left to Devon and Cornwall only, they looked upon it as a system peculiarly their own, indeed outsiders began to think of it as belonging solely and only to the West of England, while in Cornwall the Great Western Railway was looked upon with gratitude, and was thanked for their liberality in that, when other railways could not construct or work lines in consequence of the unproductive value of the traffic, the Great Western took them over and gave the country the benefit of its immense system. But although the generation directly concerned in these advantages bestowed on them by the Great Western Railway has passed away, yet the Broad Gauge vividly reminded the Cornwall folks of their indebtedness to the Great Western. This gone, the people, with their native sharpness, were not slow in taking advantage of the benefits to be derived by them from the active competition of two railways, although they well know there is not sufficient traffic to make both lines remunerative ; in fact, the Chairman of the Great Western Railway has publicly said that the West Cornwall does not pay expenses, let alone gain any profit to the Great Western, yet 'one and all' are sharp enough to encourage another line for the sake of the benefits they will receive thereby. How much the Cornishmen will invest in the line is an entirely different matter.

The London and South Western Railway entered into a compact with the Great Western that they would not promote any railway or extend their system into Cornwall. This ten years' agreement expired last year, but the arrangement has not prevented the North Cornwall Railway—a so-called independent company, but most closely connected with and worked by the London and South Western Railway—from constructing a line from the London and South Western Railway at Haswell to Padstow, a distance of 50 miles, and obtaining Parliamentary sanction to extend it to Newquay. While in the 1894 Session the North Cornwall Railway promoted a Bill for power to construct a line from Newquay to Truro, 12 miles long, with running powers over the Great Western to Falmouth and Penzance. The Cornwall Minerals Railway also promoted a similar line, not because one was wanted or would pay, but to protect their own system. This latter received the assent of the House of Lords, but the House of Commons threw it out on the ground that it was strengthening the monopoly of the Great Western Railway in Cornwall, and, if the line was made, it should be by an independent company. The result is, a line won't be made just yet. The Cornish folks, in supporting competition, have overreached themselves, and lost the benefit the Cornwall Minerals Railway was willing to give them.

In conclusion, we extract from an article in a railway paper, written by a London and South Western Railway official. His opinion is worth considering, seeing that that line is in competition with the Great Western, and he would have opportunities of comparing the two systems, while natural *esprit de corps* would not allow him to unduly depreciate his own line :—' I consider myself that the Broad Gauge is capable of great things, and I am only sorry to think that, in the interest of railway passengers, it has not become universal in preference to the Narrow Gauge. At the present time, when traffic is so greatly on the increase, and the demand for improved carriages is heard on every side, the extra width of the Broad Gauge coaches would have been found of great advantage, and I think the carrying capacity of railway rolling stock might be better increased by having more room in the width rather than length of the coaches. I maintain, therefore, that a broader gauge would prove more economical in the long run, as it is certainly much more comfortable, and it offers facilities, under an enterprising management, for the construction of cars of the American principle, which the Narrow Gauge cannot approach. I quite think that if a more go-ahead company had had the management of the Broad Gauge track, they would not now be on the point of abolishing it altogether. I have met with and spoken to a great many travellers in my time, and I have invariably heard from them that the Broad Gauge is far and away the most comfortable carriage to ride in, and I am sure numbers regret its abolition. The Midland is, I think, the company that would have given the Broad Gauge a trial, but any of the northern lines would have done it more justice than that sleepy giant, the Great Western Railway.'

Punch lamented the abolition of Brunel's gauge by a poem written in imitation of 'The Burial of Sir John Moore,' and with a cartoon representing a Broad Gauge engine being buried, with the shades of Brunel and the other Broad Gauge leaders looking on.

'THE BURIAL OF THE "BROAD GAUGE" ·

May 23, 1892.

Not a whistle was heard, not a brass bell note,
As his corse o'er the sleepers we hurried;
Not a fog-signal wailed from a husky throat
O'er the grave where our "Broad Gauge" we buried.

We buried him darkly, at dead of night,
The sod with our pickaxes turning,
By the danger signal's ruddy light,
And our oil lamps dimly burning.

No useless tears, though we loved him well!
Long years to his fire-box had bound us.
We fancied we glimpsed the great shade of Brunel
In sad sympathy hovering round us.

Few and gruff were the words we said,
But we thought, with a natural sorrow,
Of the Narrow Gauge foe of the loco. just dead
We should have to attend on the morrow.

We thought, as we hollowed his big broad bed,
And piled the brown earth o'er his funnel,
How his foe o'er the Great Western metals would tread,
Shrieking triumph through cutting and tunnel.

Lightly they'll talk of him now he is gone,
For the cheap Narrow Gauge has outstayed him ;
Yet Bull might have found, had he let it go on,
That Brunel's Big Idea would have paid him.

But the battle is ended, our task is done,
After forty years' fight he's retiring ;
This hour sees thy triumph, O Stephenson !—
Old " Broad Gauge " no more will need firing.

The " Dutchman " must now be " divided in two "—
Well, well, they sha'n't mangle or mess you !
Accept the last words of friends faithful, if few :—
" Good-bye, poor old ' Broad Gauge,' God bless you ! "

Slowly and sadly we laid him down ;
He has filled a great chapter in story.
We sang not a dirge, we raised not a stone,
But we left the " Broad Gauge " to his glory ! '

A clever acrostic appeared in a railway paper at
the time of the conversion, which we append,—

' **B**runel's pet lamb is doomed, and soon will surely die—
Relentless outstretched hands upon its head do lie ;
O'er all the world it has a famous name achieved :
Adieu ! the end has come, and 'tis by many grieved.
Down by the rocks 'twas reared, and grew a noble form—

Great Western Railway men know how it braved the storm.
A rival bold and strong put forth its claim to stand,
Upon the lamb's own ground to fix its iron band.
Grand efforts men have made to stay this giant's tread;
Each struggle fainter grew—and now "Broad Gauge" is dead!'

We have pointed out some of the disadvantages of the change of gauge, and have sought in vain for some of the advantages; but, no doubt, others can see them clearly, and will not be at all backward in introducing them to both the reader's and the writer's notice.

CHAPTER XXI.

CONCLUSION.

As a conclusion to this attempt to give an account of
the Broad Gauge portion of the Great Western Railway from its inception to the present day (a task
involving no small amount of research and labour),
we append the following statistical information, extracted from the official report of the Directors
for the half-year ending 30th June 1894, and presented to the shareholders at the One hundred and
eighteenth half-yearly meeting. As to whether the
Great Western is the leading railway is a moot point.
Some authorities assign the premier position to the
Great Western, and others to the London and North
Western, while all agree in placing the Midland third.
At all events the Great Western is first in the number
of miles worked, although much of it is single track ; it
is second with regard to receipts from passenger traffic,
and third in the amount of capital—the London and
North Western and Midland being first and second
respectively. In the matter of total income, the
London and North Western is again first, while the
Great Western and Midland both run very close for
second place.

CAPITAL RECEIVED.

Shares and Stocks, . . .	. £59,059,493	0	0
Loans, ...	. 2,350	0	0
Debenture Stock, . . .	. 18,120,884	0	0
Rent Charges, ...	. 53,700	10	0
Stratford Canal Annuities,	. 58,750	0	0
Premium on Stocks and Shares,	. 4,314,670	7	7
Total Capital received,	. £81,609,847	17	7

CAPITAL EXPENDITURE.

Lines open for traffic, . . .	£67,929,662	9	0
Lines in course of construction, .	96,050	2	4
Working Stock, ...	10,010.081	15	3
Subscriptions to other railways, viz., Abbotsbury, Alexandra (Newport) Dock, Bala and Festiniog, Corwen and Bala, Great Marlow, Limerick and Kerry, Marlborough, Oldbury, Princetown, Somersetshire Coal, Somerset and Dorset, Staines and West Drayton, Swindon Water Works, Tiverton and North Devon, Waterford and Central Ireland, Waterford, Dungarven and Lismore, and West London Extension Railways, ...	758,069	6	7
Docks, ...	648,837	0	1
Steamboats, ...	346,056	7	1
Leased Lines, ...	59,809	6	1
Canals, ...	748,091	8	0
Joint Lines, Debentures paid off or Debts assumed, . . .	471,800	0	0
Total expenditure of Capital, .	£81,068,457	14	5

MILEAGE STATEMENT.

Lines owned by Great Western Railway, . .	1925¾
Lines partly owned by Great Western Railway, .	192
Lines leased, rented or worked over, . . .	488¼
Foreign lines worked over, ...	85
Total Miles worked by Great Western Railway, .	2691

TRAIN MILES RUN DURING HALF-YEAR.

Passenger, ...	9,247,662
Goods and Minerals, ...	9,405,715
Total, .	18,653,377

ROLLING STOCK.

Engines, 1710; Tenders, 873; Royal Carriages, 3; First-Class Carriages, 228; Composites, 1067; Second-

Class, 175; Third-Class, 2288; Brake Parcel and Mail Vans, 979; Carriage Trucks, 351; Horse Boxes, 565. *Total Coaching Vehicles*, 5656.

Merchandise and Minerals.—Open Waggons, 31,525; Covered Waggons, 6034; Coke Trucks, 2322; Cattle Trucks, 1930; Timber Trucks, 2410; Brake Vans, 1139; Pilot Vans, 8; Permanent Way Trucks, 1436. *Total Goods Vehicles*, 46,804.

RECEIPTS (6 MONTHS).

Passengers, Parcels and Mails, . . .	£1,908,353
Merchandise, Live Stock, etc., . . .	1,275,366
Minerals, ...	1,142,830
Total, .	£4,326,549

EXPENDITURE (6 MONTHS).

Maintenance of Way, ...	£516,654
Locomotive and Carriage Stock, . .	869,642
Traffic and General Charges, . . .	889,107
Government Duty, Rates and Taxes, . .	169,193
Total, .	£2,444,596

Total Profit for Half-year from all sources, ... £1,999,302 7 9

PASSENGERS CARRIED IN 6 MONTHS.

First-Class,	694,190	producing	£118,931	17	5
Second-Class	2,241,573	„	131,850	6	5
Third-Class,	27,700,731	„	1,224,906	0	5
Total	30,636,494				

20,019 Season Tickets produced . 67,244 11 4

£1,542,932 15 7

During the half-year the Great Western Railway paid to forty-two other railways for rent of leased lines, etc., £143,332, 4s. 9d. The companies were, Abbotsbury, Abingdon, Bala and Festiniog, Banbury and Cheltenham, Birkenhead, Birmingham and Henley-in-Arden, Bridport, Buckfastleigh, Totnes and South Devon, Cornwall Minerals, Corwen and Bala, Devon and Somerset, Didcot, Newbury and Southampton, Ely Valley, Forest of Dean Central, Halesowen, Hammersmith and City, Helston, Herefordshire and Gloucestershire Canal Company, Kington and Eardisley, Leominster and Kington, Llangollen and Corwen, Marlborough, Milford, Minehead, Nantwich and Market Drayton, Oldbury, Princetown, Ross and Monmouth, Shewsbury and Hereford (including Tenbury), Shewsbury and Welspool, Staines and West Drayton, Teign Valley, Tiverton and North Devon, Vale of Llangollen, Vale of Towy, Victoria Station and Pimlico, Wenlock and Wenlock Extensions, West Cornwall, West London, West Somerset, Weymouth and Portland, and Wye Valley. This list does not include the many railways formerly independent, but now amalgamated with the Great Western Railway. All those mentioned above are still semi-independent companies.

These extracts from the report will show the important position held by the Great Western Railway in the railway systems of the world.

APPENDIX

APPENDIX A.

REPORT OF GREAT WESTERN RAILWAY DIRECTORS TO
SHAREHOLDERS IN FAVOUR OF THE CONTINUANCE
OF THE BROAD GAUGE.

DECEMBER 1838.

'IT may be here concisely stated that Mr Wood deduces
from experiments upon the performance of engines on the
Great Western and other lines that, although a higher rate of
speed has been attained on the former, it would appear only
to be accomplished by the increased power of the engines,
with a much greater consumption of coke when calculated
per ton per mile. He ascribes this result principally to the
resistance presented by the atmosphere to the motion of
railway trains, especially at high rates of speed. His remarks on that subject are qualified, however, by the expression of a doubt as to the value to be assigned to the single set
of experiments of each of two inclined planes, which are
quoted as the authority for the degree of atmospheric resistance supposed to have been discovered. The reduction of
friction by the employment of wheels of increased diameter,
and the benefit of lowering the carriages between the wheels,
are affirmed by Mr Wood as incontrovertible. The increased
stability, and consequent increased steadiness of motion to
carriages on the wider base are also admitted by him.

The various propositions of doubtful advantage from the
wide gauge, as well as of alleged objection to it, appear to
have been thoroughly considered in the Report in question.
The experiments on the consumption of coke at high velocities were unfavourable, and, in connection with the theory of
atmospheric resistance, appear to have influenced the mind of
Mr Wood to consider that a 7 feet gauge was beyond the
width which he would deem the best. At the same time,

325

4

upon a review of all the circumstances, and considering that there are counteracting advantages incidental to an increased width of gauge, he does not think that the result of his inquiries would justify a change in the dimensions adopted on this line, and he recommends the present width should be retained. The advice thus given by Mr Wood, upon mature reflection, being directly at variance with the conclusion at which Mr Hawkshaw had previously arrived upon an investigation similarly delegated to him, it became the duty of the Directors to consider most attentively the train of reasoning and argument which led the latter to urge such an opposite course. Naturally expecting from that circumstance to find in his Report a clear and definite statement of the positive loss or disadvantages accruing from the increased width of gauge, the Directors could not fail to remark with some surprise that he enforces his recommendation, not upon any ascertained injury or failure in the plan, but almost exclusively upon the presumption that all railways, however disconnected or locally situated, should be constructed of one uniform width. While he appears to think that it might be an improvement to have an addition of a few inches, 5 or 6 at the most, he still questions the expediency of any variation from the 4 feet 8½ inch gauge. Mr Hawkshaw, in his Report, also considers any additional expense upon the gauge, as well as upon the improvement of gradients, to be undesirable, and assumes it at a scale of augmentation far beyond the real difference of cost.

His estimates on that head are impeached in the engineer's observations, and no doubt exists in the minds of the Directors, that the subject, reduced to a mere question of figures, in its present position, would undeniably show a pecuniary loss to be borne by the Company by any such change of system as he advocates, even if it were on other grounds deemed advisable. The objection that the wide gauge might prevent a junction with other lines seems both to Mr Wood and the Directors to have but little weight, as applied to the Great Western Railway. Already has the same width been contemplated and provided for in the extension lines through Gloucestershire to Cheltenham, and from Bristol to Exeter. Any local branches hereafter to be made would undoubtedly follow the same course, and the proprietors therefore, may be satisfied that no apprehension need be entertained by them on that head.

The advantage of following Mr Wood's advice, in not making any alteration in the width of way, has been since most forcibly shown by more recent experiments, which have entirely changed the results upon which the chief objections to the gauge were founded. The performance of the engines, shown by Mr Wood's experiments in September, gave such a disproportionate result in their power upon the attainment of high velocities as to render it all but impossible that the effect could be entirely produced by the action of the atmosphere on the trains. All doubts were shortly removed by its being ascertained that a different cause (a mere mechanical defect in the engine itself) had been in operation. If Mr Wood has witnessed these recent performances of the engines, he must unquestionably have changed his opinions as to the means and practicability of carrying full average loads at a high speed, without the great increased expense of fuel. The Directors have satisfied themselves of this very important fact, by personally attending an experiment (accompanied by several gentlemen, among whom was a very eminent practical mechanic), on which occasion the 'North Star' took a train of carriages, calculated for 166 passengers, and loaded to 43 tons, to and from Maidenhead, at a mean average speed of 38 miles per hour, the maximum being 45 miles per hour, consuming only 0.95, or less than 1 lb. of coke per net ton per mile instead of 2.76, say $2\frac{3}{4}$ lbs., as previously shown. This was accomplished by a mere altered proportion in the blast pipe of the engine, in the manner explained by Mr Brunel, being a simple adaptation of size in one of the parts, which admits of a more free escape of steam from the cylinder after it has exerted its force on the piston, still preserving sufficient draft in the fire.

It must be almost needless to point out to those who have perused the reports how importantly this change bears upon the subject in almost every relation of the inquiry. It negatives the assumption that the velocity can only be attained by a ruinous loss of power. It establishes beyond doubt that the consumption of fuel, as now ascertained, in proportion to the load, is only one-third of that which from the former experiments had been the basis of Mr Wood's arguments. An analysis in the Report of the performance of the Great Western engines, with heavy loads, varying from 80 tons to 166 tons, shows in every respect a peculiarly satisfactory result at a small cost of fuel, and warrants the expectation of very great benefit to the Company from the economical transport of goods on the line. That the expenses of locomotive repairs, especially on that heavy class of repair which arise from lateral strains on the wheels and framing of the engines, have been materially less than on other lines, is ascertained by very detailed accounts, accurately made and submitted to the Board by the super-intendent of that department. The experience of some months has now enabled the Directors to witness the pro-gressive improvement in the practical working of the rail-way. A higher rate of speed has been generally maintained than on other lines, and at the same time, with that increased speed, great steadiness of motion has been found in the carriages, with consequent comfort to the passengers. If speed, security and comfort were three great desiderata in the original institution of railway travelling, the Directors feel sure that the public will appreciate and profit by any improvements in those qualities, the Company deriving ample remuneration in the shape of increased traffic. A saving of time upon a long journey, with increased comfort, will necessarily attract to one line, in preference to another, many travellers from beyond the ordinary distance of local connection, and will thus secure a valuable collateral trade which would not otherwise belong to it. It has also a decided tendency to avert competition, which may, with much reason, be regarded as the chief peril to which railway property is subjected. The Directors, upon a deliberate reconsideration of all the circumstances affecting the per-manent welfare of the undertaking, divesting the question of all personal partialities or obstinate adherence to a system, unanimously acquiesce in the abandonment of the piles, in the substitution of a greater scantling of timber, and of a heavier rail, retaining the width of gauge, with the continuous timber bearings, as the most conducive to the general interests of the Company.

APPENDIX B.

MAY it please your Majesty,—We, the Commissioners appointed by writ, under your Majesty's Privy Seal, bearing date the 11th of July, in the ninth year of your Majesty's reign, to inquire whether in future private Acts of Parliament for the construction of railways, provision ought to be made for securing an uniform gauge, and whether it would be expedient and practicable to take measures to bring the railways already constructed, or in progress of construction, in Great Britain, into uniformity of gauge, and to inquire whether any other mode could be adopted of obviating or mitigating the evil apprehended as likely to arise from the break that will occur in railway communications from the want of an uniform gauge, beg dutifully to submit, that we have called before us such persons as we have judged to be, by reason of their situation, knowledge, or experience, the most competent to afford us correct information on the subject of this inquiry, and we have required the production of such books and documents, from the various railway companies, as appear to us to be the best calculated to aid our researches. We have personally examined into the usual course of proceeding on various railways both at home and abroad, especially those which are incident to a break, or interruption of gauge; and we have personally inspected several locomotive engines, as well as mechanical contrivances invented, either for the general use of railways, or for obviating the special difficulties presumed to arise from the break of gauge, or otherwise connected with the subject of our inquiry; and as we believe we have now carried our investigation to the utmost useful limits, we feel in a position dutifully to offer to your Majesty the following Report:—

Section I. ON THE BREAK OF GAUGE.—Our attention was first directed to ascertain whether the break of gauge could be justly considered as an inconvenience of such importance as to demand the interference of the Legislature. Gloucester is the only place where a break of gauge actually exists at the present time. It is caused by the meeting at that place of the Broad or 7 feet gauge with the Narrow or 4 feet 8½ inch gauge. There are other points, however, where a transfer of goods occurs similar to that which must result from a break of gauge, and persons well acquainted with railway traffic have no difficulty in foreseeing the nature of the inconvenience that would arise from any further intermixture of gauge ; and we humbly submit the observations that occur to us as to the whole of this important part of the question.

We will divide the subject of the break of gauge under the following heads :—

1. *Fast or Express Trains.*—We believe that the inconvenience produced by a break of gauge will, in some respects, be less felt in these than in other trains, because the passengers travelling by fast trains are usually of a class who readily submit to many inconveniences for the sake of increased speed on the journey, and who are perhaps generally less encumbered with luggage than persons travelling by the slower trains ; and as it is understood to be the general practice that no private carriages or horses are conveyed by these trains, the inconveniences of a break of gauge are reduced in this instance to the removal of the passengers and a moderate quantity of luggage; and although such removal must create delay and some confusion, as well as personal discomfort, especially at night and in the winter season, besides the risk of a loss of luggage, yet we do not consider the break of gauge, in this instance, as being an inconvenience of so grave a nature as to call for any legislative measures, either for its removal or for its mitigation.

2. *Ordinary or Mixed Trains.*—In these trains the passengers considerably exceed in number those who travel by the fast trains, and they have generally a much greater quantity of luggage. To such travellers a change of carriage is really a serious inconvenience, and it is a well known fact, that persons travelling by railways in communication with each other, but under different managements, endeavour to make such arrangements as to admit of their travelling by those trains which afford them the accommodation of occupying the same carriage from the beginning to the end of their journey. The managers and directors of railways are well aware of this feeling, and in some instances where they do not allow their carriages to run through, yet with a view of diminishing the inconvenience to which this exposes their passengers, they send a luggage van from terminus to terminus, to prevent the evil of a removal of

the passengers' luggage; and some railway companies incur considerable expense in running trains of return empty carriages, in order to accommodate the public by enabling travellers to avoid a change of carriage on the journey. It is by the ordinary or mixed trains that private carriages and horses are conveyed, and the removal of either from one truck or horse-box to another, at any part of the journey, would be attended with inconvenience and delay; and with regard to the horses, it would involve considerable risk. We arrive, therefore, at the conclusion that the break of gauge would inflict considerable inconvenience on travellers by the trains now under consideration, and that this inconvenience would be much increased at points of convergence of more than 2 lines. The change of carriages, horse-boxes and trucks, and the transference of luggage of an entire train of much extent, must, even in the daytime, be an inconvenience of a very serious nature, but at night it would be an intolerable evil, and we think legislative interference is called for to remove or mitigate such an evil.

3. *Goods Trains.*—From the statements made to us by carriers on railways, and from our own observation, we are induced to believe, that not only a considerable degree of care, judgment and experience is necessary in the stowage of merchandise in railway waggons, but also that it is desirable that, when properly packed, the articles should, generally speaking, not be disturbed until the journey is completed. We find that, in the arrangement of merchandise, the heavier goods are placed at the bottom, and the lighter at the top of the load, and so secured as to prevent friction as far as practicable from the jolting of the waggons; and it is considered very desirable, with a view to prevent loss by pilfering, that the sheeting, which is placed over the load, should not be removed till the completion of the journey. Indeed, acting upon this principle, carriers find it profitable to send their waggons partially filled from various stations on the line, thereby increasing their toll to the railway company, rather than incur the risk of loss by theft, to which they would be exposed by uncovering the waggons on the journey, to fill up with intermediate local goods, waggons that may nave started with light loads from one of the termini. The stations for re-arranging the goods trains are therefore as few as possible; thus, between Leeds and London, the points for unsheeting the goods waggons are only Derby and Leicester, and between Liverpool and London, the re-arrangement is confined to Birmingham and Rugby; and even at

those stations, the proportion of waggons which are uncovered is very small; indeed, it is stated that at the important town of Birmingham five-sixths of the waggons pass without re-arrangement. In the conveyance of machinery and articles of a similar class, which are both heavy and delicate, it is of the utmost consequence that the load should not be disturbed between the beginning and the end of the journey; a change of carriage, such as would result in all probability from a break of the gauge, would altogether prevent the transport of such articles by this mode of conveyance. We believe that the traffic upon the line of railway between Birmingham and Bristol has been greatly restricted by the interruption of gauge at Gloucester. In respect to the conveyance of minerals, the inconvenience of a break of gauge would be very serious; the transfer being attended with an expense, which would be sensibly felt in consequence of the low rate of tolls charged on such articles; moreover, many descriptions of coal, such as a considerable proportion of that of the Midland Counties, are subject to great deterioration by break-age. In regard to various articles of agricultural produce, the loss by removal would be less than on other classes of goods; much inconvenience, however, would be found in the transfer of timber; and the difficulty of shifting cattle would be so great as to present an insurmountable obstacle to such an arrangement, from the excited state of the animals after travelling by railway, and the resistance they in consequence offer when it is attempted to force them a second time into a railway waggon.

4. *Conveyance of Troops.* There is another use of rail-ways which we have deemed it necessary to consider; we allude to the transport of your Majesty's troops, with their military stores, etc., either in the ordinary movements of corps through the country, in the time of peace, or in the more pressing and urgent case of their movements for the defence of the coast, or of the interior of the country. We have care-fully weighed the important information given to us by the Quartermaster-General of your Majesty's Forces, as well as by the Inspector-General of Fortifications, both officers of great experience; and we deduce from their opinions, that although a break of gauge on the line of route would produce both delay and confusion, yet, that as in time of peace it is usually practicable to give notice of the intended movements of a body of troops, the inconvenience of the break of gauge might be so reduced as not to be an evil of great importance; but, in the event of operations for defensive objects against an

enemy, the inconvenience would assume a serious character. It would appear, that for the defence of the coast the proper course would be to retain the great mass of troops in the interior of the country to wait until the point selected by the enemy for his attack should be ascertained with certainty, and then to move upon that point such an overwhelming force as should be adequate to the emergency. It is obvious that the success of such a system of defence must depend upon the means of conveying the troops with great dispatch, and without interruption on the journey. The troops should be carried with their equipments complete in all their details, and with their artillery and ammunition ; and it therefore appears indispensably necessary, in order to insure the requisite supply of carriages, where perhaps little or no notice can be previously given, that the whole should be conveyed in the same vehicles from the begining to the end of the journey. The effect of a break of gauge might, in this view of the case, expose the country to serious danger.

To all classes of merchandise, as well as to all military operations connected with railways, one general remark will apply, that, in starting from any one point, it is usually practicable to obtain a sufficient number of waggons for whatever may be required to leave that point, however irregular the traffic may be ; but, at the convergence of several lines, where the greater number might be of a gauge not corresponding to the gauge of the other lines, if it happened that all were unusually loaded at the same time, it would probably be impossible to provide on the latter an adequate number of waggons to carry off all the loads thus brought; the alternative would be, on the one hand, to submit to great confusion, delay and inconvenience on all the converging lines having the majority on the same gauge ; or, on the other hand, to maintain on the lines being in the minority a very extensive stock of carriages, which in general would be totally useless. There is one point which forcibly presses on our attention, and the truth of which must be readily acknowledged, but of which the importance is not at first equally obvious ; it is, that the greater part of the inconveniences to which we have alluded are not inconveniences of rare occurrence, and which would effect only a small number of persons, but, on the contrary, that many of them would occur several times in the course of every day to a great number of persons at each point at which a break of gauge might exist. The cumulative amount of such inconvenience would of necessity be very considerable ; and we feel bound to sum up our conclusions by stating that we consider a break of gauge to be a very serious evil.

Section II. REMEDIES FOR THE EVILS OF BREAKING GAUGE.—We are now brought to the second stage of our inquiry, which is, to discover the means of obviating or mitigating the evil that we find to result from the break of gauge

The methods which have been laid before us, as calculated for this purpose, are as follow :—1st. What may be termed telescopic axle ; an arrangement of the wheels and axles of carriages, permitting the wheels to slide on the axle so as to contract or extend the interval between them in such a manner that they may be adapted to either of the gauges. 2ndly. A form of truck adapted to the Broad Gange, but carrying upon its upper surface pieces of rail 4 feet $8\frac{1}{2}$ inches asunder, so that a Narrow Gauge carriage may be run upon these rails without any disturbance of its wheels. 3rdly. A method of shifting the bodies of carriages from a platform and set of wheels adapted for one gauge to a different platform and set of wheels adapted to the other gauge. 4thly. A proposal to carry merchandise and minerals in loose boxes, which may be shifted from one truck to another, and of which one only would probably be carried upon a Narrow Gauge truck, while two would be conveyed on a Broad Gauge truck.

1. *Telescopic Axles.*—Of these various methods, the first, if it admitted of being used safely and extensively, would be, in its application, the easiest of all. By the operations of detaching the wheels from one limiting hold, of pushing the carriage along converging or diverging rails, until its wheels were brought to the required width, and of then connecting them by another limiting hold, the transformation of the Narrow Gauge carriage to the Broad Gauge carriage, or *vice versa*, would be completed. But this construction is liable to grave objections. It is stated to us as a matter of experience (and we believe it admits of satisfactory explanation), that a very small unsteadiness of the wheels of a railway carriage upon the axle renders the carriage liable to run off the rails. A far more serious objection, however, is, that the safety of a carriage, and the whole train with which it is connected, would depend upon the care of the attendant who has to make the adjustments of the axle slide.

It is true that there are other cases, as in the attendance on the switches and signals, which depend upon the care of the person who is stationed to work them ; but the circumstances differ very widely. In these cases, the attendant has a single act to perform (or at the utmost, two acts only), he is not hurried, and his whole attention is concentrated on very simple duties.

In respect to the shifting axles, the attendant would have to adjust a great many carriages in succession (as there are sometimes a hundred waggons in a goods train), the adjustment must be made hurriedly, and often in the night, and the attendant's thoughts would probably have been partly occupied with the loading of goods, and other station arrangements.

On the score of danger, therefore, we think that this construction must be at once abandoned. But we think it proper to add, that if even there were no such essential ground of objection, a construction of this nature could not be adequately useful unless it were extended to every carriage which is likely to pass the station where the break of gauge occurs. Under the existing system of interchange of carriages, which is adopted by all the railway companies whose lines communicate, and of which the advantages are recognised in special clauses of the Acts of Parliament applying to several railways, carriages belonging to distant railways will frequently be found at the place of junction of the two gauges. This construction, therefore, would lose much of its utility unless every railway carriage were made in conformity to it—that is, unless a vast expenditure of capital, and a corresponding annual expense in replacing worn-out carriages, etc., were incurred, even on railways very distant from the break of gauge.

2. *Broad Gauge Trucks for Narrow Gauge Carriages.*— The plan of placing a Narrow Gauge carriage upon the top of a Broad Gauge truck has, on the face of it, this obvious difficulty, that a Broad Gauge carriage cannot be placed in the same manner upon a Narrow Gauge truck, and, therefore, unless not only the Broad Gauge railway, but also all others communicating with it, be furnished with trucks proper for carrying Narrow Gauge waggons, and with Narrow Gauge waggons also, and unless the loads travelling towards the Narrow Gauge be placed only in these Narrow Gauge waggons, the system effects nothing as regards the passage in one direction. But even with regard to the passage from the Narrow Gauge to the Broad Gauge, the system will not bear examination. If the trucks are supported on springs, there is practically a difficulty in running the waggons upon them; and if they are not supported on springs, they will sustain great injury on the journeys. If they are loaded singly, there will be a great delay; if they are placed in a row, and the Narrow Gauge carriages are run through the whole series, very

great caution will be necessary to secure each carriage both in front and in rear. When heavy loads are thus placed in elevated positions, and when the security of each depends upon adjustments hurriedly made, there will be the danger to which we have alluded in noticing the first proposed construction. Finally, an enormous amount of dead weight will be carried on the Broad Gauge line. We reject this proposal as entirely inapplicable to the traffic of railways.

3. *Shifting Bodies.*—The system of shifting the bodies of carriages from road wheels to railway wheels is practised successfully in France, where the diligences from Paris to distant towns, proceeding on road wheels from the Messagerie of Paris to the railway station, are carried on a peculiar railway truck as far as Rouen and Orleans, and are then again placed on road wheels to continue their journey. At the low speeds of the French railways this system is safe, but we doubt whether it would be safe with the speeds of the English railways. Moreover, it deprives the railway system of one of its greatest conveniences, namely, its readiness to receive almost any number of passengers without warning, and to carry them to any distance, small or great. Carriers' carts are also conveyed (but to no great amount) in the same manner. In France, as we understand, it is not thought likely that the system will be in any degree retained when those railways shall have been extended further. The same remarks, we conceive, would apply entirely, or in a great measure, to similar proposals for the shifting of the bodies of railway carriages ; but as this plan has never been strenuously urged, it is unnecessary to criticise it more minutely.

4. *Loose Boxes for Goods.*—The system of conveying goods in loose boxes, carried upon railway trucks, has been seriously discussed. It has been repeatedly tried, and we are able, therefore, to give an opinion on it, founded on experience. The result of this experience is, that in one instance of a temporary character, where the whole operation was under the control of one engineer, it succeeded: in other instances, although always under the control of one engineer or one company, it has usually failed ; and these failures have occurred where, from the deterioration, caused by hand-shifting, to the mineral conveyed, it was matter of anxiety to avoid transference of the load from one box or waggon to another, and where no expense was spared in the erection of machinery proper for the transference of the loose boxes. These failures, it is to be remarked, occurred in a traffic which is comparatively regular, viz., that of coal ; in traffic of

a less regular character, the causes tending to produce failure would be very much more numerous. We consider that this method is totally inapplicable to remedy the inconvenience of a break of gauge. Some of the witnesses whom we have examined are of opinion that there would be less difficulty in unloading the waggons of one gauge and 'placing the articles in waggons of the other gauge, by having two rows of waggons on the different gauges, marshalled alongside of each other ; but having witnessed this process at Gloucester, we are of opinion that such a system is totally inapplicable to an extended traffic. We sum up our conclusions on this head by stating our belief that no method has been proposed to us which is calculated to remedy, in any important degree, the inconveniences attending a break of gauge.

Section III. ON UNIFORMITY OF GAUGE.—Considerations on the general policy of establishing an uniformity of gauge throughout the country. We approach this momentous question with a full conviction of its importance, and of the responsibility that rests upon us. That an uniformity of gauge is now an object much to be desired, there can, we think, be no question. In the earlier period of the railway history of this country, the great trunk lines were so far separated as to be independent of each other, and, as it were, isolated in their respective districts, and no diversity of gauge was then likely to interfere with the personal convenience or the commercial objects of the community ; but now that railways are spreading in all directions, and becoming interlaced with each other in numerous places, that isolation is removed, that independence has ceased, and the time has arrived when, if steps cannot be taken to remove the existing evil of the diversity of gauge, at least it appears to us imperative that a wider spread of this evil should be prevented. If we had to deal with a question not affecting the interests of parties, who are not only unconnected, but who are opposed to each other in a spirit of emulation, if not of rivalry ; or if we were dealing with the property of the public, and not of private trading companies, we should merely have to consider whether that uniformity of gauge which we deem to be so desirable, would be too dearly purchased by an alteration of one gauge to suit the other, or of both to some fresh gauge which might be considered preferable to either, if any such there be. But our position is different from this, since we have to consider not only the relative length of the different systems, the comparative mechanical efficiency of each, the general superiority of one above the other, their adaptation to the wants of the

Y

country, and the possibility as well as the policy of a change, but also the pecuniary means of effecting it. We have further to look to the consequences of an interruption of the traffic during the progress of an alteration. There is still another view of the question, and that is, the expediency of having, on lines of railway, additional rails, so as to afford the facility of using engines and carriages on both gauges. This expedient, in whatever form adopted, cannot be considered as free from difficulties. If two rails, forming a Narrow Gauge way, are placed between the two rails which form a Broad Gauge way, carriages of the different gauges may run in the same train, without alteration even of their buffers, which, in the ordinary construction of the carriages, correspond exactly on the Broad and Narrow Gauges. But the expense of such an insertion would probably be not less than that of an entire change of gauge, including, in the latter, the change of engines and carrying stock ; and the complication which it would introduce at the crossings might produce danger to rapid trains, unless their speed were diminished at approaching such points. The difficulty of packing the rails, if longitudinal sleepers were used, would also be much greater than if rails of only a single gauge were employed. If a single rail were inserted eccentrically in a Broad Gauge way, so as to form, in conjunction with one of the Broad Gauge rails, a Narrow Gauge way, the expense of the insertion, and the danger of the crossings, as well as the difficulty of packing the rails, would be somewhat diminished, but it would be imprudent to run carriages of the different gauges in the same train ; and as it would probably be the policy of the railway company to adopt for their own stock of engines only one of the two gauges, and to interpose those difficulties which amount to a prohibition of the use of other companies' engines, the inconveniences of a break of gauge would exist in almost all their force at every junction of a branch railway on a different gauge. We consider, therefore, that the general adoption of such a system ought not to be permitted. We remark, however, that the difficulties to which we have alluded may be greatly diminished on any railway where the system of combined gauges is cordially taken up by the company ; and we think that great respect ought to be paid to the rights which the companies may be supposed to possess in the methods or systems which they have devised or adopted. At the same time, we lay it down as the first principle, that inter-communication of railways throughout the country ought, if possible, to be secured. If, to obtain the last-mentioned object, it should be necessary to alter or make a change in any existing railways, we think that it may be left as a matter of ulterior consideration for the Legislature, whether in these limited instances the combination of gauges may not be allowed.

ON THE BEST GAUGE.

Whatever may be the course which at the present time circumstances will permit, it will appear from the opinion we have expressed that we think, abstractedly, equalisation desirable; and we shall, therefore, proceed to consider what gauge would be the best in such a system of equalization.

1. *For Safety.*—We are of opinion that experience will, in this matter, afford a better test by which to compare the systems of the Broad and the Narrow Gauge than any theory; and we therefore have made inquiry into the nature of the accidents recorded in the Official Reports of the Board of Trade, as well as of such as have happened since the last Report was published. We find that railway accidents arise from collisions, obstructions on the road, points wrongly placed, slips in cuttings, subsidence of embankments, a defective state of the permanent way, loss of gauge, broken or loose chairs, fractures of wheels or axles, etc., and, lastly, from engines running off the line through some other cause. Of these several classes of accidents, all except the last are obviously independent of the gauge; and with reference to this last class, we have thought it right to endeavour to determine whether the advocates of either gauge could fairly claim, in regard to these accidents, a preference for their respective systems on the score of greater security to the traveller. In these lists we find only six accidents of the kind we are considering recorded from October 1840 to May 1845, whereas there have been no less than seven within the last seven months, and these are all attributable to excessive speed, the majority having happened to express trains. Of the whole number of these accidents, three have occurred on the Broad Gauge and ten on the Narrow; the former, however, differ in their character from the latter, the carriages only, in the two last cases, having been off the line, whereas, in all the ten Narrow Gauge cases, the engines have run off, and the consequences have been more fatal. We must here observe, however, that the extent of the Narrow Gauge lines is 1901 miles, and that of the Broad only 274; therefore the comparison would be unfavourable to the Broad Gauge if considered merely

with regard to their relative length; but it must be borne
in mind that the general speed of the Great Western considerably exceeds that of many of the Narrow Gauge lines,
and that some consideration is on this account due to the
Broad Gauge. The primary causes of engines getting off
the rails appear to be overdriving, a defective road, a bad
joint, or a badly-balanced engine. If, in consequence of
heavy rains or other unfavourable circumstances, any part
of the road becomes unsound, the engine sinks on one side
as it passes along such part of the rails, suddenly rises again,
and is thus thrown into a rocking and lateral oscillatory
motion, with more or less of violence, according to the
rate of speed; and a very similiar effect is produced in
passing at high speeds from one curve to another of different
curvature. A succession of strains is thus thrown upon the
rails, and if, before the rocking subsides, the wheel meets
with a defective rail or chair, which yields to the impulse,
the engine and train are thrown off as a necessary consequence; but, as far as we can see, such casualties are
equally likely to happen on either gauge, other circumstances being similar. It has indeed been stated by some
of the witnesses whom we have examined, that the Broad
Gauge is more liable to such accidents, from the circumstance that the length of the engine, or rather the distance
between the fore and hind axle, is less in proportion to
its breadth than in the Narrow Gauge engines, and that
therefore the Broad Gauge engine is liable to be thrown
more obliquely across the lines, and in case of meeting with
an open or defective joint, more liable to quit the rail; but
we cannot admit the validity of this objection against the
Broad Gauge lines. It may be, that the proportion between
the length and breadth of the engine has some influence
on its motion, and that the motion is somewhat less steady
where the difference between the length and breadth is
considerably diminished, but practical facts scarcely lead
to the conclusion that the safety of the trains is endangered
by the present proportion of the Broad Gauge engines;
for it appears that on the London and Birmingham Railway, where the engines hitherto employed have been,
generally, short four-wheeled engines, the distance from
axle to axle not exceeding 7 feet, or 7 feet 6 inches, no
such accident as we are considering has been reported;
and, we are informed by Mr Bruyeres, the superintendent
of that line, that no such accident has ever occurred. The
same remark applies to some other Narrow Gauge lines;

and if, as has been stated, exemption from these accidents has resulted from the close fixing of the engine and tender adopted on this line, the same system might be adopted on any other line, whether on the Broad or Narrow Gauge. An evil may also sometimes arise in six-wheeled engines, by the centre of gravity of the engine being brought too much over the driving-wheels, and the springs being so adjusted for the sake of the adhesion of the wheels to the rails, that the front wheels would have little or no weight to support, and would be thus in a condition, by any irregularity in the road or other obstruction, to be more easily lifted off the rails. But here, again, if this fault in the construction or adjustment has been anywhere committed, it is a fault or defect wholly unconnected with the breadth of gauge.

Another cause of unsteady or irregular motion, dangerous to the safety of the train, has been stated to be the great overhanging weight beyond the axles of some engines of recent construction, and of the weight of the outside cylinder beyond the axle bearings. So far as this construction is concerned, it certainly appertains to Narrow Gauge lines only, but at the same time we must remark that it is not essential to their working.

Upon the whole, therefore, after the most careful consideration of this part of the subject, we feel bound to report that, as regards the safety of the passenger, no preference is due, with well-proportioned engines, to either gauge, except perhaps at very high velocities, where we think a preference would be due to the Broad Gauge. On this part of the subject we would beg to point to the nature of the evidence of Mr Nicholas Wood.

2. *Public Accommodation and Convenience.*—We have now to advert to the question of the relative accommodation and convenience for passengers and goods. The first-class carriages of the Broad Gauge are intended to carry eight passengers in each compartment, and the compartments are sometimes subdivided by a partition and inside door. On the Narrow Gauge lines the first-class carriages are usually constructed to carry only six passengers in each compartment, and we find that about the same width is allowed for each passenger on both gauges. Some of the original mail carriages were adapted for four passengers, and we believe that the public had a preference for these carriages over both the other descriptions. Until lately the Broad Gauge carriages were altogether more commodious than those of the Narrow Gauge, but recently carriages have been introduced

on several of the Narrow Gauge lines nearly as lofty as those on the Broad Gauge, and equally commodious; in short, we now see no essential difference as regards accommodation and convenience to individual passengers in the first-class carriages of the two gauges.

In the second-class carriages on the Broad Gauge six persons sit side by side, each carriage being capable of holding seventy-two passengers. On the Narrow Gauge, generally, only four persons sit side by side, the total number in each carriage being thirty-two; in this respect we are inclined to consider the latter are more comfortably accommodated. With reference to the ease of the carriage, and the smoothness of the motion, we have had very contradictory evidence, and it must be admitted that great difference is experienced on the same line at different times, depending upon the state of the road, the springs of the carriage, the number of persons in a carriage, to bring the springs into action, the position of the carriage in the train, and the speed at which the train is propelled, all which conditions are independent of the breadth of gauge. We have, however, with a view of making our own observations on this question, travelled several times over all those lines having their stations in London, and after making. to the best of our judgment, every allowance for the circumstances above mentioned, we are of opinion that at the higher velocities the motion is usually smoother on the Broad Gauge.

It is now to be considered whether either gauge has a superiority over the other in regard to the conveyance to general merchandise. Under this head we class manufactured goods and their raw materials, mineral products, such as coal, lime, iron, and other ores; agricultural produce, such as corn, hops, wool, cattle and timber. On these points we have taken the evidence of persons well acquainted with the carrying trade, and from their information, and our own observation, it does not appear to be of consequence to the parties sending or receiving goods whether they are transmitted in the waggons containing 5 or 6 tons, or in waggons of larger capacity, provided that the cost and security are the same, and that the carriers undertake the responsibility of any damage that may result from the size of the load. But Messrs Horne & Chaplain and Mr Hayward, who are largely interested, and have had great experience in the carrying trade, have expressed a strong opinion that the smaller waggon is far the more convenient and economical. The same opinion is still more strongly expressed by those witnesses we have examined, who have experience of our mineral districts. These persons state that the smaller waggon can be more easily handled, and can be taken along sharper curves than would be suited to a broader waggon; that such sharp curves are very common in mineral works and districts, and that the broken nature of the ground would render curves of greater radius inconvenient and expensive.

Another important difference between the two gauges, in this commercial view of the question, would present itself in localities in which there may be a difficulty of readily obtaining full loads for the waggons at road stations. Here the defect of the dead weight, which we find to apply more particularly to the Broad Gauge, would be greatly increased, unless another evil of still greater commercial importance were created, that of detaining the waggons to receive full loads. On the whole, therefore, we consider the Narrow Gauge as the more convenient for the merchandise of the country.

3. *Comparative Speed on the Gauges.*—With a view to form our judgment on this subject, we have examined the timetables of the several companies having express and fast trains, and the returns furnished by those companies of the actual speeds attained by the express trains on thirty successive days, from the 15th of June to the 15th of July 1845. We have also, on various occasions, travelled in the express trains, and noted the speed, mile by mile. The result has been that we are fully satisfied that the average speed on the Great Western, both by the express trains and by the ordinary trains, exceeds the highest speed of similar trains on any of the Narrow Gauge lines. But some of the latter have trains which exceed in speed the corresponding trains of the Bristol and Gloucester line, and also of the Swindon and Gloucester line, both of which are on the Broad Gauge; but these latter, it is to be remembered, are still of recent construction, with unfavourable curves and gradients; and we have been informed by Mr R. Stephenson, in his evidence, that at one period the speed on the Northern and Eastern line even exceeded that of the Great Western.

In treating of a difference in the speed, other circumstances besides the mere gauge must be considered. The inclinations and curves of the Great Western Railway, between London and Bristol, and even for 40 miles beyond Bristol, are, with the exception of the Wootton-Basset and the Box inclines, particularly favourable to the attainment of high velocities; and it is important to remark that the inclinations and curves on that part of the Northern and Eastern Railway, where the competition in speed with the Great Western was the most successful, are generally of a similar character. One of the principal motives professed for constructing the Great Western Railway on the Broad Gauge was the attaining of high speeds, and the credit of the proposers and defenders of that construction has therefore been deeply engaged in maintaining them. The effect of gradients on the speed of the Great Western trains, even with the powerful engines used on that line, is shown in the time-table (page 24) where we find that, while the speed from Paddington to Didcot by the express train is 47½ miles per hour, from Didcot to Swindon it is only 41.1; and from Swindon to Gloucester only 31.7; from Swindon to Bath it is 48.2, but returning only 37.2; from Bristol to Taunton the speed is 46.3, and from Taunton to Exeter only 39.2.

We must observe, however, that while the Great Western Company have not altered in any degree the plan of their engines, the higher velocities of the Narrow Gauge lines have been attained by the introduction of a more powerful kind of engine than was employed at an earlier period, and probably the new engines now used on the Narrow Gauge lines are as powerful as they can well be made within the limits of their gauge; whereas the Broad Gauge lines have still a means of obtaining an increase in the power of their engines, and of increasing their speed provided the road be in a condition to sustain the great increased force which must result from any increased weight of the engine moving at such high velocities. Whether the permanent way is in such a state at present is very questionable, or even whether it be possible in all vicissitudes of weather to maintain it in such a condition. We ought not to lose sight of the fact that, since the introduction of express trains, the accidents arising from engines running off the line have been much more common than in former years; indeed, these accidents have been more numerous within the last seven months than within the preceding five years, and it is questionable whether this contest for speed ought to be carried to any greater length. We are, indeed, strongly inclined to the opinion stated by several engineers in their evidence, that it is the stability of the road, and not the power of the engine, that will prescribe the limits of safe speed.

On the first introduction of passenger railways, speeds of about 12 miles per hour only were anticipated : the rails then employed weighed only 35 lbs. per yard, and the engines about 6 or 7 tons. As soon as speeds of 20 and 24 miles per hour were attempted, it was found necessary to have rails of 50 lbs. per yard, and engines weighing 10 and 12 tons. Since that time the rails have been increased in weight progressively to 65, 75, and 85 lbs. per yard, and the weight of the engine on the Broad Gauge exceeds 22 tons, and on the Narrow Gauge it now approaches 20 tons ; indeed, we have seen a Narrow Gauge engine on six wheels weighing 30 tons. We doubt, however, whether a corresponding stability has been attained in the road itself. Amongst other changes for increasing the power of the engine and the speed of the trains of the Narrow Gauge lines, there have been the giving an increased length to the engine, and the placing the cylinders on the outside of the framing; but it is the opinion of some of the witnesses we have examined, that this position of the cylinders has a tendency to produce a greater wear and tear of the journals, and a consequent rocking and irregular motion of the engine on the line. This, however, while the engine is of medium length, has been denied by Mr Locke, who has had great experience in the working of outside-cylinder engines. But it is stated by Mr Gray and Mr Gooch, that where the length of the engine is greatly increased, this increased length, by causing the extremities of the engine to overhang very considerably the fore and hind axles, has a great tendency to increase the irregular motion produced by the outside cylinder. Mr R. Stephenson admits that, in some of the later engines, this irregularity does exist, but he attributes it to the weight of the piston and its appendages, observing, ' I do not believe that it is the steam that causes the irregular action, but I believe it to be the mere weight of the pistons themselves, and therefore if we could contrive to balance the piston by the weight upon the wheels, we should get rid of that very much.' At all events, from whatever cause the motion may arise, the oscillations are very considerable in some of these long engines, and such as can scarcely be considered safe at high velocities. This great length of engine is, however, by no means essential to the attainment of high speeds on Narrow Gauge lines.

We found, by timing the express trains on four different journeys on the South Western line, in both directions, that the whole distance was performed very satisfactorily in about 1 hour and 52 minutes, including the time of two stop-pages, being at an average rate of 41 miles per hour, on a line which, in one direction, rises for a length of more than 40 miles on a very prevailing gradient of 1 in 330, and in the other rises for several miles on a gradient of 1 in 250. On each occasion a distance of 5 miles on a level part of the road, was passed at the rate of 53 miles per hour. The length of the engine boiler was only 8 feet 7 inches; the driving wheels 6 feet 6 inches in diameter; the leading wheels had both inside and outside bearings. The diameter of the cylinder in one case was 15 inches, in the others 14¼ inches, both outside, and attached to the smoke-box.

In proceeding to compare the locomotive engines, we remark, in the first place, that the fire-boxes, boilers, etc., of the Narrow Gauge engines still possess a smaller evaporating power than those of the Broad Gauge engines, although recent attempts have been made to raise the former to the level of the latter; but those attempts have not succeeded; and it is indisputable that, whatever can be done for the Narrow Gauge, in this respect, can be surpassed on the Broad Gauge. And we concur in opinion with many of the ablest engineers, who have stated that the engines of both Gauges have nearly obtained the speed and power which it would be justifiable to employ in reference to the present strength of the rails and the firmness of the earthworks. We remark, in the next place, that the diameter of the driving wheels of the Broad Gauge engines is greater than that of the driving wheels of the Narrow Gauge engines; and although in many of the Narrow Gauge engines the use of the external cylinder has enabled the manufacturers to bring the boilers nearer to the driving wheel axle, and has thus permitted an increase of the diameter of the wheel, still it is always in the power of the constructors of Broad Gauge engines to make a corresponding change, and thus to maintain the superiority: for the larger diameter of the wheel is unquestionably favourable to high speed, both because the steam is used to greater advantage, and because the alternating shocks upon the machinery are less rapid. It is, however, extremely difficult to say at what speeds this advantage becomes appreciable. We think it likely that, as far as the speeds of 40 miles an hour, there is no great difference between the two, but that for speeds of 50 or 60 miles an hour, the difference may be worthy of notice. It becomes important, then, to inquire what may be the greatest speed that will probably be desired or maintained on railways for ordinary purposes.

It is certain that the wishes of the public will be limited only by considerations of economy and safety. The greater the speed the greater will be the cost, and it appears to be the opinion of many of the officers of railways that it would be difficult to maintain with safety the present express speeds upon the great trunk railways.

Impediments to maintaining the present Express Speed.—The chief of these are—1st. The difficulty of arranging the trains, where the traffic is frequent, so that the fast trains shall be entirely protected from the chance of interfering with, or coming into collision with, the slower trains, or those that stop at numerous stations. 2d. The difficulty of seeing signals, especially in foggy weather, in time to enable the engine driver to stop the fast trains. We feel it a duty to observe here that the public are mainly indebted for the present rate of speed, and the increased accommodation of the railway carriages, to the genius of Mr Brunel, and the liberality of the Great Western Railway Company. As regards the applicability of the atmospheric principle of traction, or of any other principle differing from the locomotive, we see no difference between the two gauges.

4. *Comparative Economy.*—This next demands our attention. Under this head we have to consider the cost of construction, the purchase of the plant, which consists of engines, of carriages, and of other carrying stock; and lastly, the cost of working. There can be no question that in the *first construction* of a railway the narrower the gauge the smaller will be the cost of the works. This applies to tunnels, bridges, viaducts, embankments, cuttings, sheds, workshops, turn-tables, transverse sleepers and ballast, and the purchase of land; but it does not affect the rails, fences, drains and station-houses. The exact difference, however, must depend, in a great degree, upon local circumstances, and no opinion can be given of the precise ratio of difference without going into a very minute calculation of each line on which the two systems are to be compared; for instance, in a line free from tunnels or viaducts, and in a flat country, where there are neither cuttings nor embankments, the difference would be limited very nearly to the quantity of land to be purchased (the severance and damage being about equal in both cases), the amount of ballasting, and some increase in the cost of the sleepers; whereas, in a very undulating

country the difference would be more considerable. As to the cost of the *maintenance of way*, supposing the construction to be the same, that of the Broad Gauge must be rather the greater of the two.

In respect to the *cost of the engines and carrying stock*, we have to observe that they are generally more expensive on the Broad than on the Narrow Gauge. But, on the other hand, it is asserted by the advocates of the Broad Gauge system that, as the engines will draw greater loads, as the carriages will accommodate a greater number of passengers, and as the waggons are capable of conveying a larger amount of merchandise, the work can be and is done at a less charge per ton, and that a compensation is thus obtained for the increased outlay. How far this is found to be practically the case is the next subject for inquiry. We were very desirous, if it had been found possible, thoroughly to investigate this part of the subject by means of the official data called for by us, and furnished by some of the principal companies, containing a statement of their working expenses; but we find the circumstances so different that very little satisfactory information can be thus obtained that has strictly a reference to the economy of the two gauges. There are, of course, various matters that have an influence on the actual cost of locomotive power and general traffic charges, that are in no way connected with the breadth of gauge; such as the nature of the curves and gradients, the price of coke, the general nature of the traffic, the mode of working that traffic as adopted by different companies, the employment of engines of greater or less power, that increased accommodation to the public which involves an extra expense for return carriages, etc., etc.

The London and Birmingham, and the Great Western Railway, as Metropolitan lines of great traffic and of considerable length, would, at first sight, appear to furnish the best means of comparison, and there is, in fact, no difficulty in comparing the actual expenses; but these lines differ essentially in the character of their gradients, and in the amount of traffic, estimated at per mile, and, above all, they differ in the character of the engines they employ. The London and Birminghrm Company have, from the commencement, persevered in the use of light four-wheeled engines, while the Great Western, availing themselves of the facilities their gauge affords, have adopted large and powerful engines, which are worked at nearly the same cost per mile as the former; and if such engines as those on the London and Birmingham line were essential to the Narrow Gauge, the question as to the economy of working might be at once decided in favour of the Broad Gauge, but this is by no means the case; several Narrow Gauge lines employ engines of great power, and work, in consequence, much more cheaply than the London and Birmingham; therefore the comparison between the working expenses of this line and of the Great Western can only be considered as a test of the principle of working with light and with heavy engines, and not as furnishing a test of the working economy of the two gauges.

It is a common practice with different railway companies, in their half-yearly reports to their proprietors, to state the percentage of their various expenses, under a few distinct heads, as compared with their revenue; and from these it appears that on the Great Western the locomotive charges, during a period of three years, have varied between 8.8 and 11.1, averaging 9.7 per cent. on their income, and on the London and Birmingham they have varied, within the same period, between 7.9 and 10.36, averaging about 8.6 per cent. on their income; and therefore, on a superficial view of the question, the London and Birmingham would appear to have worked their line at a cheaper rate; but valid objections have been made to this comparison on the part of the Great Western; because it is obvious, from the several returns we have received, that the London and Birmingham Company has far the more abundant traffic per mile, and ought therefore to be expected to perform its work at a less percentage on its income. It has been stated by Mr Gooch that, as locomotive superintendent on the Great Western, he is called upon to supply a certain amount of locomotive power, and that the cost of such power is almost entirely irrespective of the load or number of passengers it is made to draw; but that these numbers are of great importance in comparing the locomotive expenses with the revenue.

In page 27 of the Appendix to this Report, an abstract and comparative table are given, founded on returns furnished by the Great Western and London and Birmingham Railway Companies, showing that the revenue derived from the passengers train is 64 per cent. greater per mile worked, on the latter than on the former line. It must therefore be obvious that, as a test of economy for working, we cannot adopt the principle of a percentage on the revenue, neither will the·cost per mile run give a more just comparison as to the economy of the two systems, because it is a well-known fact that the

London and Birmingham Company have been conveying their traffic with engines of inadequate power, and that great economy would result to them by the adoption of larger engines. Other difficulties also occur in the comparison of these expenses on different lines, in consequence of the difference in the form of the accounts, and of the circumstance of one company adopting the principle of having a reserve fund for renewals, and other companies having no such fund.

Working Expenses of Great Western as a Narrow Gauge Line.—We are therefore of opinion that the most satisfactory comparison that can be made of the economy of working the two gauges will be by applying to first principles, endeavouring merely to determine what the working expenses of the Great Western line, with their present amount of traffic, would have been, provided it had been made a Narrow Gauge line, and worked with such engines as those employed on the South Western and some other Narrow Gauge lines. The average weight of a passenger train on the Great Western Railway (independent of the engine and tender, which weigh 33 tons) appears, by the returns sent to us, to be 67 tons; and the average number of passengers per train for the half-year ending the 30th of June 1845 is only 47.2, whilst the weight, including their luggage, may be estimated at about 5 tons. Mr Gooch estimates each carriage and its passengers on the Broad Gauge to weigh about 9½ tons, and therefore there would be seven carriages to make up the 67 tons above specified. The most commodious carriages on the Narrow Gauge lines, such as those on the South Western, weigh less than 5 tons; seven such carriages would therefore weigh about 34 tons, and being capable of containing 126 first-class passengers, weighing, with their luggage, 12½ tons, the total load would be only 46½ tons. Now we find that, even with a traffic as large as that of the London and Birmingham Railway, the average per train would only be 84.9 passengers, weighing about 8 tons; so that, under the supposition of a traffic of this extent, the load of the seven Narrow Gauge carriages so occupied would only be 42 tons. But Mr Gooch estimates, from his own experiments, the relative powers of traction of the Broad Gauge engines, and of the Narrow Gauge engines of the South Western Railway when working at the same speed, as 2067 to 1398, or as 67, the load of the Broad Gauge in tons, to 45 tons, which would be the corresponding load for the Narrow Gauge; so that the Narrow Gauge engine has more power over the 42 tons it would have to draw than the Broad Gauge has over its average load of 67 tons, both exclusive of the weight of the engine and tender — the Narrow Gauge carriage in this supposition being supposed to contain 84.9 passengers, and the Broad Gauge only 47.2. If, however, it were necessary, 224 first-class passengers might be placed in the seven Broad Gauge carriages, and, as it has before been said, 126 in the seven Narrow Gauge carriages; but it appears likely that this extent of accommodation would only be called for on such rare occasions that the question of providing for it, except by assistant power, cannot be taken into consideration in the present comparison.

It is obvious, from the foregoing statement, that the Narrow Gauge engine of the class we have been considering has more power over the seven Narrow Gauge carriages and a load of 126 passengers, than the Broad Gauge engine has over the seven Broad Gauge carriages and the load of the same number of passengers; and that, therefore, if the Great Western had been a Narrow instead of a Broad Gauge line, the South Western engines would have had the same command over the existing passenger traffic of the Great Western as its own engines now have with the present construction of that railway. We must remark, however, that this calculation is for trains consisting exclusively of passengers and their personal luggage. In the Great Western average trains of 67 tons there is an allowance of about 16 tons for passengers and luggage, including gentlemen's carriages. Allowing the same weight of luggage on the Narrow Gauge line, the train would still not exceed 50 tons, which is considerably within the power of the Narrow Gauge engine. For it appears, by the experiments that have been recently made on the Great Western Railway, the details of which are given in the Appendix to the evidence, that the Great Western engine is capable of propelling 83 tons at a greater speed than the average speed of that line; and, consequently, by the proportion above stated, the Narrow Gauge engine would be capable of propelling 55 tons at the same rate. We conclude, therefore, that the work would be performed at about the same expense for locomotive power. That there may be cases in which not only the full power of a Broad Gauge engine is required, but even the assistance of a second engine, is quite certain, but such trains form the exception and not the rule in railway passenger traffic, and we doubt the soundness of a principle which involves a great expense in construction, for the sake of possessing capabilities so seldom called into action.*

It is proper to observe that the foregoing comparison would have appeared to stand more in favour of the Narrow Gauge had we taken for the engine of comparison one of those engines of whose increased capabilities some of the supporters of the Narrow Gauge system have informed us; but we have preferred the comparison afforded with the South Western engine, from its being the one on which Mr Gooch, of the Great Western Railway, superintended the recorded experiments,—hence, our deductions are made from data furnished by the advocates of the Broad Gauge system, without drawing anything from the evidence on the other side; and as these deductions sufficiently demonstrate that there is no economy in the locomotive expenses for passenger trains resulting from working a line on the Broad Gauge system, even on such lines of those which have at the present moment the most abundant passenger traffic, any analysation of the evidence offered in support of the Narrow Gauge system appears to us to be quite superfluous.

There is one point, however, stated in Mr Gooch's comparative table, and repeated in his evidence, which appears so much at variance with the results obtained from other data, as to require explanation. Mr Gooch has asserted that the Great Western Company work their passenger trains at half the expense per ton at which the London and Birmingham Company work their passenger trains. The fact is, however, that Mr Gooch's calculations refer to the gross and not to the net loads : and, therefore, the comparison is not applicable so far as regards the profits of these companies, and affords no proof of economy in working the passenger traffic on the Great Western system.

There can be no doubt, judging both from Mr Brunel's evidence given to us, and from his Report to the Directors of the Great Western Railway Company, that he originally expected there would be on the Great Western Railway a demand for carrying a great number of passengers at high velocities; but from his own evidence it appears that the only heavy passenger traffic upon that railway is between London and Reading, and between Bath and Bristol, being a total distance of about 50 miles out of the 245.

---

* It appears that during the half-year ending the 30th June 1845, the number of miles run by coupled and assisting engines for passenger trains on the Great Western Railway amounted to 11,628, and for goods trains to 51,155. The total number of miles run by the former trains being 761,483, and of the latter 159,324.

On the remaining part of the line the passenger traffic per train is small.

If the convenience of the public would admit of the whole of the passenger traffic of this portion of the line being conveyed daily by two or three large trains, Mr Brunel's views would have been perfectly correct in providing such powerful means; but experience has proved that the public require passenger trains to be run many times during the day, and with this frequency of trains, such numbers of passengers as Mr Brunel has provided for cannot be expected even on railways of the largest traffic, so that practically there is a waste both of power and of means. In the case of 'goods traffic,' the circumstances are not the same; railway conveyance for merchandise seems only to be required a few times in each day, and the trains are generally large. The 'through' waggons have for the most part a full load, and the disproportion between the gross and the net weight is consequently much less than in the passenger trains; still, however, it appears from the evidence of Mr Horne, and of other persons connected with the carrying trade, that on the London and Birmingham Railway it frequently happens that waggons are forwarded to a considerable distance, to 'road-side stations,' containing not more than a ton of goods; and there can be no doubt that this must happen on any long line of railway. The same also occurs in waggons coming in from branches along the trunk line, and in all such cases the heavy, large waggon of the Broad Gauge must be disadvantageous; but although the evil is not so great with goods waggons of the Broad Gauge as with their passenger carriages, still the loss by dead weight is greater with these than with smaller waggons, and we do not perceive any advantages in the Broad Gauge to counterbalance it; for where speed is not an object, and this is the case with goods trains, we believe, from the evidence we have received, that engines of nearly the same tractive power are to be found on many Narrow Gauge lines as those in use on the Broad Gauge.

Thus far we have considered the question with reference to the railways as they now exist, and composed in a great measure of trunk lines of considerable traffic; but the railways to be made in future will in some degree be branches or lines in districts having traffic of less magnitude than is to be provided for in the existing railways; and hence, if for the greater trunk lines a superiority were due to the Broad Gauge system, that superiority would be less for lines yet to be constructed of a smaller amount of traffic; and necessarily, if the preferenc ewere given to the Narrow Gauge for the existing lines, that system would be still more entitled to the preference for the railways of smaller traffic to which we look forward.

Experiments on the Gauges.—We must here add that, towards the close of our inquiry, Mr Brunel requested, on the part of the Broad Gauge companies, to institute a set of experiments to test the power of their engines ; and Mr Bidder, on the part of the Narrow Gauge companies, undertook, in consequence of such application, to make corresponding experiments on the Narrow Gauge. After sanctioning these trials, and being present at the performance of them, we may observe, without entering into a minute detail of the results, of the discrepancies between the returns as furnished by the two parties themselves, that we consider them as confirming the statements and results given by Mr Gooch in his evidence, proving, as they do, that the Broad Gauge engines possess greater capabilities for speed with equal loads, and, generally speaking, of propelling greater loads with equal speed ; and, moreover, that the working with such engines is economical where very high speeds are required, or where the loads to be conveyed are such as to require the full power of the engine. They confirm, also, the evidence given by Mr Bidder as to the possibility of obtaining high evaporative power with long engines for the Narrow Gauge, but under somewhat peculiar circumstances. It appears, moreover, that the evaporation thus obtained does not produce a corresponding useful effect in the tractive power of the engine; a circumstance that would probably be differently explained by Mr Gooch and by Mr Bidder; but as we do not refer to the power of this description of engine in the deductions we have made, it is unnecessary for us to allude further to them.

GENERAL CONCLUSION.

After a full consideration of all the circumstances that have come before us, and of all the deductions we have made from the evidence, we are led to conclude :—

First. That as regards the safety, accommodation and convenience of the passengers, no decided preference is due to either gauge, but that on the Broad Gauge the motion is generally more easy at high velocities.

Secondly. That in respect of speed, we consider the advantages are with the Broad Gauge, but we think the public safety would be endangered in employing the greater capabilities of the Broad Gauge much beyond their present use, except on roads more consolidated and more substantially and perfectly formed than those of the existing lines.

Thirdly. That in the commercial case of the transport of goods, we believe the Narrow Gauge to possess the greater convenience, and to be the more suited to the general traffic of the country.

Fourthly. That the Broad Gauge involves the greater outlay, and that we have not been able to discover, either in the maintenance of way, in the cost of locomotive power, or in the other annual expenses, any adequate reduction to compensate for the additional first cost.

Therefore, esteeming the importance of the highest speed on express trains for the accommodation of a comparatively small number of persons, however desirable that may be to them, as of far less moment than of affording increased convenience to the general commercial traffic, we are inclined to consider the Narrow Gauge as that which should be preferred for general convenience ; and, therefore, if it were imperative to produce uniformity, we should recommend that uniformity to be produced by an alteration of the Broad to the Narrow Gauge, more especially when we take into consideration that the extent of the former at present in work is only 274 miles, while that of the latter is not less than 1901 miles, and that the alteration of the former to the latter, even if of equal length, would be the less costly, as well as the less difficult operation.

We are desirous, however, of guarding ourselves from being supposed to express an opinion that the dimension of 4 feet 8½ inches is in all respects the most suited for the general objects of the country. Some of the engineers who have been examined by us have given it as their opinion that 5 feet would be the best dimension for a railway gauge, others have suggested 5 feet 3 inches, 5 feet 6 inches, and even 6 feet, but none have recommended so great a breadth as 7 feet, except those who are more particularly interested in the Broad Gauge lines. Again, some engineers of eminence contend that a gauge of 4 feet 8½ inches gives ample space for the machinery of the engine and all the railway requirements, and would recommend no change to be made in the gauge.

We may observe, in reference to this part of the question that the Eastern Counties Railway was originally constructed on a gauge of 5 feet, and has since been converted into a gauge of 4 feet 8½ inches, to avoid a break of gauge ; and we have been informed that some lines in Scotland, originally on the gauge of 5 feet 3 inches, are about to be altered to 4 feet 8½ inches for the same reason.

Whatever might be the preferable course were the question now to be discussed of the gauge for an entire system of railways, where none previously existed to clash with the decision, yet under the present state of things we see no sufficient reason to suggest or recommend the adoption of any gauge intermediate between the Narrow Gauge of 4 feet 8½ inches, and the Broad Gauge of 7 feet, and we are peculiarly struck by the circumstance that almost all the Continental railways have been formed upon the 4 feet 8½ inch gauge, the greater number having been undertaken, after a long experience of both the Broad and the Narrow Gauge in this country ; nor must the fact be lost sight of, that some of these railways have been constructed as well as planned by English engineers, and amongst that number we find Mr Brunel, the original projector of the Broad Gauge. Mr Brunel was also the engineer of the Merthyr Tydvil and Cardiff Line, which is on the 4 feet 8½ inch gauge ; and we think that the motives which led to his adoption of the Narrow Gauge in that instance would equally apply to many English lines.

We are sensible of the importance, in ordinary circumstances, of leaving commercial enterprise as well as the genius of scientific men unfettered ; we therefore feel that the restriction of the gauge is a measure that should not be lightly entertained ; and we are willing to admit, were it not for the great evil that must inevitably be experienced when lines of unequal gauges come into contact, that varying gradients, curves and traffic, might justify some difference in the breadth of gauge. This appears to be the view which Mr Brunel originally took of the subject ; for the Great Western proper is a line of unusually good gradients, on which a large passenger traffic was anticipated, and as it touched but slightly on any mineral district, it embraced all the conveniences and advantages of the Broad Gauge system, and was comparatively free from the influence of those defects on which we have commented ; but such a breadth of gauge, however suitable and applicable it may have originally been considered to its particular district, appears wholly inapplicable, or at least very ill-suited, to the requirements of many of our northern and midland lines.

In reference to the branches already in connection with the Great Western Railway, we may observe that the greatest average train on the Oxford branch, for two weeks in July and October was only 48 tons; on the Cheltenham branch it did not exceed 46; between Bristol and Exeter 53; and between Swindon and Bristol, it was under 60 tons. With such a limited traffic the power of the Broad Gauge seems beyond the requirements of these districts.

We find, from an estimate furnished to us, and the general grounds of which we see no reason to dispute, that the expense of altering the existing Broad Gauge to Narrow Gauge lines, including the alteration or substitution of locomotives and carrying stock, would not much exceed £1,000,000; yet we neither feel that we can recommend the Legislature to sanction such an expense from the public moneys, nor do we think that the companies to which the Broad Gauge railways belong can be called upon to incur such an expense themselves (having made all their works with the authority of Parliament), nor even the more limited expense of laying down intermediate rails, for Narrow Gauge traffic. Still less can we propose, for any advantage that has been suggested, the alteration of the whole of the railways of Great Britain, with their carrying stock and engines, to some intermediate gauge. The outlay in this case would be very much more considerable than the sum above mentioned; and the evil, inconvenience, and danger to the traveller, and the interruption to the whole traffic of the country for a considerable period, and almost at one and the same time, would be such that this change cannot be seriously entertained.

PRACTICAL RECOMMENDATIONS.

Guided by the foregoing considerations, we must dutifully submit to your Majesty the following recommendations :—

First. That the gauge of 4 feet 8½ inches be declared by the Legislature to be the gauge to be used in all public railways now under construction, or hereafter to be constructed in Great Britain.

Second. That, unless by the consent of the Legislature, it should not be permitted to the directors of any railway company to alter the gauge of such railway.

Third. That in order to complete the general chain of Narrow Gauge communication from the North of England to the Southern Coast, any suitable measure should be promoted to form a Narrow Gauge link from Oxford to Reading, and thence to Basingstoke, or by any shorter route connecting the proposed Rugby and Oxford Line with the South Western Railway.

Fourth. That as any junction to be formed with a Broad Gauge line would involve a break of gauge, provided our first recommendation be adopted, great commercial convenience would be obtained by reducing the gauge of the present Broad Gauge lines to the Narrow Gauge of 4 feet 8½ inches ; and we therefore think it desirable that some equitable means should be found of producing such centre uniformity of gauge, or of adopting such other course as would admit of the Narrow Gauge carriages passing, without interruption or danger, along the Broad Gauge lines.

(Signed)   J. M. FREDERIC SMITH,   (L.S.)
                  Lieut.-Colonel Royal Engineers.
                  G. B. AIRY,   (L.S.)
                  Astronomer Royal.
                  PETER BARLOW.   (L.S.)

APPENDIX C.

MR BRUNEL'S REPORT TO THE SOUTH DEVON RAILWAY DIRECTORS, URGING THE ADOPTION OF THE ATMO-SPHERIC SYSTEM.

I HAVE given much consideration to the question referred to me by you at your last meeting, namely, that of the advantage of the application of the Atmospheric System to the South Devon Railway. The question is not new to me, as I have foreseen the possibility of its arising, and have frequently considered it.

I shall assume, and I am not aware that it is disputed by anybody, that stationary power, if freed from the weight and friction of any medium of communication, such as a rope, must be cheaper, is more under command and is susceptible of producing much higher speeds than locomotive power; and when it is considered that for high speeds, such as 60 miles an hour, the locomotive engine with its tender cannot weigh much less than half of the gross weight of the train, the advantage and economy of dispensing with the necessity of putting this great weight also in motion will be evident. I must assume, also, that as a means of applying stationary power, the Atmospheric System has been successful, and that, unless where under some very peculiar circumstances it is unapplicable, it is a good economical mode of applying stationary power.

I am aware that this opinion is directly opposed to that of Mr Robert Stephenson, who has written and published an elaborate statement of experiments and calculations founded upon them, the results of which support his opinion. It does not seem to me that we can obtain the minute data required for the mathematical investigation of such a question, and that such calculations, dependent as they are upon an unattained precision in experiments, are as likely to lead you very far from the truth as not. By the same mode M. Mallet and other French engineers have proved the success of the system; and by the same mode of investigation Dr Lardner arrived at all those results regarding steam navigation and the speed to be attained on railways which have since proved so erroneous. Experience has led me to prefer what some may consider a more superficial, and what I should call a more general and broader view, and more capable of embracing all the conditions of the question—a practical view.

Having considered the subject for several years past, I have cautiously, and without any cause for a favourable bias, formed an opinion, which subsequent experiments at Dalkey have fully proved to be correct; viz., that the mere mechanical difficulties can be overcome, and that the full effect of the partial vacuum, produced by an air-pump, can be communicated, without any loss or friction worth taking into consideration, to a piston attached to the train. In this point of view, the experiment at Dalkey has entirely succeeded. A system of machinery, which, even at the first attempt, works without interruption, and, constantly, for many months may be considered practically to be free from any mechanical objection. No locomotive line that I have been connected with has been equally free from accidents. That which is true for one railway of 2 miles in length, is equally true for a second or third although they may be placed the one at the end of the other; the chances of an accident are only in the proportion of the number, or, in other words, the length, a proportion which holds equally good with locomotives, except that a locomotive may be affected by the distance it has previously run, while a stationary engine and its pipes cannot in like manner be affected by the previous working of the neighbouring engine and pipes. In my opinion, the Atmospheric System is, so far as any stationary power can be, as applicable to a great length of line as it is to a short one. Upon all these points I could advance many arguments and many proofs, but I shall content myself with saying that, as a professional man, I express a decided opinion that, as a mechanical contrivance, the Atmospheric apparatus has succeeded perfectly as an effective means of working trains by stationary power, whether on long or short lines, at higher velocity and with less chance of interruption than is now effected by locomotives.

I will now proceed to consider the question of the advantage of its application to the South Devon Railway. It will simplify the discussion of the question very much if it is considered as a comparison between a double line worked by locomotives in the usual manner, and a single line of railway worked by stationary power, the only peculiarity of the present case being that upon four separate portions of the whole

52 miles, stationary assistant power would, under any circumstances, have been used, these four inclines forming together one-fifth of the whole distance.

It is necessary to consider it as a question of a single line on account of the expense, the cost of the pipe for each line being about £3500 per mile. An addition of £7000 per mile, or of about £330,000 in the first construction, could not be counterbalanced by any adequate advantage in the saving in the works on the South Devon Railway, and probably not by any subsequent economy or advantage in the working; but the system admits of the working with a single line, without danger of collision, certainly with less than upon a double locomotive line. And I believe also, that considering the absence of most of the causes of accidents, there will be even less liability of interruption, and less delay in the average, resulting from accidents than in the ordinary double locomotive railway.

By the modification of the gradients and by reducing the curves to 1000 feet radius where any great advantage can be gained by so doing, and by constructing the cuttings, embankments, tunnels and viaducts for a single line, a considerable saving may be effected in the first cost.

In the permanent way and ballasting, the reduction will be about one-half. I should propose to make the rails about 52 lbs. weight, and the timber 12 inches by 6 inches; the quantity of ballast would probably be rather more than half, but at the present prices of iron and timber the saving could not be less than £2500 per mile.

From a careful revision of the works generally, I consider that a reduction may be effected in the following items and to the amount specified in each, viz., ballasting, gradients and curves :—

Reduction in earth work, . .	£16,500	0 0
Reduction in length of principal tunnel, ...	14,000	0 0
	£30,500	0 0

Saving by Single Line.

Earth work, ...	£25,000	0 0
Tunnels, ...	11,500	0 0
Viaducts, ...	15,000	0 0
Carry forward,	£82,000	0 0

	Brought forward,	£82,000	0	0

Permanent Way and Ballast.

To allow for sidings, say 50 miles,
£2500, ... £125,000 0 0

	£207,000	0	0

Per Contra.

Pipe on 41½ miles, . . .	£138,000	0	0
Increase on inclined planes, 10½ miles, ...	6,500	0	0
Engines for the 41½ miles, . .	35,000	0	0
Patent right, say, ...	10,000	0	0

Total, .	£190,000	0	0

The difference in first cost, therefore, is, ... £17,000 0 0

To this must, however, be added the cost of the locomotive power, with its attendant expenses of engine houses, etc., which cannot, I think, be put at less than, ... 50,000 0 0

Making a saving of .	£67,000	0	0

I have not included in the expense of the Atmospheric apparatus that of the telegraph, because, at its present reduced cost of £160 per mile, I am convinced its use would repay the outlay in either case.

It would appear, then, that the line can be constructed and furnished with the moving power in working order on the Atmospheric System, for something less than the construction only of the railway fitted for the locomotive power, but without the engines, and that, taking into consideration the cost of locomotive power, a saving in first outlay may be effected of upwards of £60,000.

But it is in the subsequent working that I believe the advantages will be most sensible.

In the first place, with the gradients and curves of the South Devon Railway between Newton and Plymouth, a speed of 30 miles per hour would have been, for locomotives, a high speed, and under unfavourable circumstances of weather and of load it would probably have been found difficult and expensive to have maintained even this; with the Atmospheric, and with the dimensions of pipes I have assumed, a speed of 40 to 50 miles may certainly be depended upon, and I have no doubt that from 25 to 35 minutes may be saved in the journey.

Secondly, the cost of running a few additional trains, so far as the power is concerned, is so small, the plant of engines, the attendance of enginemen, etc., remaining the same, that it may almost be neglected in the calculations, so that short trains, or extra trains with more frequent departures, adapted in every respect to the varying demands of the public, can be worked at a very moderate cost.

I have no doubt that a considerable augmentation of the general traffic will be thus effected by means which, with locomotive engines, would be very expensive and frequently unattainable, particularly as regards one class of short trains, whether for passengers or goods, which, from the inconvenience of working them by locomotives, are hardly known—I refer to trains between the intermediate stations.

By many means, which the easy command of a motive power at any time, at every part of a line, must afford of accommodating the public, I believe the traffic may be increased. It appears to me also that the quality of the travelling will be much improved; that we shall attain greater speed, less noise and motion, and an absence of the coke dust, which is certainly still a great nuisance; and an inducement will thus be held out to those (the majority of travellers) who travel either solely for pleasure, or, at least, not from necessity, and who are mainly influenced by the degree of comfort with which they can go from place to place. Lastly, the average cost of working the trains will be much less than by locomotives.

With the gradients of the South Devon Railway, and assuming that not less than eight trains, including mail and goods trains, running the whole distance, and certainly one short train running half the distance, be the least number that would suffice, I think an annual saving of £80,000 a year in locomotive expenses, including allowance for depreciation of plant, may very safely be relied on.

For all the reasons above quoted, I have no hesitation in taking upon myself the full and entire responsibility of recommending the adoption of the Atmospheric System on the South Devon Railway, and of recommending as a consequence that the line and works should be constructed for a single line only.

APPENDIX D.

MR BRUNEL'S REPORT TO THE SOUTH DEVON RAILWAY
DIRECTORS, ADVISING THE WITHDRAWAL OF THE AT-
MOSPHERIC PRINCIPLE AFTER ONE YEAR'S EXPERIENCE
OF THE SYSTEM.

YOU have called upon me to report to you upon the present
state of the Atmospheric apparatus, and particularly upon the
circumstances connected with the partial destruction of the
longitudinal valve, which has lately occurred, and the probability of remedying this serious defect, and of keeping the
valve in repair and in good working order.

Such a report involves necessarily the consideration of
the whole question of our experience of the working of the
Atmospheric System, because to arrive at any clear ap-
preciation of the present state of the apparatus, I must refer
to the circumstances which have affected our working up to
the present time, and particularly to the several difficulties
which we have had to encounter, and their effects. The first
difficulty, and one which was as unexpected as it was serious,
was in the working of our stationary engines.

Upon the efficiency of these machines must, of course,
ultimately depend the economy and efficiency of the working of the whole system, however perfect in itself might be
the Atmospheric apparatus. Accordingly, great precautions
were taken—precautions which I still think such as to justify
the expectation that we should secure the best engines that
could be made.

The three first manufacturers of the day were employed—
Messrs Maudslay (who had had some experience in this particular branch, having made the engines for the Croydon
Railway), Messrs Boulton & Watts, and Messrs Rennie.
They prepared their own designs, and I know that they each
bestowed much thought in the preparation of these designs,
and took considerable interest in the results.

Mr Samuda, a man of considerable mechanical abilities,
having all the experience that could be had upon the subject,

and deeply interested in the success of the engines, was also employed to superintend their manufacture.

Notwithstanding all these precautions, notwithstanding excellent workmanship, these engines have not, on the whole, proved successful; none of them have as yet worked very economically, and some are very extravagant in the consumption of fuel, burning nearly double the quantity of others, while the average is very considerably more than it ought to be.

The apparent causes of this excess are various in the different engines, but all resulting more or less apparently from the want of experience in this particular application of power, and from the circumstance of the form of the engines being somewhat novel, and involving slight differences in the proportion and arrangement of the parts, and the consumption of steam being greater than was calculated upon, it has been obtained by a more wasteful expenditure of fuel, and the evil has been aggravated.

The difficulty of remedying this state of things has been increased by the consequence of defects in the Atmospheric apparatus, which, causing a much greater demand upon the working of the engines, has delayed, or has entirely prevented, our throwing an engine out of work, to introduce the requisite improvements. Still, so far as this defect in the engines is concerned, there is no doubt that it is susceptible of considerable, if not complete remedy, and that a reduction of one-third may be effected in the consumption of fuel. In the Atmospheric apparatus itself, our difficulties have been more numerous. We have suffered from extreme cold, particularly when it followed quickly upon wet. We have suffered from extreme heat, and also from heavy falls of rain. These difficulties have in turn been encountered and gradually overcome, and I think the effects of all these causes upon a valve in good condition may now be obviated, if not entirely, yet so much so as to render their operation unimportant. The same remedy applies to all three, keeping the leather of the valve oiled and varnished, and rendering it impervious to the water, which otherwise soaks through it in wet weather, or which freezes it in cold, rendering it too stiff to shut down ; and the same precaution prevents the leather being dried up and shrivelled by the heat; for this, and not the melting of the composition, is the principal inconvenience resulting from heat. A little water spread on the valve from a tank in the piston carriage has also been found to be useful in very dry weather, showing that the dryness, and not the heat, was the cause of the leakage; but a new difficulty has arisen, and a new defect has been discovered, one much more serious in its extent and its possible consequences, and one which renders the operation on each of the previously mentioned causes of difficulty much more powerful and mischievous. Within the last few months, but more particularly during the dry weather of last May and June, a considerable extent of longitudinal valve failed by the tearing of the leather at the joints between the plates. The leather first partially cracked at these points, which caused a considerable leakage, particularly in dry weather. After a time it tears completely through, and that part of the valve is destroyed, and requires to be replaced.

A considerable extent has thus been replaced, but the whole of the valve is more or less defective from this cause. The amount of leakage is considerable, and the working altogether inefficient. I have examined carefully portions of the valve that have been removed, and I find that at the part which has given way, the texture of the leather seems to be destroyed—it is black, and has evidently been acted upon by the iron of the plates. Upon some parts of the line, the injury seems to be more general than upon others, but it is very difficult to examine the valve in place, so as to form any correct opinion of the extent of the evil. As regards the cause of this defect, Mr Samuda, who, under his contract, is at present liable for the repair of the valve, urges that the valve was kept for a length of time in cases after it was delivered to the company, and that, exposed to damp, and the oil in the leather not being renewed on the surface, the iron may have rusted and the leather have been injured, and he refers to instances lately observed, in which valves taken out of the top of a case which has been exposed to wet do show similar signs of injury. Supposing, however, this assumption to be correct, it would not seem to affect the question of his liability. He suggests also, as a cause, that the valve remained for a length of time in place before being used, and even worked over by locomotive engines, which prevented it being oiled and properly attended to; that the evil has been aggravated by an attempt to reduce too much the use of oil to the leather; and lastly, that the piston-gear has been allowed to get out of adjustment, so that the leather of the valve has been strained. I shall not, however, here enter into the discussion of this question of liability, but confine myself to the consideration of the evil, and the possibility of remedying it. Of the extent of the evil, for the reason I have given, it is impossible to form any accurate opinion; it is impossible, therefore, to say that it does not extend more or less over the whole distance, excepting, of course, that which has been already replaced. That which has been injured cannot be repaired in place, but must be removed, and the remedy can only be applied in the new valve. It is quite possible that a valve made in the same manner as the present, if properly attended to from the first, and with our present experience, might not be subject to this destruction; and Mr Samuda states that such is the case at Dalkey, but I do not think that I could rely upon this result. By painting, but better still by zincing or galvanising the iron plates, and making them overlap a short distance, both the chemical and the mechanical action of the plate upon the leather appears to be prevented, and I believe, therefore, that this evil may be remedied at a small increased cost in any new or repaired valve that might be laid down; but of the existing valve I can say no more than I have done. It is not now in good working condition, and I see no immediate prospect of its being rendered so. From the foregoing observations, it will be evident that I cannot consider the result of our experience of the working between Exeter and Newton such as to induce one to recommend the extension of the system. I believe that, if the longitudinal valve were restored, the working expenses might be immensely reduced; that the quantity of fuel consumed, which is the great item of expense, may be diminished by one-third; that the price of the fuel, which costs 18s. per ton at the engine houses, ought to be reduced, at least, 12 per cent., and that the total cost may thus be brought down to a moderate amount, such as I had originally calculated upon. But the cost of construction has far exceeded our expectations, and the difficulty of working a system so totally different from that to which everybody— traveller as well as workmen—is accustomed, have proved too great; and therefore, although, no doubt, after some further trial, great reductions may be made in the cost of working the portion now laid, I cannot anticipate the possibility of any inducement to continue the system beyond Newton. With respect to the future working of the apparatus between Exeter and Newton, I feel in great difficulty as to expressing any opinion, seeing that a very large expense has been incurred; and believing, as I do, that the cost of working may be so very much reduced; but that the reduction can only be effected by the almost entire renewal of the valve, and by some expenditure in the engines. And unless Mr Samuda, or the patentees, undertake the first, and extend considerably the period during which they would maintain it in repair; and unless they can offer some guarantee for the efficiency of that valve, I fear that the company would not be justified in taking that upon themselves, or incurring the expense attending the alteration of the engines. I believe that for the inclined planes, as an assistant power, the apparatus will be found applicable and efficient; and as the engines and the pipes are nearly ready at Dainton, it may be found desirable to try it there, provided a satisfactory arrangement can be entered into for the maintenance and efficiency of the valve. I have not referred to our great disappointment in not obtaining the assistance of the telegraph in the working of the engines, and the greatly increased consumption of coal consequent upon the working of the engines unnecessarily, because this evil is now nearly removed; but some further reductions may still be made by using the telegraph by night as well as day, which has not yet been in our power to do, but which, I trust, will be commenced this week.

INDEX

THE END

LONDON : DIGBY, LONG & COMPANY, Publishers,
18 Bouverie Street, Fleet Street. F.C.

Printed in the United Kingdom
by Lightning Source UK Ltd.
121108UK00001B/286